BROKEN DREAMS,
BEAUTIFUL QUILTS

Broken Dreams, Beautiful Quilts

A Story of Healing and Hope

Judy Rossbacher &
Nathan Rossbacher

Library of Congress Control Number: 2011906699
ISBN: Hardcover   978-1-4628-5772-2
                 Softcover   978-1-4628-5771-5
                 Ebook   978-1-4628-5773-9

To order additional copies of this book, contact:
Xlibris Corporation
1-888-795-4274
www.Xlibris.com
Orders@Xlibris.com
82367

CONTENTS

Part Five: Piece by Piece

Part Six: Bold Designs

Dedicated to our sweet Seth

With much love from

Mommy
And
Nathan

Psalm 66:5 (NIV)
Come and see what God has done,
how awesome his works in man's behalf!

ACKNOWLEDGEMENTS

God encouraged me along the way that He would bring the necessary people for publishing this book at the precise time I needed them. And so it has been! Many thanks to the following people who have been a vital part of producing this book:

- My multitalented daughter, Kristen, for typing and editing the manuscript.
- Chris Lewis, a former pastor, also blessed with a special son, for writing the foreword and encouraging me to keep going.
- Aaron Woodard, my graphic designer, for using his artistic abilities to provide the illustrations.
- Justin Vorel, for capturing my persona on camera during my "author's photo shoot"
- My amazing son, Justin, for graciously scanning photos and providing technological assistance.
- My husband, Bob, for being the "official" printer of the rough manuscripts and also for accomplishing most of the household tasks so I could work on the book.
- Our family friend, Wayne Wright, for helping to edit and for driving with Bob on Saturdays to visit Nathan in Richmond.
- Everyone at Xlibiris who assisted me in getting the manuscript into the finished product—a published book.

Nathan and I give our heartfelt appreciation to all those who helped us in producing our *"magnum opus"*.

FOREWORD

by
Chris Lewis

Broken. Beautiful.

Two words not often found together. After all, they appear contradictory. Truth be told, they correspond perfectly. Words spoken by a sovereign God, ultimately fulfilled by a loving Savior, make the connection plain.

> The Spirit of the Sovereign LORD is on me,
>   because the LORD has anointed me
>   to preach good news to the poor.
>
> He has sent me to bind up the *brokenhearted*,
>   to proclaim freedom for the captives
>   and release from darkness for the prisoners,
> to proclaim the year of the LORD's favor
>   and the day of vengeance of our God,
> to comfort all who mourn,
>   and provide for those who grieve in Zion—
> to bestow on them a crown of *beauty* instead of ashes . . .
>
> —Isaiah 61:1-3a *(italics added)*

The broken being made beautiful. It is an eternal promise residing at the core of who God is as Redeemer. And yet, for those who receive His promise by grace, in order to experience and reflect Him more, we are often lovingly led upon a journey of being *beautifully broken.*

In your hands, you hold record of one such journey.

Beginning in 2004, I was privileged to begin serving as a pastor in the church where Judy and her family were a part. Fresh out of seminary, I was eager to serve yet humbled by the task. God in His goodness provided for me and my family a close relationship with the Rossbachers. With each shared word and moment, I grew not only in my love for this family, but I was nurtured exponentially in my faith of the One who undergirded and lived through this family.

In the wake of untold loss and extreme difficulty, I consistently witnessed the Rossbacher family being sustained, grace being displayed, and ultimately Jesus being exalted. Years later, when my family faced our own challenge of having a child born with special needs, I quickly realized not only had I been privileged to serve the Rossbachers, but I had been given the gift of seeing first-hand what sacrificially love and grace-filled living looks like. These lessons, gained from God and modeled by the Rossbachers, continue to serve me and our family well.

Broken Dreams, Beautiful Quilts offers to its readers the fruit of years walking, not just through the valley of the shadow of death, but through such valleys with a loving Shepherd. Judy, along with her son Nathan, have history with God. May all who read their book be drawn to Him.

Chris Lewis
Pastor of Discipleship
Westover Church
Greensboro, NC

INTRODUCTION

What does one do with garments or linens that have wear and tear in different spots? The first thought might be to throw away these textiles or maybe rip them into pieces to be used as cleaning rags. However, another possibility is to cut the fabrics into pieces and make a quilt. This solution requires a lot more work, but the outcome is a beautiful thing to behold.

When I was a young girl, our family took many trips to visit our relatives in Russell County in the southwestern part of Virginia. I distinctly remember Daddy driving our car down the winding gravel road, which led into Porter Hollow. I remember the car tires kicking up dust as we went along the road beside the little creek. The creek looked so small in comparison to the jutting mountains on each side of the road.

One of my favorite places in Porter Hollow was Uncle John Henry's country store. The storefront was nestled right in a curve of the gravel road with Uncle John Henry's farmland right behind it. In my mind, I can still see the cows and chickens meandering in the grass near the farmhouse.

A very special memory I have from Porter Hollow was the first time I witnessed a quilting bee. As I walked into the room behind my uncle John Henry's store, I saw a large wooden frame, holding three layers of fabric, hanging from the ceiling. Sitting around the frame, in chairs, were my Aunt Sarah and a group of women. I watched in awe as each of the ladies nimbly moved their needles up and down through the layers of fabric.

The women shared with me the purpose for each of the three layers in the quilting process. The first layer, the quilt top, provides beauty and design. They were making a patchwork quilt, which is made from colorful pieces of old fabric. The middle layer consists of cotton batting, which helps give the coverlet weight and warmth. The third layer is a solid piece of fabric, which lines the entire back side; it provides a soft finish to the quilt.

I watched the women as they sewed through all three layers. These tiny stitches not only held the layers together but also enhanced the beauty and design of the quilt. Even at a young age, I realized it took a lot of work to achieve the finished outcome. For example, to make the quilt top, a specific pattern was used for cutting out and piecing together the sections. The pieces came from different fabrics such as old feed sacks, torn or worn garments, and even some new fabrics. Each cut and each stitch was done with great care. After seeing these women perform this very intricate and detailed work, I realized a quilt of this caliber takes time and persistence.

During these quilting bees, the women created more than just a quilt; they built community. The older women listened to the concerns of the younger ones and shared what they had learned in life about being married, being a parent, losing a child, and losing a spouse. If one woman started to cry, the sewing work became secondary as the other women consoled her. These women not only sewed with one another but also cried together, laughed together, and lived life together.

Four decades later, on a lovely spring day in Black Mountain, North Carolina, I strolled into an antique store, which immediately captured my mind and my heart. Standing in the middle of the store, I perused the many quilts hanging from the rafters. I took my time in order to focus in on each quilt. As I admired the unique beauty before me, I wondered, "How many family histories are represented in these quilts?" I thought, "Maybe this blue and yellow piece of fabric was from a tablecloth, a reminder of the many happy Sunday dinners. What if this white piece of fabric is from a grandchild's baptismal or confirmation dress? Perhaps this delicate rose print is a grandmother's favorite handkerchief that she always carried on special occasions."

A patchwork quilt is like a mosaic of life because it allows for the passing of family stories from one generation to another. The quilt can be used as a guide. For example, as a child touches each block in the design, the story can be told which corresponds with each particular textile.

As I contemplated these possibilities that day, I had an epiphany: all my life experiences, good and bad, were in the process of coming together to make something beautiful. The outcome would be like a handmade quilt, something with special purpose and meaning. And so similar to a family quilt, this book tells a story. It is a story told by my son, Nathan, and me. Nathan's writing provides brief headlines, in all capital letters, throughout the book. Then I fill in the details. Together, we explain how God enabled our *broken dreams to become beautiful quilts*.

PART ONE

Fabric and Scissors

CHAPTER 1

The Beginning

MY MOM AND DAD WERE BOTH VERY INVOLVED IN CHRISTIAN WORK WHEN THEY MET.

The story begins . . .

In 1973, when Bob and I met, we were both in Christian service. Previously, I had been a high school home economics teacher and Bob had been a mechanical engineer. Both Bob and I were involved in giving spiritual help to young people in their late teens and early twenties. I was in San Diego, California, working with Navy Waves and Marine women. Bob's work was in Lexington, Virginia, with college men at VMI and Washington & Lee.

We both shared the good news of Jesus Christ with individuals we met. Then we helped new Christians learn how to share their concerns with God through prayer. Also, we showed them how to read the Bible, God's Word, so they could learn what He was saying to them. We each led small group Bible studies, trained other Christians to grow in their faith in Jesus Christ, and taught them how to share this hope they had found with others. As well, we helped lead weekend retreats and training conferences—Bob on the East Coast, I on the West.

My commitment was to do full-time Christian work, so I raised my own financial support from other Christians and churches. Bob did not raise support; instead, he worked during the day as a public schoolteacher and conducted his ministry, part-time, at night and on weekends. His last year in Lexington, Bob painted houses, rather than teach, to support himself. This change enabled him to better conserve his emotional energies for the ministry activities in the evenings.

In August 1973, I met Bob when I was in Roanoke, Virginia, for a summer vacation. When Bob first saw me, I was standing in front of a church group explaining about my work in California. When I first saw Bob the following day, he was standing in front of a group of college students teaching a Bible study at the home of one of the students. A year later, we were married on August 21, 1974. The story of how God developed our relationship is very beautiful; however, I will save that to be the subject for another book.

Judy and Bob's wedding

A Dream:

MY MOM AND DAD WANTED TO BE CAREER MISSION-ARIES OVERSEAS.

Before we were married, Bob said he would like for us to resign from our individual ministries to allow us to concentrate on building a strong marriage. Then after a few years, we would begin the process of becoming career missionaries. To me, this was a very wise idea and so I agreed. We both had enjoyed our individual ministries, and we looked forward to ministering together as a career missionary couple. Bob, for several years, had yearned to go to Eastern Europe (at that time still totally under Communist control) as a missionary. He thought we could possibly live in Austria and travel to other European countries.

To my delight, Bob thought it would be good for us to make our home in Roanoke for a few years. This way, I could be close to my mother and sister. Bob and I both loved our church in Roanoke, and we were excited about being involved in the church as a couple.

As Bob thought about what kind of work he would do in Roanoke, he chose a construction job rather than utilizing his mechanical engineering degree. He felt an engineering career might involve a longer-term commitment, and he wanted us to be ready to move overseas quickly if an opportunity came open.

A Dream:

MY MOM AND DAD WANTED TO HAVE FOUR CHILDREN.

Before I ever met Bob, I yearned to have four children someday when I was married. While I lived in California, I attended several seminars on marriage and family life at local churches. Some of the speakers at these conferences had four children. I enjoyed hearing about the dynamics of the interaction between the siblings and the parents in these families. Also, several of the families in Roanoke I spent time with, on a regular basis, had four or five children. I greatly enjoyed interacting with the children in these families.

At times, for some of the families, I stayed with the children for a few days while the parents were out of town. I loved how we worked together in a team effort to go to church. I remember sitting at the piano with one of these families and saying to eldest child, "Tricia, someday I hope to have a family like your family."

While Bob and I were getting to know each other, I discovered he too liked the idea of having four children. He was one of four children, three boys and a girl. When we became engaged and later married, it was on both of our hearts and minds to pray and work toward having four children.

A Dream:

MY MOM WAS VERY HAPPY WHEN SHE MARRIED. HER DREAM OF BEING A WIFE HAD COME TRUE.

Since I was twenty-six and Bob thirty, when we married, we did not want to wait too long to start our family. So we decided I would not look for a job, but instead stay home full-time. I was thrilled about this plan because it gave me more time to *incorporate my personal development goals* into my married life. While I was single, I had made personal goals for every area of my life. I had decided not to wait until I was married to live my life to the fullest.

Therefore, while living in California, I memorized some of my favorite verses from the Bible. I planned interesting meals for my roommate and me to eat. I used my china and placemats on a regular basis, both for us to eat on and when we hosted guests. Also, I wanted to challenge myself physically, and so I signed up for tennis lessons. As well, I made sure I did creative tasks like sewing and craft projects. Last, but not least, I intentionally used my day off to explore beautiful San Diego!

After I married Bob, these skills helped me to be a more vibrant wife and creative homemaker. I loved cooking for Bob! Every week, I planned out our menus, trying to include at least a few new recipes. At night, we ate dinner by candlelight while we lingered over our meal talking. We even, occasionally, had breakfast by candlelight.

I really enjoyed each time we had a couple over for dinner and when I had girlfriends over for lunch. Almost weekly, we invited different friends to our apartment for dinner or dessert. I had so much fun deciding what table settings and centerpieces to use. This way, I was able to combine two of my loves: being creative and spending quality time with old and new friends.

After I set up the apartment and finished writing thank-you notes, I signed up for a sewing class with my friend Deedie. Through this class, I learned many innovative sewing techniques. Each week, I made a new garment using the new skills I learned. Also, I drove once a week to the home of my new friend, Jacquie, for tole-painting lessons. I painted a floral design, using this particular technique, on a coal bucket. When I was finished, I gave it to my mom as a Christmas present. It was great to spend quality time with Jacquie and learn this new skill as well.

Twice a week, I usually went swimming at the YWCA. While going there, I met a new friend, Bryna. I was delighted to find out she was a home economics major also. After swimming, we sometimes walked back to her apartment, which was only a few blocks away from the Y. Bryna was a wonderful cook; she often had a special homemade soup ready for us to eat lunch after swimming. She shared many of her recipes with me. She also taught me how to make a special mixture for potting plants. For the first time ever, I began to grow various houseplants.

Once a week, I went to women's Bible study at the home of my friend, Phyllis. Phyllis will always be a special person to us because she is the one who made sure Bob and I met. Phyllis had teenage children; however, most of the women in the study had very young children. She taught us biblical principles to help us become better wives and mothers. After the study, we stayed and had lunch together. We each brought a dish to share as we gathered around Phyllis's dining room table. This time of fellowship was very encouraging to all in the group.

In the spring of the first year of our marriage, I talked with Bob about the possibility of our trying to start our family. My dear, sweet, character-filled husband asked his friend and mentor, Bill, and our pastor if they felt we were ready to move into this very responsibility-filled stage of life. They encouraged us by saying they thought we were ready to become parents. Soon after this conversation with Bill and our pastor, we made serious efforts to conceive a baby.

MY SISTER, KRISTEN, WAS BORN FEBRUARY 15, 1976.

To my surprise, I became pregnant the very first month. Nine months later, our sweet daughter, Kristen, was born February 15, 1976. Our Valentine bicentennial baby! She actually only missed being born on Valentine's Day by a few hours. As a newborn, Kristen looked to me like a rosebud. In fact, this ended up being one of my favorite nicknames for her.

When Kristen was thirteen months old, Bob and I found out the owners of the house we rented needed to get back into their house. This meant we needed to find another place to live. Since Bob and I were still planning on being career missionaries, we wanted to find a house to rent, again, instead of one to buy.

However, one Sunday afternoon while driving around looking for a place to live, we passed an Open House sign. It turned out to be a white two-story American Four Square house built in 1926. I immediately fell in love with the house even though it needed lots of work. I really wanted a separate dining room to be able to better entertain guests, and this house had both a dining room and a living room. Also, the house had three porches! It had a good size front porch and back porches on both levels. The front yard had a big maple tree, and the backyard was very spacious with a variety of trees and flowers.

Bob also liked the design of the house; however, he wanted to make sure it was structurally sound. He asked a close friend who was a contractor to come and check it out. The verdict was that although the interior needed a lot of work, the foundation and structure were good.

It even worked out that the monthly house payments were going to be the same as the rent we had been paying. Consequently, we became homeowners and started the remodeling and renovating process while we lived in a small apartment. Then in October 1977, we moved into our house even though we had not finished the renovations.

Kristen was now sixteen months old. Many afternoons, while Kristen took her nap in the front of the house, I was busy sanding and painting walls in the back bedroom. In the mornings, I did the laundry and special activities with Kristen, such as visiting the library to check out books, going to the playground, riding the city bus downtown, and finger-painting, etc.

After Bob and I finished the front bedroom and were almost finished with the back bedroom, I began to think seriously about trying to conceive again. However, our house was not complete: the floors in the hall, the study, and the entire downstairs were still in very poor condition. Nevertheless, I did not want to wait any longer to start our efforts to conceive another child. I still had firmly fixed in my mind the dream, the desire, and the goal to have four children by the time I was thirty-six. Therefore, I approached Bob about my idea of trying to conceive another child. When I look back at this time in my life, I am amazed at how I was able to move on with trying to have another child even when our house was far from being functional and not very aesthetically pleasing.

A Dream:

MY MOM WANTED TWINS, SO SHE PRAYED.

Bob and I both wanted to have four children, and I wanted to have my last child around the age of thirty-six. Taking these factors into consideration, I made some calculations. I originally thought about spacing our children about two or two and a half years apart. However, at some point, the thought occurred to me: if I had a set of twins I could have more years in between my pregnancies.

After the idea hit me, I became fascinated with seeing twins. Whenever I saw a woman or a couple with twins, I sat down or stood back and watched. I especially enjoyed observing the twins interact with each other. An idea, which started from the appropriateness of spacing my pregnancies, turned into a fascination with twins and then grew into a yearning to actually have twins. This yearning propelled me to pray fervently that God would give me a set of twins.

CHAPTER 2

The Twins

During the three months Bob and I tried to conceive, I prayed, "Father, if it be Your will, if You think I have the capacity to take care of twins, please allow me to conceive twins. Please give me the sex of each twin which You desire me to have. Please give me two healthy babies, if this is according to Your will."

As before, Bob and I did not have to wait very long for me to become pregnant. When the doctor's office called and told me I tested positive for pregnancy, tears began to roll down my face. They were tears of praise and thankfulness to God that I was carrying another child, a gift from my Heavenly Father.

Again, my first trimester of pregnancy was during the summer. This was particularly difficult because we did not have central air-conditioning. Nausea and high temperatures do not mix very well. Several mornings a week during the summer, Kristen and I visited friends, and then we came home and took naps in front of our electric fans. Sometimes, the temperature inside was so unbearable that I had to take a cold shower before I lay down for my nap.

On a Saturday afternoon in August, when I went to the bathroom, I saw blood. I knew the sign of blood meant that I could miscarry. Everything in my whole being did not want to lose the child I was carrying. I quickly went to the bedroom window and called out for Bob to come inside! He hurried in, and we immediately called my doctor to tell him about the bleeding! I was very upset and could not talk without crying. The doctor confined me to complete bed rest except for getting up to go to the bathroom. Also, he wanted me to come in first thing Monday morning to see him.

The idea of losing my baby terrified me! I cried out to God to save my unborn child and comfort me as only He can do. Hebrews 4:15-16 says, "For we do not have a high priest who is unable to sympathize with our weakness, but we have one who has been tempted in every way, just as we are—yet was without sin. Let us then approach the throne of grace with confidence, so that we may receive mercy and find grace to help us in our time of need." As I lay there in bed, I visualized myself right in front of the throne of grace; I was comforted by knowing Jesus understood my struggle.

I continued to bleed heavily, day after day, for the first week. Then gradually, the bleeding reduced down to just dark spotting by the end of one month. During this time, the doctor suggested that I have a sonogram to check and see if I had placenta previa, which could be causing the bleeding. I asked him if the sonogram would show if there was more than one baby. Dr. S said it would show with 90 percent accuracy whether or not there were multiple babies.

My friend Diana was also pregnant; however, her due date was little earlier than mine. Since she was new in town, I recommended my obstetrician, Dr. S, to her. Diana decided to be treated by him as well, so we always made our doctor's appointments for the same morning. As I was restricted from driving, it was very convenient to ride with her. Diana was such a special friend and blessing to me; she drove me to the doctor even when she did not have an appointment herself.

For example, Diana went with me to the hospital for my sonogram, which I did through outpatient services. I had to drink tons of water. I remember how uncomfortable it was to lie on the table for the sonogram procedure with so much water in my bladder.

As the technician proceeded to do the sonogram, she said, "I am suspicious that you are carrying more than one baby!" By the time she finished, she was sure I was carrying twins, and she thought that they might both be boys. I told her that there was nothing she could tell me that would make me happier than this special news! I was elated and felt as if I was floating on cloud nine as I left the sonogram room. I told Diana my special news, and then she drove me by Bob's office so I could tell him. When I told Bob, I saw a tear roll down his cheek. He gave me a big hug and told me how happy he was.

Diana drove me home. I walked up the stairs of the porch, then up the stairs to my bedroom, and I climbed into bed with the phone beside me. I called several of my friends. I told them, "We now need to pray twice as hard . . . because I am carrying twins!"

GOD HEARD MOM. MOM WAITED TWO YEARS. THEN IT CAME TRUE. MOM WAS GOING TO HAVE TWINS, AND SHE WAS HAPPY.

The Elders Pray for My Pregnancy

After we found out about the twins, Bob and I asked the elders of our church to come to our home and pray for me because the bleeding had not stopped. The elders gathered around my bed, anointed me with oil, and prayed for God to stop the bleeding and enable me to continue carrying the babies safely. This was done in accordance with the passage in James 5:13-16: "Is any one of you in trouble? He should pray. Is any one of you sick? He should call the elders of the church to pray over him and anoint him with oil in the name of the Lord. And the prayer offered in faith will make the sick person well: the Lord will raise him up. If he has sinned, he will be forgiven. Therefore confess your sins to each other and pray for each other so that you may be healed. The prayer of a righteous man is powerful and effective."

Although there was no known sin to confess, there was someone, even perhaps a total of three persons, who was sick and needed God's healing. My prayer was, "Dear Father, thank You so much for sustaining me during the last three weeks of uncertainty. Hebrews 4:16 has meant so much to me lately. 'Let us then approach the throne of grace with confidence, so that we may receive mercy and find grace to *help* us in our time of need.' Even though the times of heavy bleeding have been very emotional for me, I will give thanks in the midst of them. Having to cry out to You for grace in times of need has richly deepened my relationship with You."

Finding out there were two babies was thrilling for both Bob and me! It was particularly special, though, for me, because I realized God had positively answered my prayer for conceiving more than one baby! Also, I remembered how I prayed God would choose the sex of each baby and for each child to be healthy if it be His will. I asked the Lord to enable me to give every concern over to Him in regard to the growth and delivery of my babies and other areas of my life too.

I remained on bed rest until the bleeding stopped. Once I was allowed to be up and about, my doctor had certain restrictions for me to follow. He was concerned that early dilation might take place if I was too active.

My restrictions were as follows:

- Only to walk down and up the stairs in our house one time per day
- To lay down and rest once in the morning and once in the afternoon
- Not to drive or go shopping
- To only go to church once a week
- Not to lift anything heavy (not even a laundry basket with clothes in it)

October 15, 1978

Dear God, thank you so much for this time that I can develop a better relationship with my neighbors Cindy and Sharon. (Kristen has stayed a lot at their houses.) I see this as one reason for setting me aside with these restricted activities. I know too that I am developing a closer relationship with Kristen, who is two and a half. I pray, Father, that You would give me wisdom as to the kinds of things I can do with her to develop her physically, socially, emotionally, mentally, and especially spiritually. Please enable us to start family devotions soon. Help me during this time to get more direction on my role as a wife and mother. Show me more ways I can be efficient and creative!! Show me what things to work on during the time I have before the babies are born. Help me to first and foremost, to be ready spiritually for the birth of the babies.

Preparing for the Babies

During the duration of the pregnancy, I kept a very detailed prayer list in a notebook. I drew a line down the middle of each page. On the left side, I wrote the prayer request, and on the right side I wrote the answer. Every time something came up that I was concerned about in regard to the twins, I recorded it in my prayer journal. In total, I made sixty-five entries. As I saw how God answered my requests, I made an entry under the answer column.

After my bed confinement ended, I started making plans for the nursery. I bought a counted cross-stitch pattern to stitch for each twin. Using light orange and green yarn, it read, "Dear little baby born today, may God be with you all the way."

My sister-in-law, Kathie, had made a lovely baby quilt for Kristen when she was a baby. I still had it and planned to use it for one of the twins. I decided to make a different, yet complimentary, quilt to go with the one from Kathie. This way, each twin could have one. The color scheme of Kathie's quilt was light orange and white. For this reason, I chose to use light orange and white gingham-checked fabric, but in a different pattern.

On the quilt squares, which were white, I appliquéd either a puppy dog, a ball, or a block made out of the gingham check and trimmed it with white rickrack. I made a coverlet for the changing table out of the light orange and white gingham-checked fabric that I was using to make the quilt. I also made cushions from the fabric to go on an old white wicker rocker that I had bought at a yard sale.

Over the years, sewing has been a wonderful hobby for me. During my single and early married years, I loved sewing all different kinds of garments. It was such fun to pick out the patterns and carefully select the fabric to go with the pattern. Ever since I was a young child, the world of color, texture, and design has brought me a lot of comfort and joy.

The nightmare of a seamstress is that she might accidentally cut the fabric the wrong way. When I was teaching home economics, I once had a student who accidentally cut off the length of her dress she was constructing. We either had to turn the dress into a tunic top or add decorative trim to connect the length back to the garment.

Two Beautiful Garments

When I was pregnant with my twins, it was as if I was sewing two beautiful garments. In reality, it was God who picked out the pattern and fabric for each of my two babies, and He was constructing them inside my womb. The psalmist David spoke to God in Psalm 139:13-16, "For Thou didst form my inward parts; Thou didst weave me in my mother's womb. I will give thanks to Thee, for I am fearfully and wonderfully made; wonderful are thy works, and my soul knows it very well. My frame was not hidden from Thee, when I was made in secret, and skillfully wrought in the depths of the earth. Thine eyes have seen my unformed substance; and in Thy book they were all written, the days that were ordained for me, when as yet there was not one of them."

I wanted to do everything possible spiritually and physically to ensure that both garments (babies) would be successfully constructed (knit together) for the glory of God. So I strove to do the following:

1.   Provide the best environment possible in my womb for my babies to grow by eating well, resting, following my doctor's instructions and praying.

2.   Carefully and prayerfully prepare our house to be the best atmosphere possible for my babies to come home to from the hospital.

3.   Prepare myself spiritually to be the best mother I could be.

Bed Rest Again

When I went for my checkup at thirty weeks, my doctor decided to do a pelvic exam to see if any cervical dilation had taken place. Again, he was concerned because women carrying multiple babies tend to dilate early. Sure enough, I had dilated 3 cm.

I was, once again, confined to total bed rest; the difference this time was that the Christmas season was upon us. We were blessed to have people from our church bring us meals as well as come and help take care of Kristen. Also, we hired a teenager to come over to watch Kristen and to wrap our Christmas presents. Then on Christmas Day, I came down and reclined on the sofa downstairs while we opened presents. I did not mind any of these restrictions because I wanted to do everything possible to bring my twin babies into the world safely.

MOM WENT TO THE HOSPITAL. SHE CHOSE THE NAMES NATHAN AND SETH FOR THE TWINS.

Two weeks later, at thirty-two weeks, I went for my weekly checkup. They informed me that I had dilated to 7 cm and my blood pressure was up. I was surprised because I had not felt any contractions. Dr. S told me I needed to go straight to the hospital.

My doctor hoped that by being in the care of the nurses, the arrival of the babies could be delayed as long as possible. Also, my blood pressure could be monitored and lowered. There was a concern as to whether I would be able to make it to the hospital before the babies were born. By being in the hospital already, I would only need to be wheeled to the delivery room when I went into labor. Diane offered to drive me over to the hospital; Bob left work and met us there. The nurses instructed me to let them know as a soon as I thought I was in labor. This way, they could get me downstairs to labor and delivery as quickly as possible.

On the second day I was in the hospital, I made this entry in my prayer journal:

January 3, 1978

Dear Father, I have been so scared today! Enable me to focus my eyes upon You. Please give me peace and strength. It is so frightening to be dilated 7 centimeters. Please enable the babies to stay in my womb as long as You see they need to be there. Enable them to be born safely and to be healthy if it be Your will. Enable them to weigh 5 lbs. each, if it be Your will. When I go into labor, enable me not to panic and to be able to use my Lamaze breathing if necessary. If it be Your will, please let Bob be here and see the babies be born. Enable me to talk to my roommate, Kathy, about spiritual things.

On January 4, the nurses indicated they were having difficulty finding the second heartbeat. However, eventually as they moved the stethoscope around, they would say, "Oh, now I found the other heartbeat." Each time, I was very relieved to hear them say this!

Then on January 5, my friend Diana went into labor. She actually became my new roommate after she delivered Danelle. This was great because we could enjoy talking to each other while in the hospital room.

On January 6, I began looking through my name book again. Bob and I had picked Nathan out for our firstborn son's name as we drove back from our honeymoon. We loved the name Nathan, which means "gift of God." Also, we admired the prophet Nathan, of the Old Testament, who helped King David turn back to God. However, we did not have a name yet for our other son. After months of reading through names and their meanings and after months of praying for another boy's name, I finally found it! My eyes had settled on the name Seth, which means "the appointed." It was the name Adam and Eve gave their third son after Abel was killed. I loved the name Seth and sensed it was the right name for our other son. This was the answer to one of my sixty-four prayer requests that God would lead us to the right names for our babies.

A few minutes later, Bob came to visit me. Eagerly, I showed the name Seth to Bob, and he loved it also. We talked about how the line of Jesus came through Seth. Neither of us could come up with a middle name to go with Seth, but we had already selected Lee to be the middle name with Nathan.

Later that day, around suppertime, I began to feel a lot of pressure in my lower abdominal region. When the pressure became more intense, the nurses sent me down to labor and delivery for observation. However, I could not feel the coming and going of my contractions. The nurse attending me said I was having partial contractions, but she did not think I was in labor. She called Dr S, and he said to keep me downstairs overnight for observation. Bob had not been called since it did not seem I was going to be in labor.

When Bob came to visit me in the evening, he was sent down to labor and delivery. Very soon thereafter, my water broke and I was definitely in labor, so the doctor was called. He arrived as I was being hurried into the delivery room. Bob was already dressed in the green scrubs when he got the word he could *not* come into the delivery room.

The Delivery

With my feet in the stirrups and my eyes closed in great concentration, I pushed the first baby out. Immediately, a gas mask was put over my face, and I went under anesthesia. When I became conscious, I heard the doctor say, "Look over here at your son, Judy." I turned my head and saw Dr. S holding one of my sons. Immediately, I called out, "Where is my other baby?" My doctor said, "Your other son was born dead." (My stillborn son had been taken out of the delivery room while I was unconscious.) When I was told he was born dead, I *screamed*!

A Broken Dream:

At this moment, it was as if I knew *one garment of my twin pregnancy was shredded* and there was nothing I could do to change what happened. It was an irreversible situation. Unable to focus emotionally on the baby I lost, I began to immediately focus on the baby who was living, but in distress. We had just been told that he had hemorrhaged in uterus and was receiving a blood transfusion.

As the staff transferred me from the delivery table to the gurney, I looked over and said to the nurses, "I was planning on only being pregnant one more time, but now I am planning on two more times." Then while being pushed down to the recovery room, I said to Bob, "I think I want to wait until heaven to see our stillborn baby when he has his perfect body." It will be like having a special present waiting for me in heaven. I was concerned about how he might look since he died a few days before I actually delivered.

In the recovery room, we were told that our other baby's transfusion was complete. He had lost 50 percent of his blood, and the transfusion was necessary for that reason. As Bob and I held hands, we discussed which names to give our babies. I said, "Let's call our living son Nathan, which means 'gift of God,' since his life was spared. Let's call our stillborn son Seth, which means 'the appointed,' because we know his short life in my womb was appointed by God to accomplish great things." Bob quickly agreed.

After I left the recovery room, Bob pushed me in a wheelchair down to see Nathan in the nursery. He was lying in an incubator with all kinds of hookups: a heart monitor, oxygen, and an intravenous feeding tube, etc. As I looked at Nathan in the nursery for the first time, I felt such a surge of love!

SO WE WERE BORN SEVEN WEEKS EARLY. SETH DIED INSIDE MOM. I HAD TO STAY IN THE INCUBATOR AT THE HOSPITAL FOR A COUPLE OF WEEKS. MOM STAYED THERE TOO. DAD WAS AT HOME WITH KRISTEN.

In order to be ready to breastfeed Nathan, I used an electric breast pump to express milk. The breast pump was placed next to my bed, and I had a schedule to follow for pumping my milk. By the third day, Nathan was off with all the hookups, and I was able to breastfeed him. It took several days to work through various problems: Sometimes Nathan would fall asleep while nursing—sucking was difficult for him—and I became painfully engorged with milk. Nathan was losing one ounce a day in weight. The pediatricians told me this was normal for a premature baby, but it was still hard for me not to blame myself for his weight loss. Also, Nathan developed jaundice and so had to be placed under the bilirubin light for three days. After each precious time of nursing, he was placed back into the incubator because he was not able to maintain his own body temperature without help.

January 12, 1979

Dear Father, I need you so much right now. I have written each concern in regards to Nathan down on my prayer list as it comes up. But, I still get uptight. I want to have a divine perspective. I confess my worry as sin and I ask that the Holy Spirit give me power right now, Father, so that I can be relaxed for my nursing. Nathan needs all the nourishment he can get for weight gain, which is so important for a premature baby. It is so obvious to me that I cannot have the power by myself. I must be enabled by You.

Psalm 20:1-4 says, "May the LORD answer you when you are in distress, may the name of the God of Jacob protect you. May He send you help from the sanctuary and grant you support from Zion . . . May He give you the desire of your heart and make all your plans succeed."

A few days after I delivered, Seth was buried next to my father in a little town about one and a half hours from our house. My mother bought a heart-shaped grave marker for Seth. I was not at the graveside funeral service because I was still in the hospital. Before the service, our associate pastor, Randy, came to the hospital and read the entire eulogy to me and asked me if I had anything to add. Then Betty, my friend, came to stay with me while Bob went to bury Seth. Betty had been my roommate when I was single and taught high school. She and I talked, but I did not say very much about Seth.

In preparation for writing this book, I have read through all the journals I have written over the years. As I read the journal entries I made while I was in the hospital, I realized that I was not able to write about Seth until eleven days after the delivery. The night I made the entry about Seth was the same day Nathan gained weight for the first time. The entry is very short. In retrospect, it seems that I was not able to write about Seth until I knew Nathan was doing well.

January 17, 1979

Until now I have not been able to write anything down concerning the death of Seth. I'm not sure if I can write anything now. You know Father, how much I wanted twins and how I eagerly awaited their arrival, except I didn't want them to come too early. I remember distinctly praying for twins before we tried to conceive. When I had my first sonogram, I was so elated to find out You had answered my prayer. Someday maybe You will give me insight into why You allowed Seth to die. Oh, Father, the pain due to his loss was so great the first 2 ½ days. Yet, I was so thrilled with Nathan and I felt such a surge of love for him from the first time I saw him. What an unusual time in our lives to feel the depth of sorrow and the peak of joy simultaneously.

Each day, I hoped Nathan would gain weight and that his body temperature would stabilize so that we could go home together. I was glad I was still at the hospital because it made breastfeeding easier. Finally, my obstetrician said, "Judy, you *must* go home." So I left the hospital on January 22.

In order to be ready for Nathan's homecoming, I used an electric breast pump to keep my milk flow steady. To my surprise, Nathan's body temperature stabilized, and he was able to come home the very next day. Our health insurance did not cover the extra days that I chose to stay in the hospital to be near Nathan. As a result, we ended up having to make monthly payments to the hospital to cover the bill.

CHAPTER 3

Life with Nathan

I WAS A HAPPY BABY, BUT I WAS SLOW IN DEVELOPING.

At home, we settled into a routine. We had a great time because Nathan was a content, happy baby and Kristen enjoyed being the big sister. Yet at times, as I walked through the house, a profound sadness came over me. I experienced an intense awareness that there was supposed to be another child, my dear Seth, in our household. Whenever I reached my destination in the house and became involved with a task, the sadness lifted. As the days turned into months, I continued to have these fleeting moments of sadness.

Kristen next to Judy holding Nathan

However, most of the time, I felt fairly normal. In fact, in the spring, I gave two special parties in our home. The first celebration was to welcome back a couple, Becky and George, who had recently returned to Roanoke. We invited as many of our friends as we could think of to come. We asked each couple to bring a snack or dessert. Bob and I had recently put an island counter in the middle our kitchen, and this served as a perfect place to serve the refreshments. The party was a lot of fun, and our friends were very touched by how many people came.

The other party was a dinner to say good-bye to a couple that was moving away. Tommie, the wife, was the person who had coordinated people to bring meals to us when I was confined to bed rest during my pregnancy. She also lined up the women who took turns taking care of Kristen in their homes while Bob was at work. As well, Tommie took a turn watching Kristen in her home once a week. Since she had done so much to help our family, I wanted to do something really special for her. With the help of another friend, I planned an elegant dinner party for Tommie and her husband. I put two tables together and covered them with a lovely long pink damask tablecloth. I set the dinner table with my white silver-rimmed china and our monogrammed pewter goblets.

During the summer, I also had a luncheon for two women who were serving as missionaries in different countries. They were home in the states for a visit, and so I thought it would be nice to have something special for them. During the luncheon, both women enjoyed sharing about their individual ministries. I really was excited to be able to do these special things for others. It was great to be able to further develop my hospitality and homemaking skills and strengthen friendships at the same time.

Concern for Nathan

At Nathan's fourth-month checkup, I had to check no on the pre-exam list of questions in regard to almost everything. Because he was born almost two months premature, I figured that Nathan was really at a two-month level of development rather than four. For this reason, I was not very concerned at this point and neither was our pediatrician. However, after the four-month checkup, I began to watch him closely for further development.

At the six-month checkup, the pediatrician, Dr. B, walked into the examining room and asked how I was doing. I answered, "I am not doing well because I am concerned about Nathan. He does not reach for objects. He does not even hold a rattle!" Dr. B recommended the Denver Diagnostic Test be given to Nathan to obtain an objective view of his development. The results indicated that Nathan was behind in several motor skills.

A few days later, an X-ray showed that Nathan's skull development was abnormal. Our pediatrician recommended waiting until Nathan was nine months old and then administering the test again. If there were no significant improvements, then Dr. B would refer Nathan to a pediatric neurologist.

At eight and a half months, I could see no progress in Nathan's development. Without delay, I called Dr. B and the Denver Diagnostic Test was given again. It showed he was now considerably behind in development. As a result, an appointment was made to see the pediatric neurologist on October 8. Before the visit to the neurologist, I wrote this in my journal:

September 25, 1979

Dear God, these days seem to be very difficult for me emotionally. I am fighting back tears so much of the time. My emotional make-up is very fragile right now. The last year has been hard. First, came the threat of miscarriage, then dilating early, then going early to the hospital, then losing Seth, and then the pain that continues in my life due to the loss of Seth. And now over the last few months, we have the increasing concern over Nathan not reaching important developmental milestones.

Psalm 63 has been so encouraging to me.

Verse 1: "O God, Thou art my God; I shall seek Thee earnestly; My soul thirsts for Thee, my flesh yearns for Thee, In a dry and weary land where there is no water."

The psalmist in this passage is King David. I am not sure if David is only speaking of a literal land, but in my present situation I feel emotionally like I am a dry and weary land. Tears often mount up behind my eyes and I feel nervous and tense inside.

Verse 2: "Thus I have beheld Thee in the sanctuary, To see Thy power and Thy glory."

Just as David realized that he must spend time intimately with You to see Your power and Your glory, I too must meet with You daily to see Your power and Your glory.

Verse 3: "Because Thy loving kindness is better than life, My lips will praise Thee."

I need to meditate more on Your power, Your glory and Your loving kindness. It would be good to review the ways You have manifested Your loving kindness to me in the past and to praise You.

Verse 4: "So I will bless Thee as long as I live; I will lift up my hands in Thy name."

I need to spend more time in prayer blessing You for who You are. In addition, throughout the day, I need to praise and thank You in the circumstances of my life.

Verse 5: "My soul is satisfied as with marrow and fatness, and my mouth offers praises with joyful lips."

Only in God can my inner being be satisfied, just as food satisfies the body. Once again, I see how important it is for me to be praising God.

Verse 6: "When I remember Thee on my bed, I meditate on Thee in the night watches."

Sometimes it seems that at night my fears hit me the hardest. This would be a good time to review verses and meditate on them. I wonder when he says, "night watches," if David was keeping watch for his enemy to approach.

The Appointment

The morning of the appointment with the pediatric neurologist, I dressed in a gray wool skirt, a wine-and-gray tweed jacket, and a white blouse. I had all my questions written out and placed in my clipboard. Bob was to meet me at the neurologist's office. When it was time for me to go into his office, Bob had not arrived yet. So I had to go into the doctor's office alone with Nathan. As I sat across from Dr. S, I held my clipboard on my lap so I could take notes.

While we were in his office, Dr. S began by asking me several questions about Nathan. When he finished, I said, "May I ask you a few questions now?" Looking at his watch, he said, "You may, if you make the questions quick." As tears formed, I looked down at my clipboard trying to decide which questions I should ask him.

After I asked my questions, it was time for me to take Nathan into the examining room. When the neurologist walked in to examine Nathan, I knew I had to say something about how I felt; however, I was still undressing Nathan. So with my eyes still on Nathan, I said, "Doctor, it was very difficult for me emotionally when you indicated to me that I needed to ask my questions quickly. I just experienced Nathan's twin brother's death almost nine months ago and now I am faced with the possibility of something being terribly wrong with Nathan." He apologized and said, "I am due to be at the television station soon. You can come back at a later time and we can talk more." Bob arrived at the very end of the appointment, and we agreed to both return the next day to the doctor's office.

WHEN I WAS NINE MONTHS OLD, THE DOCTOR FOUND BRAIN INJURY.

The next day, Bob and I met with Dr. S. He told us that there appeared to be an even dispersal of brain injury throughout Nathan's brain, and he was not sure what Nathan would or would not be able to do as he grew older.

Nathan had not lost the infantile tonic neck reflex, and his other reflexes were abnormal. An electroencephalogram, or EEG, showed that he had a tendency for seizures. Also, Nathan's head and brain growth were very slow.

His motor development was severely delayed. The neurologist felt there was significant damage to the motor cortex and perhaps to the entire brain. This prognosis did not look very encouraging, but our neurologist was careful not to say exactly what he thought Nathan would or would not be able to do in the future.

As Bob and I walked out of the building, I leaned on Bob's shoulder and cried as if my heart was breaking in two. Bob put his arm around me, and we walked toward the car. All the way home, I wept.

A Broken Dream:

When I heard Nathan's diagnosis, it was as if I was looking down at the remaining garment of the twin pregnancy and realizing it was not whole, as I had hoped, but instead cut into pieces. Time alone would show us just how damaged, in other words, how extensive, the brain injury was. I was up the whole night dealing with the deep emotional pain that was stabbing at my heart. I sat on the living room sofa talking out loud to God, writing in my prayer journal, and reading my Bible.

October 8, 1979

Oh Father, I hurt so much on the inside. I can't sleep and I am here applying Psalm 63:6, "meditating of Thee in the night watches." I'm so scared. It was very hard for me to hear what the doctor had to say today. The possibility of Nathan not eventually developing is so frightening to me. I know You love us, but my emotions are so out of kilter right now. Psalm 63:8 is once again so precious to me. "My soul clings to thee; Thy right hand upholds me." Also, Hebrews 4:16 means a lot to me: "Let us therefore draw near with confidence to the throne of grace, that we may receive mercy and may find grace to help in time of need." Oh Father, You have promised to give me grace in time of need. I must lay hold of the promise now.

My desire, Father, is that Nathan could develop into a mature man (spiritually, mentally, socially, and physically). At this point, I have no way of knowing that he will develop this way. But, I guess no parent really does know, even when his or her child is very normal.

I feel so torn inside. Please give me wisdom, Father, daily as to the things I should do to help Nathan and the things I should do with Kristen and Nathan. Please enable me to have a divine perspective and emotional stability.

I know I must thank You and praise You, in the midst of this situation with Nathan, and I do. I feel there is special grace imparted to us when we thank You and praise You in the midst of difficult situations.

You may think that Nathan could bring much more glory to Yourself by being severely handicapped the rest of his life. I must accept this if it be Your will. I feel, though, at this point Bob and I should cover all the bases possible, at least spiritually and humanly speaking, to help bring about healing for Nathan. Please show us every effort You want us to make, at the point You want us to make it.

Next Day after the Diagnosis

Early in the morning, I called my friend Jan and asked her to come over as soon as possible. Jan arrived soon after I phoned her. She was a great encouragement to me during her visit. We talked and prayed for several hours. I praise God for this precious time to share my heart with Jan. Later the day, I made this entry in my journal.

October 9, 1979

Oh Father, I hurt so much on the inside. The possible thoughts of what the future may hold are so scary. So many things have come to my mind. Seeing Nathan as a man and yet still being a baby. Yet, I know I should not dwell on these thoughts because this may not be the future. I need to be meditating on Your promises. There are so many scriptures that speak of meditating on Your Word during the night as well as during the day.

Psalm 1:2-3 "But (her) delight is in the law of the Lord, and in His law (she) meditates day and night. And (she) will be like a tree firmly planted by streams of water, which yields its fruit in its season, and its leaf does not wither. And in whatever (she) does, (she) prospers."

I have substituted "her" for he in these verses so that I can more easily lay hold of this promise. If I am meditating on YOUR word day and night, You will prosper what I do.

In James 1, You say that if we ask for wisdom with faith that You will give it to us. Everyday and several times a day, I must come to You and ask You for Your wisdom as to how to best help Nathan.

The First Week

The first week after we received the diagnosis, I continued to pour my heart out to God in my journal writings. I also went to the library and checked out a huge stack of books on brain injury, and I feverishly began to read them. Some of the books were strictly factual, and others were stories parents had written about their brain-injured children.

October 11, 1979

Oh Father, I still ache on the inside. I need so much to be heavy in Your Word, so I will have the perspective You want me to have. We always need Your strength, grace, and wisdom, yet it is not always so obvious to us. I think more than ever in my entire life I see my need greatly; I must cling to Your promises.

I would not be honest with You God if I didn't say I want so very much for my little boy to be well. Years ago when I was single and struggling with the desire to be married, You brought Psalm 27:4 to my attention. "One thing I have asked from the Lord, that I shall seek; that I may dwell in the house of the Lord all the days of my life to behold the beauty of the Lord and to meditate in his temple." My desire to know You, Father, must be far greater than my desire for Nathan to be well. Just as my desire to know You intimately must be far greater than any other desire in my life now or anytime in the future.

By Friday, we had received the CT scan report.

October 12, 1979

Psalm 28:1 describes how I have felt this week. To Thee, O Lord I call; my rock, do not be deaf to me, lest, if Thou be silent to me, I become like those who go down to the pit.

Oh Father, Monday, Tuesday, and Wednesday I felt that I was deep down in the pit and that the dirt was going to cover me up. Toward the end of this week I began to feel like I was coming up to the edge of the pit. I was feeling much stronger emotionally and spiritually. Then after hearing the CT scan report last night, things started looking more on the really bleak side. The report says that Nathan's brain does not fill the skull cavity. Yet, this condition is in Your perfect control.

I know, Father, You are all powerful and You could instantly heal Nathan supernaturally if You so desire. I believe with all my heart You could do this. I know too that You could, over time, build up his living brain cells to partially heal him or completely heal him.

Asking for Prayer

Over the weekend, Bob and I composed a note to send to our friends and relatives explaining Nathan's diagnosis and asking them to pray. We shared the following:

Knowing God desires us to pray, we ask you to pray with us that:

1. We would know God better through this.
2. The doctors would have wisdom.
3. We would have wisdom in planning and carrying out a stimulation program for Nathan.
4. Kristen who is a 3 ½ year old would adjust and help.
5. God would give us emotional stability.
6. If God wills, Nathan would develop motor skills (picking up objects, crawling, etc.)

October 14, 1979

After the Sunday night church service, upon our request, the elders anointed Nathan with oil and prayed for his healing according to James 5:14. We sat in our pastor's office, and I held Nathan on my lap. While the pastor put oil on his head, all the elders stood around him, placed their hands on him, and prayed for him. As I heard their prayers, I felt like my heart was breaking into pieces.

On Monday morning, I made the following entry in my journal:

October 15, 1979

Father, please show me how to organize my time. I think I should have the postcards printed today. Then, I would like to address them to our friends and relatives. I guess next I should start to listen to the Institutes for the Achievement of Human Potential tapes that Kris loaned me. I think this will take me quite a while to do. Father, please show me if I should do things differently.

After I mailed the postcards, I turned my attention to listening to the tapes that I had borrowed from our friends Kris and Jerry. They had a daughter, Dana, who was brain injured, and they were doing an intense stimulation program with her in their home. The Institutes for the Achievement of Human Potential in Philadelphia, Pennsylvania, had designed the program for Dana and had trained Kris and Jerry in how to carry out the program. I had just finished reading a book, *What to Do about Your Brain-Injured Child*, written by Glenn Doman, the founder of the Institutes. Every day, I listened to the tapes while the children were napping. The tapes included all the speakers for the orientation that Kris and Jerry went to when they made their first trip to the Institutes with Dana.

The Second Week

After I finished listening to the tapes, I spent a big portion of a day observing Kris as she carried out Dana's stimulation program, which was called patterning. Bob and I were impressed by the gains Dana had made thus far doing the patterning program. So we wanted to look very closely at this program to see if it was something we wanted to consider for Nathan. As I researched about the patterning program, I shared my findings with Bob at night after the children went to bed. I also shared with Bob what I was learning from the many different books I was reading that covered more traditional ways of treating brain injury than the Institutes' patterning program.

I also spent a half day observing a public school program called REACH. This was a preschool program for children two years and older who were developmentally delayed. Nathan was not old enough for this program, but I wanted to see what it had to offer him for the future. I was impressed with the love the staff had for the children, but I knew when I left that I wanted Nathan to have much more stimulation than what the REACH program had to offer.

After much discussion and prayer, Bob and I decided that the best direction for us to go in with Nathan was to fashion a program similar to Dana's initial patterning program. The symptoms of Dana's brain injury were similar to Nathan's. We decided to start doing this program with Nathan on our own and to continue to pray about actually applying to the Institutes.

Bob and I felt that we needed to do all that we could to build up Nathan's good brain cells so that they could take over for the dead brain cells while he was still young. We did not even know how many brain cells were dead, but we wanted to give it our best effort. *It was as if we were striving to sew back the pieces of our cut-up garment of the twin pregnancy not even knowing how many pieces there were lying on the floor.*

PART TWO

Extraordinary Measures

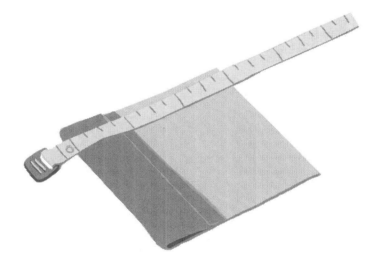

CHAPTER 4

Patterning

WE DID PATTERNING TO HELP ME. EIGHTY PEOPLE HELPED ME DO THIS. MANY OF THESE PEOPLE BECAME SPECIAL FRIENDS. THEY HELPED ME CRAWL ONE THOUSAND FEET IN ONE DAY.

In preparation for the beginning of the patterning program, we took the furniture out of the dining room so that we could make it into a therapy room. Since there were going to be so many people in our house every week, we felt we needed to help it look more attractive to the eye. There were quite a few remodeling projects we had started when we first bought the house but had not completely finished. We had torn out parts of several walls between a few of the rooms. We did this to make our house look more spacious, but as a result, it left some holes in the wood floor. Bob thought we would eventually put carpet in, and so he just used mismatched wood planks to fill in the gaps. However, now that we had received Nathan's diagnosis, we knew it would be a long time before we could think about investing in carpet for our house. So instead, we painted the floors of the dining room, living room, and the entrance hall with a dark brown paint in an effort to make the boards all the same color.

While we prepared the house, we recruited volunteers. Chris helped me find some people for Nathan's therapy program. She primarily did this by asking her patterning volunteers if they could work with Nathan as well as her daughter Dana. Also, she asked them to put a write-up in their church bulletins about our need. I quickly realized we needed someone to help coordinate the volunteers, so we included this specific position in the write-up. It was not long before people began to contact us about volunteering.

One day, a lady named Annette called me about the notice she had seen in her church bulletin. She explained that she did not drive and so could not come to our home, but she wanted to use her telephone as a way to help Nathan. Annette ended up assisting me in getting the schedule set up for the volunteers, who we called patterners. As well, we established a substitute patterner list. This way, if someone was unable to come, he or she called Annette, preferably in advance, and then she lined up a substitute using the list. Whenever Nathan or I was sick, I called Annette and she called the patterners for that day and told them not to come. She also placed articles in the newspaper to recruit more volunteers. Annette was such an answer to our prayer: her personality and interpersonal skills were absolutely perfect for being the coordinator for the patterners!

Patterning Program

Once the house was prepared, we officially started our program. As each new patterner came, I trained them in the procedures we used in Nathan's program. Bob helped train any of the patterners who came only in the evenings.

In the middle of the dining room, which became the patterning room, there was a table that we used to teach Nathan how to crawl. This waist-high table was padded with cotton batting and then covered with an oilcloth. We sprinkled cornstarch over the oilcloth to prevent Nathan from getting abrasions. Then we placed Nathan on the table flat on his stomach. Next, we moved Nathan's limbs across the tabletop in a crawling fashion. We were sending the message of "THIS IS HOW IT FEELS TO CRAWL" to Nathan's brain.

It took three people to take Nathan through these movements. One person moved Nathan's head from side to side, and the other two each moved an arm and a leg. A timer was set for five minutes, and Nathan was put through the patterning exercise until the bell rang. The patterners often sang to Nathan as they worked with him. After each five minutes of patterning, we showed Nathan a set of word cards, written in large red print. While we did this, he was simultaneously wearing a respiratory therapy mask for thirty seconds.

Next, we placed Nathan on a slide, called an inclined plane, which was located in the corner of the dining room. As Nathan moved his limbs, we cheered him to move down the inclined plane. Gravity helped him move forward. Our goal was to move the slope of the inclined plane gradually lower until Nathan was crawling flat on the floor.

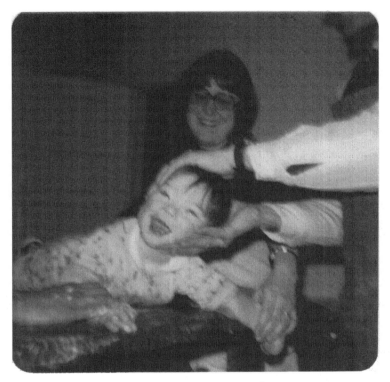

Patterning Nathan

Our daily schedule, Monday through Friday, included four sessions. Three different patterners came for each session. Our day began at 7:30 a.m. We had two sessions in the morning, and then we took a break for lunch and Nathan's naptime. At 3:30 p.m., our afternoon session began, followed by a dinner break. At 7:00 p.m., the evening patterners came for a session. We did not have any sessions on Friday night or Saturday night or any at all on Sundays.

During Nathan and Kristen's naptime, I went to my bedroom to read my Bible, to pray, and to rest. It was a good time for me to process my thoughts by writing in my journal. The following are some of the entries I made in my prayer journal:

November 19, 1979

Thank you so much, Father, that the patterning has gone well so far. Please enable me to manage the house effectively. Enable me to be kind and sweet with Kristen and constant with discipline. Use this time to strengthen her to one day be a child of Yours.

Oh, Lord, may I keep my eyes on You. Some days, I wonder if I will ever see Nathan crawl and reach out for objects. The important thing is to do the program as You direct and to leave the results of the program in Your hands. By Nathan's birthday, I want so much to see him do something new such as reaching or crawling. If it be according to your will, I am asking you to bring this about for him and for me.

November 21, 1979

Thank you, Father, for allowing Nathan to move his arms forward. Thank you, too, for the way he rubbed his fingers across the spokes of the baby bed. May we appreciate every new aspect of Nathan's development.

December 15, 1979

Dear Father, it was so hard for me tonight to see the babies in the church nursery and to see how far behind Nathan is. By an act of my will, I will say thank you to You in the midst of this situation. Show me things we ought to do with Nathan and how best to organize our time to do these things. Father, enable Nathan to not be stiff when we pattern him. I know You are all powerful and if You desire for Nathan to crawl by his birthday, You will enable him to do so.

January 3, 1980

I was so excited when Nathan crawled a little on New Year's Day. Even though it occurred while he was mad, he did move. I know for sure because he moved off the masonite board I had placed under him to make it easier for him to crawl. I cried with much joy! I continue to praise You for answering my prayer request.

The last two Sundays have been very hard for me emotionally. Please help me, Father. It hurts very much for me to see how far behind Nathan is compared to the other babies.

I keep wondering and, at times, worrying as to whether we should apply to the Institutes. At this point, You have not made Bob's heart positive concerning applying to the Institutes. When I am angry with him about this, then I am angry with You. You will direct us as to whether we should apply through Bob, because You have ordained him to be the head of our family.

This morning, verses 1 and 2 of Psalm 131 are very encouraging to me. "Oh Lord my heart is not proud, or my eyes haughty; nor do I involve myself in great matters, or in things too difficult for me. Surely I have composed and quieted my soul, like a weaned child rests against his mother."

Contacting the Institutes

On February 25, 1980, we wrote the Institutes for the Achievement of Human Potential, asking them to give Nathan an appointment to be evaluated. At this time, Bob felt this was the next step for us to take with Nathan. We received a letter back from the Institutes dated March 28, 1980, stating that we had an appointment with them in Philadelphia for the month of April 1981. There was going to be a wait of almost one year for us, but the letter also stated we were on the waiting list for an earlier appointment. A few months later, our appointment date was moved up to September 15, 1980.

While we waited for the time to come for us to go to Philadelphia, we continued on with our own program. It was a very difficult time for us because we did have the support of the trainers at the Institutes; we were all on our own. The day I made this following entry in my prayer journal, I was feeling discouraged that Nathan was not progressing with crawling.

July 10, 1980

Dear Father, as I read 1 John 5:14 and 15, I am pondering how these verses tie in with Your ultimate will concerning Nathan's crawling. "And this is the confidence, which we have before Him, that if we ask anything according to His will, He hears us. And if we know that He hears us in whatever we ask, we know that we have the requests, which we have asked from Him."

Usually, when I have prayed about something a lot and the thing I have prayed about has not occurred, then I say to myself, "It was not God's will for this to take place now." This time though, it is so much harder for me perhaps because I feel I have not prayed enough and I have not used my time with Nathan as wisely as I could have. Yet, I do know for sure, at this point I must thank You in this situation with Nathan, whether it seems good or bad to me. It hurts me deeply that Nathan is 18 months old and he cannot crawl. But, in obedience, I will thank you in this time of uncertainty and emotional pain. In I Thessalonians 5:18 the apostle Paul says, "Give thanks in all circumstances, for this is God's will for you in Christ Jesus."

There are many positive things I can focus on. I thank You that:

1. *Nathan can now use his arms and hands to touch my nose, eyes, mouth, and hair and that he can patty cake and clap with his hands.*
2. *He is very alert, enjoys people and responds well socially.*
3. *He can see, hear, and make jabbering noises.*
4. *He does occasionally move 2 or 3 feet.*
5. *Also, I thank you for all the patterners who are working with Nathan and for all the sweet, thoughtful things they do for us.*

Preparing for First Trip to the Institutes

September 4, 1980

Dear Father, I thank You for the many marvelous things you have done for us. Today, though, I am very tired, both physically and emotionally. The situation with the refrigerator really unnerved me earlier. I am not taking the demands from Kristen very well. Please help me to regain a divine perspective and have more emotional stability.

Please work out all the details concerning our trip to Philadelphia. Please provide us with a comfortable and friendly Christian home to stay in while we are there.

Answered Prayer

The Lord provided two wonderful couples who gave us a portion of their homes and a portion of their hearts each time we went to Philadelphia. The use of their home was quite a financial help, and their listening ears were of great spiritual help to us. Bob and I really enjoyed coming up with ideas for thank-you gifts for our hosts.

The Institutes

It was with great hope and excitement that we set off for our first trip to the Institutes in Philadelphia for our September 15 appointment. The staff thoroughly evaluated Nathan's neurological development, and they designed an individualized therapy program for Nathan. The program was similar to the one we had been performing with Nathan in Roanoke, but it also included tactile stimulation activities, respiratory therapy (masking), and a nutritional program.

An absolute requirement of the program was that it would be seven days a week, so we recruited more volunteers for the time slots on Friday night, Saturday, and all day Sunday. With all the patterning, it took a total of eighty people a week. Every three to six months, we took Nathan back to the Institutes in Philadelphia to be reevaluated. Each evaluation would change the program somewhat, which included *new and higher goals* for Nathan to reach.

The Institutes outlined the route of Nathan's motor development in four different levels:

Level 1: Crawling on his stomach one thousand feet in one day on a smooth surface with bare arms and legs.

Level 2: Crawling one thousand feet in one day on carpet with long pants and long sleeves. The friction caused by crawling on carpet and over obstacles will bring his rump in the air.

Level 3: Creeping up on his hands and knees one thousand feet in one day.

Level 4: Nathan begins the process of learning to walk.

Nathan was always working ahead of time on certain skills, which would help him on down the road with a higher level of motor development. Learning how to hold a quadruped position was preparation for learning how to creep. Learning how to hold on to a rung of a small vertical ladder, which we made, was preparation for holding on to an overhead bar. Holding on to this bar with feet touching the floor was preparation for learning how to walk.

In addition to the motor program, there was an intelligence program. Through showing him large reading cards, we taught him to recognize thousands of words. Using these words, we made homemade books for Nathan, which he loved to read. Also, we cut out pictures of different kinds of birds, dogs, cats, flowers, etc., and pasted them on individual pieces of cardboard. After each interval of patterning, we showed five of these cards, called bits, at a time to Nathan. This group of cards would all be related, for example, five kinds of birds. He thoroughly enjoyed this part of the intelligence program as well as the books.

The world of Nathan's pattering room was ideal for him during the early years. He was surrounded, throughout the day, with a wide variety of people who enjoyed working with him. Nathan's days were filled with social, intellectual, and physical stimulation. Everyone who worked with Nathan talked to him as if he understood everything they said. As they interacted with him, they constantly affirmed him.

Special Journal

In March of 1981, I began a special journal for Nathan that he could look back at when he grew older. My entries were addressed to Nathan as if I was writing him a letter. When I filled out Nathan's progress reports for the Institutes, I used the journal entries to document his progress.

First Entry

March 17, 1981

My Dearest Nathan,
    I am beginning this journal today so one day you can go back and read the miracles God has done in and through your life. It is my constant prayer God will use the situation of your brain injury to manifest His power and His love to us as a family and to all the many people who enter our home.
    By now, there have probably been about 100 plus different people who have worked with your patterning program. Some of the people are Christians and some are not. I pray God will use you and the rest of our family to show those who are not Christians how they can come to know Him through Jesus Christ. My prayer for the Christians who pattern you is God will use us to encourage them to trust him with their concerns.
    It seems, Nathan that almost everyone who comes to help us, falls deeply in love with you. And, oh, how you love your patterners. As soon as someone enters the door, you are saying "hi" and you have a great big smile for him or her. You flirt and tease a lot and we all enjoy you so much.
    Oh, Nathan, how God has blessed us through the lives of our beloved patterners. Many people help make your bits, word cards, and your books. Some of the patterners have given us money to help with the expense of our trips to Philadelphia. Many bring us special treats, such as homemade soup, homemade breads and pastries, and gifts of books and toys for you and Kristen.
    Grandmamma comes almost everyday, Monday through Friday, to help us. She washes clothes, vacuums, mends, and cooks our dinners. It would be so much harder to carry out your program if we did not have Grandmamma's help and love.
    Nathan, before I close for today, I want to tell you what a privilege and joy it is to work with you in the many facets of your program. There are times I am so weary and tired Daddy must take over. It seems after I have rested, I get back in gear. Whenever possible on Sunday afternoons I take time to go to art galleries, music concerts, and flower gardens in order to be refreshed for Monday mornings.
    I love to kiss you and I kiss you many times during the day. You now know how to give kisses back. You give me many kisses, too, all through the day. You and Kristen, both, are special gifts to Daddy and me.
    I pray that in the future God will give us more children. Daddy and I have desired, since our engagement, to have four children and this desire has never left my heart. I am praying that the intenseness of our program will only last for a few years if it be God's will, so we can have a little brother and or sister for you and Kristen.

My heart's desire, Nathan, is for God to bring you to the point of being totally well. I constantly pray for this. Yet, I must wait on God and trust Him with each individual step. Right now, we are praying hard that you will reach your crawling goal of 150 feet in one day by April.

With Much Love,
Mama

The journal entries were a way I could express my prayer requests to God. As God provided, I would write it down. Having the answers to specific needs documented helped me be more aware of God's provision in our lives. This allowed me to give praise to God at that particular time and also for years to come.

April 21, 1981

God did many special things for us over the past few weeks. Before we went to the Institutes, Jan F. gave us two hundred dollars to buy a mattress. She did this because she heard me tell one of the patterners that I was not sleeping well at night because the springs in our mattress were poking me. I called a bunch of stores in town trying to find a Serta mattress because that was the kind Daddy wanted us to get. None of the stores, I called, carried a Serta so we didn't get a mattress.

We left for the Institutes a few days later. Our car broke down on the trip and it was not fixable. We had to use the $200 to rent a car and to get a motel room. Now, we need a car and a mattress.

April 29, 1981

We have bought a mattress on sale for about $145. We still do not have a car. Nathan, I am praying that God will literally give us a very good small car or enable us to buy one for a low amount of money. (A few months later, a couple in our church gave us their old car when they bought a new one.)

I am also praying that people will help us paint our house trim and porches if it be God's will. Even if they are not painted and the wood rots, it is of no great loss compared to the importance of working with you, Nathan. The porches are replaceable, but your life is not replaceable. We feel before God that we must work hard and intensely now to build up your good brain cells so that someday you will be able to walk and run.

Also, the letters to Nathan were a way for me to follow Nathan's growth. I was able to see his developmental progress in several different areas. This was particularly helpful because, often, Nathan's improvements were so incremental they could be hard to detect on a daily basis.

Speech and Language

Speech has been the one area where Nathan has made steady, albeit slow, progress. This trend started when he was a baby and has continued all the way up to the present. Nathan said many words before he ever said *mom*; in fact, he said *chimpanzee* before he ever said *mom*. Frequently, Nathan responded with a new word when someone was reading him a book, showing him picture cards, or holding up word cards.

August 27, 1981

A few weeks ago, you said "puppies" very clearly when you were looking at a book about baby animals. You said puppies again yesterday. Nathan, you also said "bir" (bird) over and over while Kristen and I were looking at a bird book. I got very excited that you could say bird. You said bird many times before you went to bed.

September 3, 1981

You said "bull" after I said bull when I was showing you your word cards. You said "bloom" when I held up the word, bloom.

September 17, 1981

We got out your old books about dogs and you were so excited. It was like you were seeing old friends. You are trying to say "dog," except you start the word with a "b" sound.

The routine of the program also helped stimulate Nathan's speech development. He often used words to interact with us as we did the patterning exercises. Some of the phrases were tied to the repetitive activities we did, and other times he expressed his desires spontaneously.

September 24, 1981

Nathan, you are starting to be able to communicate a little what you want to do. When you want to go outside, you can say "outside." Several times, when coming down your crawling track, you have said, "ball" seeing the ball on the floor. You were saying to us, "I want to play ball when I get down the slide." Several times, you have asked to read a book by saying, "boo."

October 14, 1981

When Evelyn was here yesterday, I said, "Crawl and you can play with Evelyn." You said, "Ball, ball." (The week before you and Evelyn played ball together.)

March 23, 1981

Monday, this past week, you started saying "go" very clearly. We can count 1-2-3 and often you will say, "Go!" right before we start patterning you. We praise you bunches for saying "go" and you love it. Sometimes, you say "go" to get our attention.

Communicating with the patterners was an excellent format for facilitating language growth. Nathan would use speech to greet people and to say good-bye to them. The names of some of the patterners were a part of Nathan's early vocabulary. The interaction with all the volunteers who came to our home helped him become a very social person.

April 29, 1981

Monday, you were so happy to see everyone come to pattern. You repeated "Jim n Mary" and "Hi Frank" after you heard us greet the patterners. You smiled and laughed lots all through the day. Today, as each group left the house you said, "Hi da" for "bye-bye" and blew kisses to everyone.

May 22, 1981

Yesterday, when Daddy pulled up in the driveway, I said to you, "Nathan, listen, Daddy is pulling up in the driveway." You said, "Go, go, go, hi." To me it seemed as if you were in your own way saying, "Daddy is coming home in the truck and I want to see him."

August 27, 1981

The last few days, you seemed so much more aware of things, people, and situations. I have noticed that you start to say "bye-bye" even before people say bye-bye to you. Marge picked up her pocketbook today and you said bye-bye.

Motor Development

April 29, 1981

The Institutes gave us extremely high goals for your crawling and for your intelligence program during the last visit. It will take miracles from God for us to accomplish these goals. We know God can work these miracles. Daily, we must cry out to God asking Him to give us His power and His strength so we might reach our weekly goals. Yesterday, I thought I was going to crack up mentally and emotionally. Today, even though I slept very little last night, I am much more at ease. The pressure on Daddy and me is very great right now as we organize our new program for you.

Up until now, you have crawled in order to follow a toy. You use almost exclusively your arms. You like to pull up to the toy and put your mouth on the toy. Then we move the toy ahead of you a few inches and you pull up to the toy again. The only time you will use your legs along with your arms to crawl is when you are angry.

At this point, you don't realize you can crawl on your own to get things. So, we are working to teach you to crawl in order to obtain things you want. We have at least 8 crawling sessions a day lasting 15 minutes each. As you reach the session goal you receive a reward such as finger-painting, playing a drum, reading a book etc. Right now, I sit on the other side of the room encouraging you to reach your goal so you can receive the reward. In a sense, I am your own personal cheerleader as I say things like, "You can do it; you can do it! Go! Go! Go!" Oh, how I pray God will soon show you that you can crawl and you can move from point A to point B to get something you want.

The Institutes wants you crawling 300 feet by your July 13th appointment. Everyday, your crawling distance is increased and you are not to go to sleep until you have reached the daily goal. In the evening, we are to have you crawl down the inclined plane to make up the difference if you have not reached the goal for the day.

We must claim God's strength and power:

Jeremiah 32:27 "I am the Lord, the God of all mankind. Is anything too hard for me?"

Mark 10:27 "Jesus looked at them and said, 'With man this is impossible, but not with God; all things are possible with God."

Job 42:2 "I know that you can do all things; no plan of yours can be thwarted."

May 19, 1981

Nathan, your crawling on the floor up until a few days ago has been very good! Saturday you did not meet your goal, but Sunday you crawled 156 feet and met your goal. Sunday morning you moved 70 feet before 9:00am. You were very mad and you furiously moved your arms and legs as you crawled. However, yesterday and today have not gone so well. I feel very low inside right now so I am going to write what I feel now to God and perhaps I will regain a divine perspective.

Dear Heavenly Father,

I have been having such a difficult time emotionally since Saturday night. I can see many factors contributing to my emotional weakness—1. Pushing myself too hard last week 2. Not resting enough last week 3. Not getting out of the house enough for a change of pace 4. My time with you not being quality enough 5. The pressure of motivating Nathan to crawl.

Oh Father, I feel uneasy about Nathan's crawling. I am unsure about the way I have been trying to motivate him. I have been touching his body some to agitate him and I pull his arm out when he lays on it sometimes. I really don't know if I should do this! Also, yesterday I began to feel uneasy about using food to agitate Nathan into crawling. The food seems to work better for me than anything else, though.

Father, I acknowledge that Your wisdom is perfect. You know every possible way to motivate Nathan to crawl and You know the absolute best way to motivate him to crawl. According to James 1:5 and 6, You will give Bob and I wisdom with this concern, if we ask in faith. James 1:5-6 "If any of you lacks wisdom, he should ask God, who gives generously to all without finding fault, and it will be given to him. But when he asks, he must believe and not doubt, because he who doubts is like a wave of the sea, blown and tossed by the wind."

I am sitting here asking myself if I have doubts about You giving Bob and me this wisdom. I don't want to doubt, Father. I want to believe, with all my heart You will give us Your perfect wisdom. Father, the question comes to my mind, what if our techniques of trying to motivate Nathan don't change and/or his style of crawling doesn't change, do I say then the present techniques are the best? It seems according to these verses I must say yes.

June 6, 1981

Nathan, after crawling 200 ft. a few Sundays ago, you lost your zeal to crawl. We are calling the Institutes today and oh how I pray that they will know the right things for us to try. I have been praying God will give them wisdom in what to tell us.

June 7, 1981

Nathan, when we talked with the Institutes Wednesday night, we discussed your decreasing desire to crawl with Holly, your advocate. She said you should have to earn the privilege of the patterners talking with you, since you love to interact with your patterners. If you crawl, then they can talk with you. If you don't crawl, then they can't talk with you.

The next morning, we started the new reward system. It is going to take several days to see if this strategy will work. I am concerned that Daddy might not do the same thing I do concerning this. I am crying out to God to give us grace to be consistent.

Because of the increased demands of the program, I have not been able to rest much at all in the evenings. I have been making sentence cards, word cards, etc. upstairs while Daddy carries out your program downstairs. There are, also, other pressures, not pertaining to your program, I have been dealing with lately. By the end of this week, Daddy and I decided I needed to get away from the house to have an uninterrupted time of rest.

I am, now, at the Holiday Inn. I came early yesterday morning and I will go home today at noon. My time has been very relaxing. I am reading and meditating in God's Word. I went swimming yesterday afternoon and I will go again this morning. I ate supper last night at Belle's Restaurant. The atmosphere was beautiful and my meal was delicious. I had fried chicken, baked potato, green beans, tossed salad, and a blueberry muffin.

Nathan, several verses mean a lot to me today. In particular, Psalm 62:5-8 which says, "My soul, wait in silence for God only, for my hope is from Him. He only is my rock and my salvation, my stronghold; I shall not be shaken. On God my salvation and my glory rest; the rock of my strength, my refuge is in God. Trust in Him at all times, O people; pour out your heart before Him; God is a refuge for us."

Oh, Nathan, I must constantly pour out my heart to God about my concerns. He alone can make a difference in the situations I am concerned about and He alone can give me a divine perspective!

July 12, 1981

My dearest Nathan, things have changed a little today. We were supposed to go to the Institutes this weekend, but our trip was postponed because the Institutes want you to crawl 450 feet before you go for your appointment.

We also are working on getting you to crawl without us touching you. This is quite a task and we need to pray a lot. The next possible time we can go is August 10th. We need God to work a miracle with your crawling in order for you to reach your goal of 450 feet by then, with us not touching you. God is all-powerful though and He can do this in your life if He so pleases.

Last week, we gave you a party in honor of you exceeding your 300 feet goal. We invited all the neighbors who pattern and the people who pattern on Thursday night. We served homemade ice cream. Patty made vanilla, Jean made chocolate, and I made a special banana ice cream for you. Everyone had a good time, especially you.

August 2, 1981

Nathan, last weekend we went to the Mink's farm. We have gone there for the past three summers. We always have such a marvelous time—swimming, boating, walking, and looking at the horses, cattle, ducks and swans. We eat out some, which is a treat especially for me. The last 2 times, we have eaten at "Harbor's Landing" and we eat seafood, except for you. You eat something else because of the salt.

God is so good to have worked out these wonderful opportunities for us to go to the Mink's farm. Our visits there are always very, very relaxing for us. Each time, we make many special memories and take photos to remind us of these trips.

We are very excited tonight because you crawled 500 feet today. This is a new record for you! You are half way to our end goal of you crawling 1,000 feet in one day. Praise God, He is constantly pouring out His loving-kindness to us.

January 3, 1982

Nathan, I am praying hard God will enable you to start using your legs when you crawl. I am also praying you will start to use crawling for transportation: to take yourself from one room to another. You still don't realize you can use crawling to take you into the kitchen to see what Kristen is doing.

I have also been continuing to pray that you will sleep through the night. Now, you are sleeping many more nights straight through and so this is encouraging.

Birthday Letter

January 8, 1983

My dearest Nathan,

You celebrated your fourth birthday a few days ago on the 6th of January. We had a wonderful day on your birthday. We ended the day with your birthday party. Aunt Kathy, your cousin Joel, Ray (one of your patterners), his wife Lenora, and their daughter Debbie came for dinner. We had spaghetti, tossed salad, and French bread.

Aunt Kathy baked you a chocolate cake and iced it with chocolate icing. You love chocolate! When you were to blow out your candles, Sissy helped you. You cried a little, so we lit the candles again and you asked Joel to blow them out with you again.

After eating cake and ice cream, you opened your presents. You received all books, which you so dearly love. Blanch sent books. Ray's family, Aunt Kathy and Grandmamma gave you books too. Then Ray, accompanied by his sound track presented a birthday concert to you. You sang your heart out along with him. Oh, what a good time we all had.

Nathan, I also want to tell you about a very special Christmas present you gave us on the 22nd of December. On this day, you were sitting on my lap at the kitchen counter. You had just finished your crawling session and your reward for meeting the session goal was to color with Kristen's crayons. I wrapped your fingers around the crayon and then I wrapped my hand over your hand so that the crayon would be positioned straight up. I asked you to make dots and then straight lines. While you made straight lines, I happened to ask you if you could make the numeral 2. You immediately made a 2. I proceeded to ask you to make other numerals, which you did. When we reached 10, I began to cry tears of joy. We continued on to the numeral 20. You made each number correctly. I was so excited I thought I was going to go "through the ceiling!"

After your nap, I decided I would see if you could write words. For the first word I asked you to write, I dictated each letter to you. However, for the second word I asked you to write, I didn't dictate the letters and you spelled the word correctly. Every word I asked you to write you spelled 100 percent correctly!

That evening, I called several of my friends to tell them what I witnessed you do. Not since I heard I was carrying you and your brother Seth in my womb, have I experienced such an intense excitement and joy. Both times, I realized that the events were brought about by my Heavenly Father.

Since that day, we have had you write many different words. So, for example, if it is a word you have had on a word card, you have spelled the word correctly 100 percent of the time. Words you have not had on a card, it seems that you try to spell them phonetically.

We have placed objects in front of you and asked you to count them and write down the answer. You have done this perfectly so far. As well, we have asked you to write down the answers to different questions. I asked you to write the name of your favorite color and you wrote blue. I asked you what your favorite thing to drink is and you wrote juice.

What a very special Christmas gift to find out that our four-year-old brain injured son can not only read, but spell, write, and do basic math. Thank you, Nathan, for showing us this. We are so very proud of you.

Love,
Momma

Last Trip to the Institutes

February 1, 1983

My dearest Nathan, it is time for us to make our last trip to the Institutes. This visit will mark the end of our initial commitment. Daddy and I do not plan to sign up for another stint. You have accomplished level 1, which is crawling 1,000 feet in one day. Also, you have worked your way up to crawling 1,000 feet in one day on carpet. Now, with level 2, you are having great difficulty crawling over obstacles with your arms and legs behind you. If you used your legs to help push yourself over, there would be more hope for us that you could learn to creep up on your hand and knees in the near future. Then, maybe Daddy and I would consider continuing on with the Institutes.

However, at this point, Daddy and I plan to work with you on our own, using the patterning program. This way, we can move at our own pace. The intensity of working with the Institutes has been very exhausting for us.

CHAPTER 5

Burnout

Day after Returning from the Institutes

To my surprise, the day after we arrived back from our last trip to the Institutes, I awakened feeling emotionally exhausted. I cried off and on all day long. The next day, I thought I would be all right, but I cried off and on all day long that day too. Day after day, I cried and poured my heart out to God as I wrote in my prayer journal.

February 28, 1983

Dear Father, oh how I love You and I need You so very much. I do not know how to cope with what has happened to me gradually over the past months. Ever since we have been doing the program from the Institutes, I have had periodic crying spells. I think the crying may be a result of the intense pressure which comes with the program. As the months progressed closer to the last visit to the Institutes, my times of crying grew closer together. One Thursday morning Glena, one of the patterners, questioned whether Nathan was really doing the writing when I had my hand over his hand to hold the marker. After this conversation, I cried the whole morning. In fact, I was still crying when Glen, Priscilla, and Jean arrived to help with the next patterning session.

I felt tears behind my eyes the week prior to the Institute's and I knew that I needed to have a hard cry so I would be somewhat on even keel when we arrived at the Institutes. When I was watching the Waltons on television and I saw Mary Ellen in labor with her baby, the tears began to flow. I cried through the whole show. There was a woman on the show whose baby died and she kidnapped Mary Ellen's baby. This hit me very hard.

Now, here I am back from the Institute's and I cry almost every time I talk with someone. I think I partly understand what is wrong with me, but perhaps there is far more which I don't understand. I think I have pushed so hard with Nathan's program that I am all pushed out. I have talked and explained with so many people that now I am all talked out. I can hardly bear the thought of talking with people, especially about the program. I guess I have or perhaps I should say I am experiencing burnout!!

How do I get over this, Father? Will I ever be a stable person emotionally again? Will I always have to guard myself emotionally, constantly measuring out how much I'm giving of myself? Before the trip to the Institute's, I felt I was fighting to keep what was left of my slight emotional reserves. Now, I feel as if I don't have any emotional reserves left.

Ever since my second pregnancy and delivery, I seem to have a particular emotional fragileness. I think this is contributed to by the stress of the possible danger before delivery, the fact one son died, and then six months later we realized something was wrong with Nathan. O Father, that was four years ago and the pain is still so great! Perhaps the pain is more intense because I have pushed myself so very hard to work with Nathan. I do not think bitter thoughts about these events. I acknowledge Your right to bring these events to be or to allow them to be, whichever the case may be. In the midst of the pain of Seth's death, coupled with dealing with the pain related to Nathan's brain injury, I will give thanks to You. I know you are accomplishing many great things through Seth's death and Nathan's brain injury.

Yet, I am sitting here wondering if I will ever be emotionally strong again. I want to be stronger; I'm asking You to make me stronger. I am going to thank you in the midst of all my tears, but also I'm pleading with You to give me strength!

I don't know enough of what to do to help make myself stronger. Please show me. Ideas are coming to my mind.

1. *Review Scripture.*
2. *Listen to the Christian radio station music.*
3. *Listen to Christian tapes.*
4. *Have a lot more time by myself (I need more ideas of how to do this . . . Turn the phone off? What if Kristen needs me?*
5. *I think I need a variety of activities (decorating Kristen's doll house, painting my house walls and doorknobs)*
6. *Ask some of my close friends to pray for me.*
7. *Stop drinking coffee, tea, etc. for now.*
8. *Cut way back on sugar. Try to eat lots of protein.*

9. *Start going through my prayer cards again.*
10. *Watch less television*
12. *Memorize new verses (Perhaps Psalm 61:2-4)*

Psalm 61:2-4

"From the end of the earth I call to you when my heart is faint;
Lead me to the rock that is higher than I.
For You have been a refuge for me,
A tower of strength against the enemy,
Let me dwell in Your tent forever,
Let me take refuge in the shelter of Your wings."

Bottoming Out

No matter where I was, when someone asked me the question "How are you?" I would burst into tears. My first Sunday back to church, our family was talking with our pastor in the foyer of the church. We were one of the last families leaving that day. When our pastor shook my hand and said, "How are you?" I burst into tears. Another Sunday morning, Terry E., a friend who helped make visuals for Nathan, was talking with me in the church kitchen. When she said, "How are you?" I burst into tears.

Whenever I went to a shopping mall, I kept an eye open for people I knew. If I saw someone from a distance, I headed in the opposite direction to avoid talking. I never knew whether I might start crying if I entered into a conversation.

I was unable to talk more than a few minutes on the phone without crying. We purchased an answering machine so I would not have to answer the phone. For several years after this, whenever I needed to call someone back, I'd call them five minutes before Kristen was to come home. I did this so I would not talk longer than five minutes. If I talked longer, I often felt emotional fatigue.

A Yearning

I yearned for something to do that was fun, a beautiful experience to lift me up from the darkness of the burnout pit. This yearning became very evident to me one day when I was standing in the kitchen talking with my friend Priscilla about her upcoming wedding plans. Priscilla was a young nurse we got to know through her coming to our house to pattern Nathan. She became a friend to our entire family. She frequently brought books and other gifts for

Kristen and Nathan. One time, Priscilla took Kristen and me as her guests to see a ballet, *Cinderella*.

During the time she was coming to our house to help with Nathan's program, Priscilla met her future husband. Each time I saw Priscilla, I loved hearing about how her relationship with Don was developing. I was thrilled when she told me Don had proposed and she said yes.

On this particular day in the kitchen, I asked Priscilla if she had chosen her bridal attendants. After she finished naming her attendants, I began to cry uncontrollably. Without realizing it, I had hoped she would want me to be one of her attendants.

In my early twenties, I had been a bridesmaid in three different weddings. I loved going to bridal showers and luncheons and helping my friends in whatever way I could with their wedding preparations. Over a period of months, there's a lot to do from the fitting of the dress to the activities of the wedding day. If I had been one of Priscilla's attendants, I would have had a few months to focus on a happy, joyous occasion. I stood there, caught off guard by this desire, unable to talk, unable to explain my tears.

A Broken Dream:

At this moment, it was as if I was looking down at the floor and *seeing the garment of my personhood cut into pieces*. I did not know how many pieces were barely hanging on and how many pieces were lying on the floor. I did not know if I ever would feel like my old self again, emotionally whole and stable.

Would I ever be able to talk with my friends without crying? Would I ever be a vibrant wife again to my husband, Bob? Psalm 32:4b expresses how I felt, "My vitality was drained away as with the fever heat of summer." How did I get to this point? My plummet into burnout was not just a result of my efforts to help Nathan.

The first few years of working with Nathan were therapeutic for me; I was doing something to make a positive difference in his life. I enjoyed interacting with the patterners as we worked with Nathan. Then with the last couple of years of working with Nathan, I progressively found the demands of the program harder and harder. Simultaneously, I was dealing with responsibilities not related to the program.

My Personal Life

My father died several months before I met Bob. My mother moved to Roanoke when Nathan was one year old because she wanted to live closer to my sister and me. In fact, she moved only four blocks from us. Mama living this close allowed her to help us at our house, therefore making it easier for me to focus on Nathan. I do not have any brothers, but I do have one sister, Kathy, whom I love dearly. She and her husband, Danny, have one son, Joel, who is about eight months older than Nathan. Even though my family is not very large, we are close and really enjoy doing things together. In fact, my nephew, Joel, grew up almost like a sibling to my children rather than just a cousin. Saturday, in particular, was when we would usually get to spend time together. Bob was able to stay home with Nathan and oversee the patterning sessions so we could go out. We would take my mother with us and do things like roller-skating, swimming, and going to the park.

Throughout the patterning years, I put a lot of energy into parenting Kristen. Several nights a week, I read to her before she went to sleep. We read books like the *Bobbsey Twins* and *Winnie the Pooh*. Once a week, I walked her one block over to the Grandin Court Recreation Center to take tap and ballet lessons. Also, Kristen enjoyed taking art classes from several different teachers. As well, I planned playdates with her friends. I strove to consistently discipline Kristen when she disobeyed and/or had a bad attitude. Also, I worked hard to regularly affirm her when she obeyed and/or had a good attitude. These affirmations included hugs, kisses, and verbal praise.

My Church Life

My church life gradually became a source of stress instead of a refuge. Somewhere in the middle of the patterning years, the senior pastor of our church experienced a period of emotional struggles resulting in him taking a sabbatical. During this time, I was concerned about his total well-being and that of his family.

Our senior pastor and his wife had been spiritual mentors for me starting back to my single days as a high school teacher. It was through our pastor's teaching I learned about the wonderful attributes, or characteristics, of God. Knowing God is sovereign, nothing happens outside of His control, and knowing God's love for me is unconditional has been a continuous help to me in dealing with difficult circumstances in life.

Through my interactions with our senior pastor's wife, Carol, I began to contemplate, as a young single woman, the beauty of Christian femininity. I loved her enthusiasm for all she did. For example, the way she decorated her home and the way she interacted with her young sons.

After our senior pastor had come back from his sabbatical, we received a letter in the mail from our associate pastor telling us he was resigning. He resigned without, yet, having another church where he was going to be employed. Getting this news was very hard for me emotionally. Our associate pastor conducted the funeral service for Seth, and he was one of the first people to volunteer to help pattern Nathan.

The next evening after we received this letter, I went to church. As I entered the back of the church, the first hymn was being sung. I thought, "How can the people of our church sing when we have lost one of our beloved pastors?" The emotional pain I felt was similar to the pain one feels when a loved one has died. I was unable to stay; I turned around and walked out of the room.

In the months that followed, several families progressively left the church fellowship. When it was a close friend of mine who left, I felt like I was being abandoned and grieved the loss. After experiencing many of these smaller losses, I experienced a permanent loss.

I received a phone call telling me my dear friend, Catherine, had been in a car accident. We had been close friends throughout high school and college. I was even a bridesmaid in her wedding. Every few years, we got together in our hometown. In between those times, we kept up with each other through Christmas newsletters.

Not only did I find out Catherine had been killed in the car accident, but also all three of her children and both of her in-laws lost their lives! The only survivor from the car accident was Catherine's husband. I poured my heart out to God as I wrote in my prayer journal.

October 19, 1982

I couldn't go today, Father, to the funeral home to see Catherine's parents and brothers. I felt that going to the funeral service would throw me over the edge of the narrow emotional line I operate on a daily basis. It seems I have been barely hanging on emotionally for such a long time. I guess it started when I was pregnant, but the intensity of my emotional tightrope came when I delivered my twins. By your grace, Father, I have continued to carry out my responsibilities at home. Also, I have come to know You in a more intimate way.

CHAPTER 6

Help Is Coming

Our senior pastor moved to North Carolina to pastor another church. Dr. H became our interim pastor. He drove into Roanoke every Sunday from Lynchburg, where he lived and worked at Liberty University. Once a pastor, he now was a counselor. His sermons from the book of James were so encouraging and comforting to me. I so wished he could be our full-time, permanent pastor.

One Sunday night, I lingered after the service hoping I could speak to Dr. H. As I reached out to shake his hand, he asked, "How are you?" I burst into tears. One of the deacons saw me crying. He directed us out into the hall and then into a small Sunday school room.

It was very hard to tell him about my last pregnancy: how I prayed for twins, how God answered my prayers, and how, when I delivered, one baby was stillborn and the other baby was brain injured. I told him about the intense stimulation program we had done with Nathan. I shared with him that ever since we came back from our last trip to the Institutes, I cry every day.

As I talked, I would get one sentence out and then stop to cry. When I stopped crying, I would begin again until I needed to stop and cry. When I finished, Dr. H gave me his phone number and asked me to make an appointment to come and see him at his office at the university. Dr. H said, "You have pushed your body *beyond* what it was designed to do, but I believe I can help you."

I went home and shared with Bob this conversation. However, he was not very eager for me to go see Dr. H since he was not exactly sure what he thought about the practice of counseling. For this reason, I did not call to make an appointment. A few weeks later, one of the elders, a long-time friend, called me up and said, "Judy, Dr. H says he has not heard from you." It was not until this happened that Bob agreed to go with me to see him. With Bob there beside me, I shared my entire story with the counselor. At the end of the counseling session, Dr. H said to me, "Judy, have you ever heard of stress management?" I replied, "No." Then he told me to go home and read as much as I could on stress management.

My Research

The next day, I went to the library and looked up books on stress management and left carrying a huge stack of books home to read. As I read the books, I began to understand more about what had happened to me. In one of the books on burnout, Dr. F shares about his own experience with burnout. His story helped me see what had happened to me after we arrived back home from our last trip to the Institutes.

Dr. F worked during the day with his private practice, and at night, he volunteered at a free clinic. He had not taken a break from his work in a very long time. Finally, he agreed to go on a vacation. He went to sleep the night before he was to leave and slept for the next forty-eight hours straight. After this happened to him, he began to analyze the factors that brought about this response in his body. He discovered that when people push, push, push and then stop abruptly, strange things can happen to their bodies.

After I read this story, I began to analyze the physical manifestations of burnout. Dr. F slept for forty-eight hours. For me, I started crying uncontrollably. Another person I know lost her ability to walk for a while. I questioned why these things happened.

When one keeps pushing and pushing, a lot of adrenaline is used. The adrenal gland is the "fight or flight" gland. Its hormones are always released when we are under stress. After periods of chronic stress, one's adrenaline can become depleted. This can have very serious consequences like extreme fatigue and more vulnerability to depression and mood swings.

While patterning Nathan, I was, in a sense, fighting to build up Nathan's good brain cells to take over for his dead brain cells. With the day-after-day cheering on of Nathan to motivate him to reach his many goals, my body had an ongoing release of adrenaline. In the process of trying to help Nathan build up his good brain cells, I threw off the chemical balance in my own brain by using up so much adrenaline. The chemical imbalance in my brain contributed to the uncontrollable crying spells and the depression. When there was no more pressure to push, push, push in order to accomplish the high goals of the program, I bottomed out with adrenal fatigue. The adrenaline I needed in order to function was not there, and the effect was devastating. Instead of having sporadic crying spells and occasional depression, I was crying off and on all day—*every day*! I now realized what had happened to me, but I did not know how to recover.

The Nehemiah Approach

One day, in the midst of reading the books from the library, I heard a radio program that intrigued me. I listened intently to the woman on the radio as I was walking up the stairs to the second floor of our house. She was talking about the prophet Nehemiah and how he approached the rebuilding of the wall around Jerusalem. When I reached my bedroom, I sat down on the edge of my bed and continued to listen. As I heard the speaker describe how the wall around Jerusalem was in ruin and how the people were in great distress, I thought, "That sounds like my life."

I knew I was in great distress. No matter where I was or with whom I was talking to, the questions "How are you?" or "How is Nathan?" would trigger a flow of uncontrollable tears. Proverbs 25:28 described my condition, "Like the city that is broken into and without walls is a man who has no control over his spirits."

In chapter 2 verse 17, Nehemiah presents a plan to his people. He said, "You see the bad situation we are in, that Jerusalem is desolate and its gates burned by fire. Come let us rebuild the wall of Jerusalem that we may no longer be in reproach." As I studied Nehemiah, I began to get a basic plan for my recovery from burnout. The plan combined what I had learned about stress management with the principles I gleaned from Nehemiah's approach to rebuilding the wall around Jerusalem. I wanted to rebuild the wall of my life so I would no longer be in reproach.

I wanted my life to be like a fortified city as spoken of in Jeremiah 1:18-19. "Now behold, I have made you today a fortified city and as a pillar of iron and as walls of bronze against the whole land . . . They will fight against you, but they will not overcome you, for I am with you to deliver you, declares the Lord."

Sitting at my writing desk, I drew a large circle in the middle of a piece of paper. The circumference of the circle represented the size of my emotional capacity, and the space inside the circle corresponded to my emotional reserves, which are fluid. My emotional reserves are connected with my having joy in the Lord, zest for living, creativity, and physical energy. To indicate the various components of my life, I drew smaller circles around the larger circle. By labeling each of the smaller circles, I identified all the responsibilities in my life that required my emotional reserves. How far each smaller circle overlapped into the big circle was determined by how much of my emotional reserves I gave to that area of my life.

The first thing I noticed was that Nathan's circle came really far over into my emotional reserves! I realized I needed to set some boundaries so that I would not be giving such a large amount of my emotional energy and time in helping him. In a sense, I felt it was necessary to move his circle further outward. Also, I discovered that with some responsibilities, even though I was not giving a lot of time to them, they were still requiring a lot of emotional energy. Drawing this diagram helped me recognize there were also other areas of my life that were using up too much of my emotional reserves.

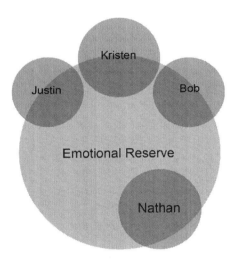

Just as Nehemiah examined the ruined wall of Jerusalem, I prayed around the ruined wall of my life, asking God to give me wisdom as to how to rebuild the wall of my life. I asked him to show me what changes I needed to make in order to restore my emotional reserves. One of the first changes I made was to drop the Friday afternoon patterning session.

Opposition to Rebuilding

Just as Nehemiah encountered much opposition from his enemies as he rebuilt the wall, I encountered opposition as I worked on rebuilding my life. Where did my opposition come from? It came from two different directions: from outside of myself and from inside of myself. However, I realized that any opposition ultimately came from Satan. He is the enemy. He did not want me to rebuild the wall of my life; he wanted me to remain in reproach!

Sometimes, it was hard for me to get the courage to tell certain people that I wanted to do things a different way or not at all. I had trouble knowing exactly how to express myself. Also, I had difficulty when I encountered negative response from some people as I began to make certain changes in my life.

An example of this is when my aunt was visiting my mom. An all-day outing was planned that involved a lot of driving. When I told my aunt that I was not joining the group for the day, she was not happy and responded, "Why not?" I said, "I believe an all-day event may be too tiring for me." With an attitude of "shame on you," my aunt said, "I am 70 years old. If I can do this trip, you can too!" This demonstrates an occurrence of an outside pressure.

I did not go on the trip, but it was difficult for me to emotionally handle my aunt's negative response. As I compared myself with my aunt, I thought, "I should have more energy. I am a lot younger than my aunt and in relatively good health." Comparing myself with other women almost always led to discouragement. This was a common type of internal pressure for me.

To get help with how to handle these types of situations, I went back to my counselor one hour away in Lynchburg. Dr. H directed me to work on being more assertive. So once again, I went to the library. This time, I was looking for books on the subject of assertiveness. As I read the books, my goal was to learn how to be more graciously assertive.

Studying Psalm 139 helped me combat my tendency to compare myself with others. I realized that just as God uniquely designed my physical makeup, he also uniquely designed my emotional makeup. God impressed upon me: First, I need to remind myself that each woman's emotional capacity is uniquely created by Him, just as hair color, eye color, height, etc., are uniquely created by Him. Second, the demands made on each woman's emotional reserves vary as does the level of her emotional reserves at any given time. And lastly, it would be unwise for me to compare myself with other women. I need to prayerfully make choices as to what I can or cannot do based on the level of my emotional reserves.

Another opposition to my "recovery" was the habit of negative self-talk. When I experienced relapses, I tended to say to myself, "You failed, you can't do it, why even try?" I knew Satan would be delighted for me to forsake the rebuilding of the wall of my life. Instead of succumbing to this negative self-talk, I learned to prayerfully regroup. I did this by resting, evaluating what to do differently, and then making the necessary changes to keep on keeping on.

Also, another thing I learned in my research is that there are two kinds of stressors: both positive and negative. Positive stressors can be events like birthday celebrations and holidays. They are usually happy, but they take a lot of energy to plan and to execute. In our family, birthdays come every few weeks starting after Christmas until the end of February. Negative stressors—death of loved ones, illnesses of children, car accidents, etc.—require significant energy to deal with their ramifications.

Often, negative stressors just come and one cannot stop them. However, I can strive to space the activities I choose to do in a way that allows me to have more time to regroup between them. By doing this, I will have more emotional reserves to deal with the negative stressors that I cannot control. Also, I made myself a worksheet that helped me think through possible solutions to certain stressors in my life. Later, I ended up using this worksheet as well as the circle diagram when I taught stress management seminars.

CHAPTER 7

A Time of Joy

Yearning Fulfilled

In June 1983, I realized I was pregnant for the third time. I was very happy about my pregnancy. Bob was delighted also. I had something happy to focus on—getting ready for our new baby. I was experiencing an emotional springtime just four months after I had bottomed out with fatigue and depression.

We decided not to announce that I was pregnant until the end of the first trimester. Bob and I wanted to cover the first three months of my pregnancy in prayer, just the two of us. We knew most miscarriages happen in the first trimester.

Early in my pregnancy, I found the name Zachary in my name book. *Zachary* means "whom Jehovah remembers." My prayer was that God would remember my baby in a very special way—that my baby would be born alive and healthy and that he would have a heart for God as he grew.

To celebrate our ninth anniversary, Bob and I were able to get away, just the two of us, for a few days. We traveled to North Carolina for a complimentary stay at a time-share resort. Our vacation was filled with swimming, boating, hiking, sightseeing, and eating dinner by candlelight. While we were gone, Jerry, one of our patterners, kept Nathan at her house. She took such good care of him. Nathan had a great time interacting with Jerry's three children. Kristen stayed the first few days with one of our patterners, Jan, who pampered her like a princess, and then the last few days, she stayed with the family of her friend Katie.

When school started, we continued on with Nathan's patterning program. However, since I was pregnant, I made changes whenever and wherever needed.

One change was that on Thursdays, I did not have any patterners come to the house; I used this day to do creative sewing projects. Thursday was now my favorite day of the week! On the other days of the week, I enjoyed being able to share my happy news with each patterner that came to our house.

In preparation for our new baby, we moved Kristen into the room that was our study; we moved Nathan from the nursery into Kristen's old room. We bought a secondhand trundle bed and red rug for Nathan's new room. Using fabric remnants I already had and also newly purchased calico print fabric, I made a patchwork round tablecloth to go on a bedside table. I also made a co-coordinating pillow and wall hanging. Nathan's new room was bright and cheerful. If we had a baby boy, he would eventually sleep in the other bed.

Kristen's new room had a pale blue, pale pink and white color scheme. So I made a special pillow to go on Kristen's bed, out of pink and white gingham-check fabric with a counted cross-stitch insert with her name stitched in the center and then underneath that was the meaning of her name. I trimmed the pillow with white eyelet lace. For the nursery, I made fabric balloons of different bright colors like ones I had seen in a very nice baby store. I hung them on the wall next to the baby bed.

During the fall, I was a helper, one night a week with a group Kristen was in called Pioneer Girls, which is a little bit like the Girl Scouts. Every week, I looked forward to going to the Wednesday-night meeting with Kristen. It was great fun to do the crafts and to sing the songs with the girls in the group. I occasionally taught the Bible lesson. I laughed a lot with the girls and the other leaders.

During my pregnancy, I was much more even emotionally, but I did have a few times of plunging downward. One of those times was when Bob and I took a refresher course in Lamaze childbirth. The first night of classes, we were asked to share about our previous deliveries. When it came to our turn, I began to weep. I went to the bathroom to work on regaining my composure. The assistant instructor came in to talk with me. While we were in the bathroom, Bob told about our last delivery.

After this happened to me, I went out to dinner with a friend, Sharon, who also had a baby die. I shared with Sharon my upcoming concerns, and she understood because she gave birth again after losing her previous baby. We discussed our feelings. I asked Sharon to pray for me and my unborn baby that the delivery would be safe. The reality of having a baby die or a baby to have problems was ever so real to me.

Another difficult time for me was when the school board of our church's day school was in the process of reconstructing the school budget for the current year. There was deep concern over the financial status of the school. In many ways, I felt like the school was one of my children. To see it struggle was like seeing one of my children struggle. This was because I had prayed for the conception of the school, along with several other women. After the school was established, we continued to meet and pray for the school to have healthy growth.

During the middle of the school year, the headmaster position was eliminated. A dear friend of mine had held this position. He and his wife had been good friends of mine since right after our college years. I understood that there was a need to adjust the school's budget, but it was very hard for me to deal with the emotional ramifications of the decision made by the school board.

In the midst of this same period, our church was searching for a senior pastor. One of the potential candidates for this position was someone I knew personally. He and his wife, Betsy, had been very close friends of mine since our college days. I had been a bridesmaid in their wedding. As I considered that my friend might be called to be our pastor, I could not bear the thought of possible future events or circumstances related to our church in which he and his wife might experience duress. I was unable, emotionally, to talk with my friends about my concerns. But I did fast and pray fervently, asking God to only allow my friend to be our church's senior pastor if it was His direct will. Our church did not call him.

As the time of my delivery drew nearer, Bob and I still had not settled on a boy's name. We had chosen Megan Ann for a girl's name. *Megan* means "strong," *Ann* means "grace." So for us, the name Megan Ann would mean "strong by the grace of God." Zachary, being a three-syllable name, was really too long to go with Rossbacher, and we did not want to shorten the name to Zach.

One day, when we were driving home after eating Sunday dinner at a restaurant, I said, "This morning I found another boy's name I like in the name book. It is Justin, which means 'righteous and just.'" Immediately, I heard Bob, Kristen, and Nathan say, "We like it!"

One of the patterners, Jerry, who had become such a good friend to our entire family, had a son named Ty. She told us that she and her husband used the meaning "pure" for Ty's name. Their son, Ty, had a winsome personality and a temperament I was drawn to. So we chose Ty as a middle name to go with Justin.

I WAS HAPPY WHEN MY BABY BROTHER, JUSTIN, WAS BORN.

Justin's birth came at a special time for our family. While I was cutting the cake for Kristen's lunchtime birthday party at school, I felt the first strong labor contraction. Before I left the school, I called Bob and asked him to meet me at home.

When Bob arrived, I told him my contractions were coming hard and heavy five minutes or less apart. So Bob called the doctor and we left the house around 4 o'clock in the afternoon. We entered the birthing room around five o'clock, and at 6:11, Justin Ty Rossbacher was born weighing in at nine pounds even. Eight years before, on the same date, February 15, I had given birth to our daughter, Kristen Lynne Rossbacher, at 2:00 a.m.

Bob was with me the whole time just as he had been when Kristen was born. Not only was Bob a wonderful coach, but our nurses, Betsy and Betty, were also absolutely terrific. They held my hand while Bob rewet the washcloth to place on my forehead. They cheered me on when it was time for me to push. In appreciation, we sent them flowers the next day.

After Justin popped out and my doctor caught him and cut the umbilical cord, I immediately wanted to know how he was. Was he breathing? Did he have all his body parts? When Justin was put into my arms, I felt like having a big party! Bob and I started calling our friends and relatives, telling them our good news. In the midst of our celebrating, I looked over to Bob and the nurses and said, "I would like to do this one more time." Still firmly fixed in my heart and mind was my desire to raise four children.

Two days after Justin's birth, I wrote the following in my journal in prayer while I was in the hospital:

February 17, 1984

Oh Father, how I praise you that Justin was born safely and that he is such a healthy baby. I do not take Justin for granted at all. I praise you and thank you so much for saying yes to my prayers. You have blessed me with a wonderful, sensitive, loving husband and three beautiful sweet children.

Psalm 146:1-2 Praise the Lord! Praise the Lord, oh my soul! I will praise the Lord while I live, I will sing praises to my God while I have my being.

Justin at Home

In retrospect, I believe God gave me the name Zachary early in my pregnancy to encourage me that He was remembering my baby in a special way. Then near the time of my baby's birth, God gave me the name Justin Ty to describe the type of character my son would have as he grew older: righteous, just, and pure.

Justin's birth ushered summertime into my life. I am not talking about a literal summertime because he was born in February, a winter month. I am talking about an emotional heartfelt summer.

The next few months were great for me with Justin. I felt better than I had in five years. When people who did not know me saw me with Justin, they thought he was my first baby. I think they thought this because of the way I glowed when I showed him off. I loved singing to Justin when I nursed him, gave him his bath, and changed his diaper. While rocking him, I received so much pleasure looking into his beautiful eyes. Also, when I attended the festivals we are famous for here in Roanoke, I really enjoyed carrying Justin in the front-pack carrier. As I walked around, I was thrilled to introduce him to people I knew. I experienced what Proverbs 15:30 talks about when it says, "Bright eyes gladden the heart and good news puts fat on the bones."

Judy holding 4 month old Justin

CHAPTER 8

Winter Returns

Downward Spiral for Me

Summer 1984

My emotional summertime started to disappear in the middle of June; this was because I began to focus once again on how to best help Nathan. I was very aware of the reality that I could not work as intensely with Nathan as I had prior to my burnout in February 1983. Yet I did want to give a certain amount of time and energy to help Nathan be able to hold a full quadruped position. His achievement of this developmental position was a prerequisite for later learning how to creep up on his hands and knees.

However, the pieces of equipment we needed to use in facilitating this next level of development were very large in size and would not fit in our dining room. Plus, I was eager to have my dining room back for family meals and entertaining. I thought I could better continue or resume Nathan's therapy/patterning program if it was not carried out in the main part of our living area. As well, we knew that as Nathan's body grew, there would come a time when Bob could not carry Nathan upstairs to sleep at night. We prayed to God asking Him if we should begin building the addition soon.

As the summer progressed, I found that the harder I worked on plans for Nathan's stimulation program, the more winter crept back into my life. I was crying at unexpected times. A gray cloud seemed to be pushing in on me. I was in an emotional wintertime. I poured my heart out to God in my prayer journal.

August 12, 1984

Dear God, what are we going to do with Nathan? Are the results of my efforts of laboring with Nathan significant enough to merit that I keep on giving of my emotional, mental, and physical energies? Can I keep asking people to help me if Nathan is not going to move upward with his gross motor development?

Father, you know how much I have prayed about this all summer. I have been praying around myself and around Nathan, as if we are two separate circles that intersect each other. How much should our 2 circles interlock?

For months, I have been asking You to lead me in how I can best help Nathan and yet be an emotionally stable person at the same time. I want to be able to minister to my entire family! Sometimes, I think I have it almost together—how I am going to continue patterning Nathan, and then I am so unsure of myself. I told Bob this morning that I can't live with myself if I stop working with Nathan and I presently cannot live with myself working with him. Father, this situation is very discouraging for me.

I have worked all summer trying to get Nathan to hold a good modified quadruped position. This position involves him leaning back on his haunches and pushing his torso up with his arms straight out. When one method did not work, I tried another. But I still have not attained getting Nathan to hold a good modified quad position. This is important because being able to hold a full quad position is a prerequisite to Nathan learning how to creep up on his hands and knees.

With the Institutes' methods the mother is usually the key person. Here I am Nathan's mother, so very weak. If I push really hard, I will be back to where I was a year and a half ago—severely burned out. I cannot set myself up for this to happen to me again, Father. I realize my emotional reserves should be used wisely just like money and time should be.

Father, do you want Nathan to go to a public school with a special education class? Do you want him in school this fall and then resume his stimulation program when we have finished building his room? Bob and I feel you are leading us to start building the addition very soon. Perhaps by the time the addition is finished, I will feel like resuming Nathan's program.

August 13, 1984

Dearest Father, over the summer I have become increasingly aware that we need to do something different with Nathan this fall. At first, I thought a special education class within the city school system was our only option.

This morning while I was talking on the phone with Kris I said, "If I could have what I really want, it would be to have Nathan in a regular kindergarten and have an aide to help him. Saying this set me off to pursue this direction.

Lord, I do believe you gave me the idea of looking into Nathan being a part of our church's preschool program. When I called Cindy, the teacher of the class, this morning, she said my idea would work as long as Nathan had his own aide to help him. When I talked with Bruce, the school administrator, he thought it would work also. He suggested I contact Gina, a college age young woman he knew, about the position of being Nathan's personal aide.

Also, I believe you gave me the idea of calling the adult education department of the City School System to the see if there was a Home Economics course I could teach in the evenings. The Home Economics adult education co-coordinator told me that the person who was scheduled to teach an eight-week interior design class in the fall recently said she was no longer available. Also she said that the course description listing this woman as the teacher had already been sent to the newspaper. But the coordinator told me if enough people sign up for the class by the deadline I could be the instructor.

The subject matter of the course is perfect for me. Recently, while I was in a nearby fabric shop, I noticed two women looking for fabrics to go with several paintings they were carrying. The women appeared to be interior decorators. I came home that day and told Bob I thought it might be fun for me to work part time in something related to interior decorating.

CHAPTER 9

Up and Down

I WENT TO PRESCHOOL AT MY CHURCH. GINA AND NANCY HELPED ME. MY DAD STARTED BUILDING A NEW ROOM FOR ME.

Nathan was moving out of the world of the patterning room into the world of a regular preschool. This new world was ideal for him at this point in his life. The stimulation of being with the other children was great for Nathan's overall development.

During this time, he was no longer in the umbrella stroller but rather in a travel safety chair. This was a little bit more like a wheelchair, but the back wheels were retractable. This allowed us to put him in the backseat of the car while he was still in his chair. Then to secure him, all we had to do was put the seatbelt over him and the chair.

Also, as Nathan was exploring preschool, I was moving from the patterning room into the beautiful world of interior design. This new world was ideal for me at this season of my life. The stimulation of preparing for my teaching opportunity was great for my overall development.

In fact, that fall of 1984 proved to be eventful for our entire family! The same week that Nathan began preschool, Bob started working on building the addition and I began preparing for my interior design class. Also, Justin reached quite a few motor developmental milestones. For the first several months, I kept a record of many of our endeavors in a letter to Nathan.

My Dearest Nathan,

We have all been very busy! Daddy cut down several bushes in the yard. He also marked off the footers for the addition, which will be your future room. Your baby brother, Justin, can stand himself up if he holds on to something. And you did something new: you crawled over to the bathroom door and exclaimed, "bathroom, bathroom!" When I opened the door, you crawled over to the commode and asked to get on by saying, "that-on!"

Each day I pick you up from preschool, Gina, your aide, shares various tidbits with me. I think you are making friends! For example, I learned that one of your classmates Hannah sometimes stands next to you and whispers in your ear. Also, one day a little boy, named Jaime, put a truck in your lap and told the other children not to touch the toy because it was just for you.

I think you really enjoy going to preschool, Nathan. Daddy and I have noticed your whole disposition changes from negative to positive on days that you go to school. Often when I pick you up, you tell me you have colored when you get in the car. Once, you moved your arms around and licked your fingers to show me how you had finger painted with pudding.

Dad has been working on the floor of the addition. I have been studying and preparing to teach my Interior Design class. You continue to blossom at school. One day, I asked you who held the flag and you said, "me." You, also, had a chance to be the line leader! I know because I saw Hannah pushing you at the front of the line and Ben was walking right beside your wheelchair.

I can see progress in your language development as well. Once when Daddy said your brother Justin is cute, you said, "I cute too!" You have begun to talk about your school friends at home. On one occasion, you told me, "I want to call Jaime and Ben." Another time, you asked, "Where is Ben? Where is Jaime?" I think you were trying to ask me where they live.

At one point, it looked like I might not be able to teach my decorating class because not enough people were registered. However, Daddy had the idea to call the names of the people who signed up and see if they would be interested in me teaching the class on my own. Praise God that they said yes and even a few other people I knew joined us.

Nathan, I am also encouraged to see you growing spiritually and intellectually. Gina told us you prayed a long prayer at school. When your teacher, Cindy, asked you what you prayed about, you answered, "Daddy." Another day, during prayer request time, you asked the class to pray for Mama, Daddy, and your sister Kristen. However, when Cindy asked about Justin, you said, "No!"

Love,
Mommy

Life as a Mom

Over the Christmas holidays and on into the beginning of January, my children had chicken pox, one right after another. Kristen had the worst case. Nathan had a medium case. Then Justin only ended up with a few spots.

After the holidays, while I was talking on the phone with Becky, the mother of one of Kristen's classmates, she told me that Jessica seemed to be in a slump period at school, and she needed something to look forward to doing. While we were talking, the idea came to me to teach a music appreciation class. I called Kristen's teacher and she loved the idea. We decided I would teach it once a week for six weeks.

For George Washington's birthday in February, I taught the children how to dance the minuet, a traditional dance from that time period. Later that day, another mother had the children over to her house to watch a video about our first president, George Washington. Since there is a famous story about George not being able to lie about chopping down a cherry tree, she had cheesecake topped with cherries for the kids to eat. Nathan, Justin, and I joined the class in this special outing, and it was so much fun.

Then in March, we celebrated the three hundredth birthday of Johann Sebastian Bach from Germany, one of the greatest composers of all time. We enjoyed going to a special musical program where they played well-known music written by Bach. Afterward, we returned to the classroom and the children celebrated by eating a birthday cake made by one of the moms. I loved volunteering in this very special way in Kristen's class while she was still in elementary school.

Stress Management Seminar

During the winter on a Sunday morning, while I was chatting with my friend Sharon, I mentioned to her that I would be interested in presenting a stress management seminar for women. Sharon was on the Women's Ministry Committee for our church. She said she would pass this idea along to the committee. She is also the same friend I talked with before Justin was born.

Later, I received a phone call from the chairman of the women's committee asking me to do the seminar. We set it up to be on a Saturday with two morning sessions, then lunch followed by two afternoon sessions. We met in the conference room at the church. The women sat around the table, and I stood up at a podium and presented the information.

Prior to the seminar day, I made a notebook for each participant, which included an outline for taking notes, informational sheets, and worksheets to help the women in identifying and managing their stressors. On the first page of the notebook was the purpose for seminar:

Help each woman glorify God by learning how to
- identify areas of stress in her life;
- manage these areas of stress;
- recognize, prevent, and, if necessary, cure the burnout syndrome;
- be a good steward of her emotional reserves.

After I presented my stress management seminar, I turned my attention, once again, to my love for interior design. I prayed for insight into how else I could use my knowledge and the teaching materials I made for the eight-week class I taught during the fall.

Business Seminar Idea

In the mid-1980s, seminars were being offered here in Roanoke by businesses such as paint stores, clothing stores, department stores, etc. These seminars were instructional for the patrons while, at the same time, promotional for the services and goods offered in the store. Many of the seminars were advertised in the newspaper. As I spotted the ads, I cut them out and placed them in a file folder. Whenever possible, I attended them.

As I prayed, an idea crystallized in my mind—to offer a promotional service to stores that sold interior decorating items. My idea was to teach, in the store, seminars on how to plan a successful color scheme and how to use accessories to add personality to a room's decor. In my presentation, I planned to highlight different pieces of merchandise in the store. The store would advertise the seminar and pay me a flat fee for my work.

One morning, after I dropped Nathan off at preschool, Justin and I went downtown to the historic market area where there are lots of unique shops; one of which was an art gallery I greatly admired. Justin and I were viewing the paintings when we came upon the owner of the store, whom I slightly had an acquaintance with at that time. I shared with him about my promotional idea. He, in return, shared my idea with his wife and the store manager. Then a time was set up for me to come into the store and present a mock presentation of my seminar in front of the three of them. I was thrilled I was getting the opportunity to develop my seminar concept.

This first thing I did was select two paintings at the gallery to use in my mock seminar. Each painting was to be the focal point of a color-scheme presentation. Using paint sample chips, I identified the colors in each painting. Then I took the paint chips to fabric stores to help me in the process of selecting fabrics for each color-scheme presentation. Next,

I selected other art objects in the gallery, which picked up the common colors in each painting. To help the patron decide what direction to go in for making decorating changes in their homes, I developed a worksheet. I made posters that illustrated how to use symmetrical (formal) and asymmetrical (informal) balance in hanging paintings and in arranging other art objects.

When the big day came, I carried the bolts of fabric into the store, set up my displays, and presented my seminar. The storeowners and store manager really liked my presentation, but they were not ready to move on having me do a seminar for their patrons. They had a limited amount of advertising money budgeted for the year. Also, they wanted me to have experience with other businesses before they used me. After hearing this, I decided I needed to present my decorating seminars wherever and whenever I could—clubs, churches, etc.—for free, if necessary.

While I was preparing for the gallery presentation, Justin was hospitalized because he had become dehydrated as a result of having the flu. I stayed with Justin during the day, and Bob spent the night with him so I could conserve my emotional energy. Bob can sleep anywhere, anytime and I cannot. Nathan stayed with our friend Maria during the day. Her son, Aaron, was in the same preschool class as Nathan. Maria has been a dear friend to our entire family throughout the years.

In hindsight, I realize I was able to handle my children's illnesses during the school year because I had sufficient emotional reserves to meet the demands. The creative outlets I had in my life, at that time, were adequate to replenish my reserves. This observation reaffirmed to me the importance of having creative outlets in one's life. Putting this into practice has been so instrumental in helping me maintain a more balanced life.

End of School Year

Right before the school year was over, I visited the multidisabled class in one of the city schools. Bob and I needed to decide what direction to go in with Nathan for the next school year. So I wanted to see this class in action. We were also looking into another preschool opportunity as well. One of Nathan's former patterners, Mary Lou, was the director of a very innovative program at a nearby church. She told us that she would love for Nathan to be a part of her program if he had his own aide to help him.

As the day drew near for Nathan's current preschool year to end, I began to feel heavy with sadness. Throughout the school year, I had really enjoyed getting to know the children and their mothers. The thought of those relationships ending was heartbreaking. I poured my heart out to God in my prayer journal.

June 2, 1985

Oh Father, what am I to do next with Nathan? Everything changed so quickly at the end of last summer when I knew Nathan and I needed to do something different. Our church's preschool has been the perfect stimulation for this year. It is so very difficult for me to see the year come to an end.

In my heart, I so wish that Nathan could continue on with the children in a once a week environment conducive to him excelling academically. I have ideas, in my head, for how I could set this up. But, I am concerned I might expend too much of my energy. Perhaps I could offer a class at my house one afternoon a week for Nathan's preschool alumni. The class could be about music and/or art appreciation. Since I already have a good beginning on the music appreciation; it would not be too difficult to expand the curriculum. I could have guest musicians come show and explain their instruments. I have the bits, picture cards of instruments, composers, music notes, etc. which we used during the patterning years. Also, I could buy the visuals I saw at the school supply store.

Could I make the class exciting enough for the children? How much of my time and energy would this endeavor take? I want a way to keep Nathan with his friends on a consistent basis. If I don't, the children will forget about him. They don't realize how much he loves them and how, in so many ways, he thinks and feels as they do. Nathan's life needs to be exciting and different—so as the children grow older, they will want to be with him.

If you want this idea of a special interest class to be a means of keeping Nathan with his friends, please bless my efforts. Perhaps this summer I could get the class organized so that it would not take too much of my time when school starts. Oh Father, what do I do for Nathan during the day this next school year? Deep inside of myself I know Nathan and I need to be apart at least two or three mornings a week.

Making a Decision

After visiting the multi-disabled class at Preston Park, I now know that they do not offer the social and intellectual stimulation I think Nathan needs. Neither am I very excited about pursuing a placement in a regular kindergarten class for Nathan in the public school system because of the incredible amount of effort needed to make this happen. Also, there is no assurance the kindergarten teacher would even be open to this idea. Based on all these considerations, I still think Mary Lou's preschool is the most stimulating option for Nathan at this time. My only concern, other than the money, is the fact he is two years older than the rest of the children.

The last day of preschool, after I picked up Nathan, I drove to an educational supply store where I bought some visuals that I could use in teaching a music appreciation class for young children. One of the other preschool moms, Karen, lived near the store, so I stopped by with Nathan and Justin to chat with her about my idea. When I showed her my newly purchased music appreciation visuals, Karen said she liked the idea. It turned out that I never did teach the class, but working on the idea was a way for me to cope with the grief I felt.

A few days after Nathan's last day of preschool, Kristen's school year ended. On the last day of school, I met with Kristen's teacher to express my appreciation to her. At the end of our time of talking, I learned there were at least two key families not planning to return the next school year. I left feeling very low emotionally. I viewed these departures as a potential crisis for our small school because of the loss of financial and volunteer support.

Early in June, we made our decision in regard to Nathan's next school year. Bob and I knew a special education program in the public school system would probably be the place for Nathan in a year or so. But for this time in his life, we wanted him to do all the neat things children do in regular preschool as long as he could. So we enrolled Nathan in the Rosalind Hills preschool program. With this decision behind us, we now focused on making plans for Nathan's summer.

A Downward Spiral

Summer 1985

I made a schedule of possible activities for Nathan to do out in the community and at home. We hired two teenage girls to take turns helping him participate in weekly story time at the library and in week-long Bible schools at area churches. At home, they also helped Nathan do creative activities like finger painting.

Early in the summer, my mother was diagnosed with a health condition in which part of the treatment involved medication. She was experiencing a lot of anxiety that she did not have before she started the medication. One day, after talking with my mom on the phone, I emotionally felt like I was a puddle of water on the floor. So I contacted my mom's doctor to see if the medication she was taking could be the cause of her anxiety. He said yes and changed the medication; after which, she felt much better.

As the summer progressed, I increasingly felt heavy laden. I was walking on an emotional tight rope. Some of my friends' lives were still filled with complex situations. By the middle of the summer, our two teenage girls were no longer able to help us with Nathan, and it was really hard for me not to have their help. Bob's parents were scheduled to visit us in July; we changed the date for their visit to a later time.

A neighbor told me about an hourly babysitting business that an acquaintance of hers had opened near our neighborhood. My neighbor had used the service and was pleased with the care her daughter received. So one morning, while Kristen was with friends across the street, I decided to try out the babysitting service for a few hours. I took the boys by, filled out the forms, and then went on to the library to work on my interior design studies. The boys were very happy when I picked them up. However, to my surprise, I was told not to bring Nathan back again because he was considered a special-needs child. I was very disappointed to hear this because I had hoped this service would enable me to have a little time to myself on a regular basis.

I knew I really needed some time to myself because I could sense the beginning of a downward spiral. At the end of each day, I was physically and emotionally worn-out. If I sat down to watch the evening news, I often found myself crying. So I stopped watching and listening to any news programs.

Burnout in My Prayer Life

One summer evening while at church, I experienced a deep sadness coming over me as I listened to the prayer requests of people who were ill or in distressing situations. Tears formed in my eyes and rolled down my cheeks. Unable to stay, I slipped out and drove home crying.

After this, I avoided being in group prayer sessions. There were also significant changes in my private prayer life. For many years before, I had prayed very intensely and very specifically about my concerns and those of others. I loved to record how God answered whether it would be no, wait awhile, or yes. Praying in this manner was a vital part of my intimacy with God.

Now it seemed I could hardly pray any prayers of petition without crying, especially regarding topics dear to my heart. I could no longer make the emotional investment to pray in this manner. Many of the sick people I was praying for were not getting better. The troubled marriages I had been praying for were now ending in divorce. Our church's day school continued to experience financial strain.

One day, during my prayer time, I finally said to God, "I can't keep praying for these situations. If you want them to, in a sense, 'bomb out,' so be it." This is how I was honestly feeling at the time.

God's Grace through Nature

Not long after I prayed this prayer, I was nearing my house when I noticed the flowers on the corner in a special way. The thought came to me. "No matter how much pain and suffering there is around me, every spring, the leaves come out on the trees and the flowers bloom." It was as if God was saying to me, "Judy, I want you to focus on the beauty and constancy of my creation and I will give you grace. I will give you grace."

The rest of the summer, when I was driving around the city, I focused on the flowers and trees in people's yards. Whenever I was close to the Fishburn Rose Garden, I would drive by it. And in my prayer life, I focused mainly on praising God and giving Him thanks.

A New Opportunity for Me

Right before school started, Bob came home one afternoon and asked if I would like to help one of his customers, the Johnsons, pick out the paint color and the wallpaper for their new Florida room. I was both excited and nervous about this new opportunity. However, I decided to accept the challenge; so that same evening, I called the Johnsons and set up a time to meet with them.

The day of the appointment, I borrowed my mom's car. I wore a periwinkle blue linen suit I had recently bought on sale. Underneath the blue suit, I wore a fuchsia top. As well, I carried a clipboard. I wanted to look as professional as possible pulling up in front of their house and going in the front door.

While there, I asked the Johnsons if they had any other decorating needs. They told me they needed window treatments for their new Florida room. Then Mrs. Johnson also said, "I really need new draperies for the upstairs master bedroom!" So we walked up the stairs and I took a look at the bedroom so I could get an idea of what she might want.

The next day, I went downtown to a paint store where I had attended a seminar. Using an arm cover from the Johnson's new sofa, I selected a paint color and wallpaper. While there, I learned about a local business that makes custom window treatments. So we decided this business should make the sheer draperies for the sliding glass door in the Florida room and for the bedroom. We also ordered, through them, soft pleated shades for the many windows in the Florida room. Before placing the order, I took the Johnsons by my friend Katie's house to show them how this type of shade looked and worked. I wanted the Johnsons to be very satisfied with their decision.

When the window treatments were installed, I helped the Johnsons hang their pictures on the walls. They were very pleased with how the paint, wallpaper, and window treatments looked. This meant a lot to me to help make the new room comfortable and pretty since they planned on spending a lot of time in it. The Johnson interior decorating job was a happy, upbeat project for me. Working on this project helped me to be more emotionally ready for the start of the school year.

CHAPTER 10

Up and Down Again

NEXT, I WENT TO ROSALIND HILLS PRESCHOOL. KATIE AND CAROL HELPED ME THERE.

Nathan was off and going with his new preschool program. Katie, one of his former patterners, was his aide. The year before, Katie had come one morning a week to our house to work with Nathan on his crawling. She did a great job motivating him to crawl, then rewarding him when he reached his goals. Katie was equally as good at helping Nathan make the most of the many stimulating activities Mary Lou had planned—looking through a magnifying glass at various objects, listening to sounds, making fresh butter and orange juice, doing a wide variety of artistic activities like music, dance, and drama.

New Dreams:

With Nathan happily settled, I turned my attention to how I could use my love of interior design to make money. In my journal I wrote,

September 10, 1985

Father, I am asking you to lead me as to how I can make money to help with the expenses entailed with Nathan's preschool experience. There are so many other things I desire for Nathan which require a lot of money.

- *The addition on our house for his therapy/bedroom and special bathroom*
- *A computer system*
- *A musical instrument he can play and an instructor*
- *A foreign language instructor*
- *And someday, a van to transport Nathan*

If You chose to bless my interior decorating seminar and consultation ideas, I will give You, Father, all the credit. What name should I use for my seminar service? Show me each step I need to take. Lord, give me just the right experiences to prepare me for my Interior Design mini-career. Oh, how I would love to do more design consultations! I so enjoyed the work I did for the Johnsons. However, if I am to do more consultation work, please provide a nicer car for me to drive. Don't let me go any faster or slower than what You think is best.

Decorating Dynamics

Not long after I made this entry in my journal, Bob came home and said, "Judy, look out the window." There sitting in front of our house was a nice used station wagon that Bob's bosses decided to give us. They had previously used it for company business. God had answered my prayer; now, I felt good about pulling up in front of a client's house. I felt this answer was a confirmation to me that God wanted me to move on with my ideas. So, I began to make plans.

In preparation for doing interior design consultations, I had business cards printed. I also designed a flyer and had copies made to advertise my decorating seminar service, which I called Decorating Dynamics. I finished making my teaching posters, and I had them laminated along with the other visuals I had made the year before for my eight-week interior design course. I so enjoyed working on these projects, and I anticipated more opportunities to teach decorating dynamics.

Once a week, during the fall, I went to a women's Bible study at my church while Nathan was in preschool. Justin stayed in the church nursery. At the first Bible study meeting, I told the women about my Decorating Dynamics seminars. I let them know I was available to teach a four-week basic course and a variety of individual seminars. That very day, Betsy volunteered to hostess a four-week decorating class in her home. A few other women said they would like to take the class as well. Another woman, Peggy, asked me to schedule a one-time seminar presentation for her craft club. After she and I discussed the possibilities, we decided the topic would be on how to make wise decorating decisions.

Early in the fall, while attending a women's program at my mom's church, I learned that the coordinator of the women's special interest programs was looking for possible future programs. Later in the evening, I spoke with Carol, the coordinator, and told her I was available to do a program on some aspect of interior decorating. Within a month, she called me to set up a late-winter date for me to do a presentation on how to use accessories to add personality to your home decor.

I now had several dates lined up for teaching. Two of the mornings Nathan was in preschool, I worked on preparing for my seminar presentations. After dropping Nathan off at preschool, I usually stopped at a coffee shop. While Justin ate a biscuit and I drank coffee, I worked on my decorating lesson plans. Then before picking up Nathan, Justin and I went to various places: paint stores, fabric shops, office supply stores, and the library. I pushed him around in a stroller while I looked for items to use for my seminars and classes, which I taught in the evenings.

A Friend for Justin

Justin was now nineteen to twenty months old, and I felt like he needed to play with another child his age on a regular basis. I also wanted to have one morning a week to be all by myself. My neighbor, Cindy, had a little girl, Heather, who was just a few months older than Justin. Cindy and I decided to do a babysitting exchange so that we each could have one morning free each week.

Besides the one morning a week, I also kept Heather on Wednesday afternoons for three hours while Cindy taught piano lessons at her church. I did this in exchange for Cindy giving Kristen a weekly piano lesson. Heather was a wonderful playmate for Justin, but I found it progressively harder and harder to coordinate their playtimes. I also knew I needed more time alone.

By or before the end of the school year, our exchange of services had ended. Cindy and her husband bought a larger house on the other side of the city because they were expecting another baby. Thus, the opportunities for Justin and Heather to play together ceased.

Women's Bible Study

All throughout fall, I looked forward each week to my women's Bible study. It was an excellent study written by Kay Author on the names of God. I, particularly, enjoyed the fact that our teacher encouraged us to participate in the discussion. On the day we studied the name Jehovah Rapha, "God who heals," I shared in our large group session the experience Bob and I had of asking the elders of the church to anoint Nathan with oil and pray for his healing. When we divided into our smaller groups for prayer, I shared my concerns about getting Nathan into the best possible educational setting for the next school year. Although both of these topics were very emotional in nature for me, somehow I managed to talk about each without crying.

After the Bible study, I went to pick up Nathan. His aide, Katie, and I stood and chatted for a short time. However, when Katie brought up the topic of Nathan's educational future, I burst into tears. I cried all the way home; I cried all the way through feeding the boys lunch and putting them down for their naps.

While I was resting in my bedroom, I asked God to totally heal me from my emotional infirmity or, at least, bring me to the point where I could function better emotionally. I was concerned the stress in my life was now affecting my body, not just my emotions since I had recently discovered a bald spot on top of my head the size of a dime.

Answer to My Prayer

A few days later, I was talking with my friend, Sonny, on the phone. In the course of the conversation, Sonny shared with me about a period of sleeplessness she recently went through; her doctor diagnosed a chemical imbalance as the cause and prescribed an antidepressant. Now she was sleeping well at night. I asked Sonny who her doctor was; then, I called his office and made a consultation appointment.

Bob accompanied me to the appointment. I told Dr. W about my hair loss and the uncontrollable crying and that after talking with my friend, I wondered if I could have a chemical imbalance. Once again, I told my story. I shared how I had prayed for twins, how God answered my prayers on conceiving twins, how one baby died, and how the other baby became brain injured. I was only able to get a few sentences out at a time because I was weeping. I would compose myself and then start again with my story.

Dr. W prescribed an antidepressant for me. Within just one day, I could see a night-and-day difference. Bob could see the dramatic difference in me; in fact, he thought he had his original wife back! I felt even, calm, and rested and I was able to laugh. Sometimes, I laughed with total abandonment like I did in my younger adult years.

I continued to feel this wonderful sense of well-being until the night of our church's Christmas program. I sat in the middle of the worship center so that I could better see the faces of the children in the program. However, after the program, I found out there was a possibility that our church's day school might close down. This was very painful for me to hear. Tears mounted in my eyes; I hurried to the car. As soon as I closed the door to the car, my tears flowed and flowed. I cried all the way home.

The next day, I was still crying off and on. Dealing with the possibility of the school closing was similar to my dealing with the possibility of one of my children dying. Not only had I prayed for the conception of the school, but also I was even more bonded to the school after years of praying for the students and the faculty. All of Kristen's teachers had made such a positive impact on her life, and I enjoyed relating to them.

The evening I learned that our beloved school might close down was the last time I was emotionally able to sit in the main worship center. After this, I always sat in the overflow area behind the glass windows. I would slip in right after the service started and slip out just before it ended so I could minimize my amount of personal interaction.

My Church & Ministry

A Broken Dream:

The night of the Christmas program, it was as if I was looking down at the garment of my church involvement and seeing it, the garment, so cut into small pieces that I did not even recognize what it had been originally. Now not only was Bob's and my dream of being career missionaries in Europe shattered, I was also not even able to be a part of our church that I loved so dearly.

The next day, Bob and I talked with my doctor about my relapse. He ordered blood work to be done to see if I was getting a therapeutic amount of the antidepressant. Upon receiving the report, he increased the dosage. In the days that followed, the antidepressant helped me cope, but I did not return to the same degree of well-being that I had before the evening of the Christmas program.

In January, we found out that our church's day school was not going to close. However, the school planned to reduce the number of grades it could offer. This meant Kristen needed to go to another school the next year. I purposely did not talk with any of the other parents about the possible educational plans they were making for their children. I focused solely on what we needed to do for Kristen. Immediately, I called and made an appointment for us to visit another Christian day school in the city. When Bob, Kristen, and I visited the school, the principal took us on a tour and spent quality time with us explaining the school's system and answering our questions. We were able to sit in both fifth-grade classes and observe the teachers and students in action.

All three of us were very pleased with what we saw and heard that day, so we did not schedule visits to any other schools. When the time came to turn in

Kristen's application to the school, Bob and I had the forms already completed and turned in on the first day.

My Medical Problems

Also in January, I started seeing a dermatologist about my hair loss. The bald spot on top of my head had grown to a size of a quarter. Fortunately, after a series of cortisone shots over a span of months, my hair gradually grew back.

During this time, I was also seeing another specialist about a precancerous health problem. After several months of the prescribed treatment, the condition disappeared. These medical appointments were very draining for me. At each initial appointment, I shared with the new doctor briefly about my burnout.

School Options for Nathan

On January 30, 1986, Bob and I met with the director of special education for Roanoke City Schools. In preparation for the meeting, I decided to wear a navy blue wool suit, navy heels, and matching purse. Bob wore a suit, a dress shirt, and a necktie.

Earlier that day, I came up with the idea of writing a profile about Nathan. It included as follows:

- Basic description of Nathan
- Areas of development (physical, language, speech, emotional, social, and intellectual)
- Educational background including home therapy program and two different preschools

After I wrote the rough copy, I typed up the profile, which I photocopied on the way to the meeting. I also took along a picture of Nathan so that the director could see what Nathan looked like as he read the profile. I carried a clipboard folder to hold the profile, Nathan's picture, and paper for me to take notes.

Before the meeting, I was concerned I might have tears build up in my eyes and need to suddenly exit the director's office. I did not want this to happen, but if it did, I at least hoped I could get out of the room before completely bursting into tears. In my mind, I thought the more we can look like and act like professional parents, the better my probability would be in remaining even emotionally during our session.

During the meeting, Bob and I sat across from the director. He looked up and said, "How can I help you?" We stated, "We are ready to enter our son who has cerebral palsy into public school." As I handed the director the profile and picture, I said, "We would like to know what the possible educational options are that might be available for our son." After he read the profile and asked us a few questions, the director handed us a brochure and indicated which programs might be a possible considerations for Nathan. He reminded us that a thorough evaluation would need to take place before a placement could be proposed by the school system.

We told the director that we understood, but we wanted to go ahead and visit the programs he had mentioned. He said this would be fine, but we needed to contact the principle of each school and make the plans through the school's office. On the way home, I expressed to Bob how relieved I was that I did not cry during the meeting. Having the profile reduced the amount of talking we had to do, and it helped the meeting to go more smoothly.

Over the next few months, Bob and I visited each one of the possible educational options. When we visited the Roanoke County Occupational School (RCOS), the principal introduced us to Mr. King, who would be the teacher for the multi-disabled class the next year. He bent down on one knee and talked to Nathan. Seeing the way Mr. King interacted with Nathan meant a great deal to me. In the end, Bob and I felt the multi-disabled class at RCOS was the best choice for Nathan because of the computer opportunities it offered. We believed that technology would be the key to Nathan's intellectual stimulation and development. So we called the director to tell him what we thought.

During the winter, we also made several trips downtown to the Child Development Clinic to work on Nathan's required evaluation for school. There were four major components to the evaluation: educational, social, psychological, and medical. The results of these tests would help to provide an appropriate placement and educational plan.

The day Nathan was to be tested by the clinical psychologist, I decided, at the last minute, not to go with Bob and Nathan. I asked Bob to drop me off at a nearby coffee shop. Bob was to go into the psychologist's office with Nathan to help interpret his responses. The idea of sitting outside the testing room at the clinic was very daunting for me. So instead, I was busy working on my upcoming interior decorating seminar and drinking coffee a few blocks away. I had made the agreement to do the seminar in early fall before the surge of stressors began. The topic was on how to use accessories to add personality to your decor. The morning of the day of my seminar presentation, I felt weary. I thought, "Will I be able to get up in front of the women tonight and talk?" In the afternoon, as I set up my display tables in the church fellowship hall, I felt encouraged. I enjoyed trying out different ways of arranging my display items.

Crying Again

The winter months had been very hard for me. Making the educational decisions for Kristen and Nathan involved lots of observations, meetings, and discussions, especially in regard to Nathan. Interspersed between the educational appointments were my frequent medical appointments. The demands on my emotional reserves far exceeded the replenishment of them. By spring, I found myself, once again, crying at unexpected times.

Increasingly, I was concerned about the possibility of becoming pregnant again. Each time a new child comes into a family, there also comes the possibility of health problems, behavior problems, and educational difficulties, etc., that require special attention. I was afraid that if I had another baby, I might totally deplete my sparse emotional reserves and that I might not remain sane.

After much discussion and prayer, Bob and I decided to move in the direction of one of us having a surgical procedure done to prevent us from conceiving again. One day in the spring, something happened that confirmed to us that we had made the right decision. I was at the mall with Kristen and the boys. Nathan and Justin became unhappy within seconds of each other. It was very hard for me to simultaneously meet their needs. Realizing it would not be wise for me to remain at the mall, I quickly ushered us to the car. I put the boys in the car, fastened their seat belts, and drove home.

During this whole process, I was progressively feeling more and more stressed. When I got home, Bob helped me get the boys out of the car. Then I went straight upstairs, turned the water on at the bathroom sink, shut the door, leaned over the sink, and wept. I cried out, "Please, dear God, don't let me go crazy! Please don't let me go crazy!" I hoped the running water would muffle the sound.

A Broken Dream:

On the day I cried in the bathroom, it was as if I was looking at the garment of my motherhood and seeing the mother I had once been seemingly cut into little, tiny pieces. Not only was my dream of raising four children broken, but also I was now no longer a joyful mother for my three living children. I did not have the energy to do with Justin the kind of activities I had done with Kristen and with Nathan. There were days that I was not even able to make it through dinner without crying.

Bob and I called my doctor; he asked me to come into the office for another blood test to, once again, find the therapeutic amount of the antidepressant for me to take. In my journal, I wrote, "Enable my doctor to know how much medicine to give me or whether to give me a different antidepressant. I await the results of my blood work concerning the dosage. Father, bring about the right dosage and the best results."

While we waited for the results of the blood work, Bob suggested that I immediately do more relaxing activities to replenish my emotional reserves. That week, I went to a women's conference at Hollins College in Roanoke, and I also drove to Lexington, which is one hour away. The town is filled with quaint shops and lots of history. The campuses of Washington and Lee University and Virginia Military Institute are side by side right in town. The weather was beautiful, clear, crisp, and sunny. I enjoyed walking around the two campuses and going in and out of historical museums.

The following weekend, Bob and I went to Winston Salem, North Carolina, which is two hours away. We left on Friday afternoon and came back on Sunday afternoon. My mom and sister stayed with the children at our house. Our neighbor, Bob, came over to carry Nathan up and down the steps.

The weather was beautiful. On Saturday, we enjoyed walking around historic Old Salem and going in some of the buildings to learn more about the Moravian way of life. On Sunday, we toured an old mansion and its grounds in another part of Winston Salem.

When we got back home, I felt replenished enough to work on a plan for long-term regrouping. When my blood work results came back, the dosage of the antidepressant was increased. The new dosage made a significant difference in how I felt.

Bob and I thought it would be good to have Justin in a situation where he could play with other children during the times that Nathan was in preschool. This would give me time alone to relax and regroup. The one-morning-a-week babysitting exchange that Cindy and I had been doing was not enough time for me.

First, I tried, on a trial basis, Justin going to the home of a new friend I had made through my Bible study. Her little boy had difficulty sharing with Justin though, so she said that this arrangement would be too much for her to handle. Knowing I did not have sufficient emotional energy to keep trying out home-based childcare, I started thinking in terms of day care centers. I made a list of what I wanted for Justin, and then I began to research different day care centers on our side of town. After I observed different settings, I wrote out the pros and cons of each setting.

Bob and I decided to use Young World. The teacher of Justin's class had a wonderful touch with the children. There was a playground with green grass and a sandbox right outside the door. Also, by having Justin in a day care center, I did not have to chitchat when I picked him up like I would if a friend was keeping him. This helped me conserve some emotional energy.

Seeking Counsel

Once Justin was settled, I turned my attention to how I could get help in becoming more emotionally well. Bob was getting more and more weary being the mainstay in our family. He did not have the emotional energy to listen to me. Plus, it is hard for someone, who is right in the middle of the same crisis, to give insight to the burned-out person.

I was emotionally unable to talk with my friends to gain perspective and insight into my struggles. Friendship is a two-way street, and I was easily weighed down by what was going on in their lives. Many of my friends had difficult situations like dealing with aging parents who had health problems while they themselves had health problems. At times, just seeing my friends from a distance reminded me of their pain. I did not even have enough emotional energy to explain to them why I had become so distant.

I felt seeing a professional counselor could be a great help to me. My doctor thought this was a good idea. With a professional counselor, I would be able to share about my struggles without having to hear about the problems of the person listening. And I could receive help in gaining perspective and insight into my emotional infirmity. I wanted to see a Christian counselor who used biblical principles in his counseling. I found out our church was offering supplemental financial help for members who went to a particular Christian counseling group. So I prayerfully studied over this list of counselors and John G. stood out to me.

April 1, 1986

Today is Bob's birthday. Oh Lord, Bob and I both are so tired physically, emotionally, and mentally. Bob needs spiritual refreshment right away, but I believe he also needs a lot of time to himself—a change of pace and change of surroundings. Please help him Father.

I am so weak and tired; there is little I can do for Bob. You know how I am, Father, I tend to want to solve people's problems for them. I have such a low emotional capacity at this point, and yet I find myself wanting to solve Bob's problems.

Oh Father, even though Bob is not fully convinced that I need to see a counselor, I think after reading Scripture that it might be a good idea to see a Christian counselor. Proverbs 12:15 says, "The way of a fool is right in his own eyes, but a wise man is he who listens to counsel."

Proverbs 14:1 "The wise woman builds her house, but the foolish tears it down with her own hands." I truly want to build my home as a wise woman. I don't want to tear down my home with my own hands. This tearing down would be so easy for me to do because of my fragile emotional framework.

April 21, 1986

After much prayer and talking with Bob, we really believe the next step for me is to see John G., a Christian counselor here in town who we feel is the best. So, I'm going today to see him. Please use the session today in a mighty way in my life. Help me to communicate my story clearly and distinctly to him. Enable my counselor to give the right counsel for today.

I ended up going to counseling once a week while Kristen and Nathan were in school and Justin was in day care. In one of our sessions, John asked me to make a list of situations where I overextend myself emotionally. As I thought about it, I could see a pattern: situations that involved multiple demands being made on me were very difficult. If these types of situations were accompanied with multiple noises, I had even more difficulty trying to cope.

Typically, dinnertime was very hard for me. It was difficult to get the food on the table and get the family to the table. Usually, there were several demands being made on me with a lot of background noise. Someone might spill milk. The boys might fret, and Kristen liked to talk a lot and act silly. It was not unusual for me to cry during dinner.

Once, while standing in the line at Hardy's, I started to cry. My children were having a hard time deciding what they wanted to eat, and I was having a hard time hearing them because of the high noise level. Then, there was uncertainty about where we would sit once we got our food.

Another day, I was working on getting ready to go to a dermatology appointment when I heard both boys crying. I wasn't able to get dressed and deal with the boys at the same time. I started to cry. Kristen was downstairs with the boys. I called my sister to come and help me, and I asked if she would call and cancel the appointment for me.

One Saturday, my children and I along with my mother and sister were downtown for a festival. There was confusion over whether Nathan was going to do a certain activity. The street was crowded with people. There were a lot of different activities and noises going on around us. I stepped into a store and dropped my head over on a stack of men's pants and wept.

I also realized that certain topics were extremely painful for me to discuss, like Seth's death, Nathan's diagnosis, and my children's well-being. While reading *Happiness Is a Choice*, a book about depression by Frank Minirth, MD, and Paul Meier, MD, I gained insight into why particular topics were very distressing for me. The authors explain how stressful memories are recorded and stored in the brain. This means they can be replayed in as vivid a form as when they initially occurred. Current-day stress can be a trigger for remembering these disturbing memories.

Another Downward Spiral

Summer 1986

When summer came, Justin continued going to Young World every morning until noon, Monday through Friday. I did not set up activities for Nathan to do like I did the summer before with the two teenagers who helped us. Instead, Bob and I made arrangements for our neighbor, Karen, to work with Nathan several mornings a week. Karen was a single mom raising three young sons.

Being a teacher, she was at home during the summer with her boys. Karen planned activities that she could do with Nathan along with her children. Kristen pushed Nathan down to Karen's house in his chair and stayed to help with him. Then she brought him back home. She enjoyed doing the activities. Nathan loved being one of five children laughing and having a good time together; I enjoyed having time alone at home.

Either Bob or I picked Justin up at noon. We all had lunch and the boys took their naps in the afternoon. Several afternoons a week Kristen went swimming with one of our neighbors who lived across the street. She had a daughter, Lindsay, the same age as Kristen, and they had a family membership at a private swim club in our neighborhood.

Things were moving along fairly smoothly, then somewhere in the course of the summer, Karen told us that she could not continue working with Nathan because her sister was coming to live with her for a while. Karen's sister was also bringing her young children along. The dynamics of Karen's summer dramatically changed and so did mine. After this point, my remembrance of the summer is rather hazy. I began to cry more often, especially in the afternoons, when both boys were awake and Kristen was not home to help me. Nathan complained that he was bored without Karen's stimulating activities to do, and I did not have the energy to do very much with him.

God's Grace through a Long-time Friend

Bob told me to call him if I felt I could not cope, and he would come get Nathan and take him back to work with him. A few times, I did call Bob to come get Nathan. When our long-time friend, Phyllis, learned of this difficult situation, she approached the church leaders about using money from the "helps fund" to enable us to get all-day childcare for Nathan and Justin.

Bob talked with the director of Young World about the possibility of Nathan coming to the center with Justin. She, in turn, talked with the teacher of Justin's class. Justin's teacher said yes, she could handle Nathan. So both boys stayed all day. Each day, Bob took them there and then picked them up. This gave me the entire day to be by myself except when Kristen was home.

Bob wanted me to get away for a change of pace for a few days. It was difficult for us to come up with a way for me to do this. Earlier in the summer, my mother and I traveled to Ashville to pick up Kristen and her friend from summer camp. By leaving two days early, we were able to enjoy a full day touring the Biltmore Estate in Ashville. Upon traveling down Interstate 40 by the Great Smoky Mountains, the majestic beauty of these mountains seemed to beckon me to come back at a later time and travel into them.

So the thought came to me to plan a trip to into the Great Smoky Mountains. Some people are drawn to the seashore for rest, relaxation, and reflection. They love to hear the ocean waves, to put their feet in the sand, and to walk on the beach. I like the seashore, but I am drawn to the mountains filled with lush green trees and cool nights and creek waters rippling over rocks when I need to find rest, relaxation, and reflection.

My mother traveled with me again, and we shared the expenses of the trip. I had a very relaxing time in the Smoky Mountains just as I had earlier in the summer in Ashville. But with both of these trips, I arrived home frayed. With the first trip, Kristen's friend accidentally slammed the car door on my hand when we made a stop about one hour from Roanoke. I had intense pain and swelling, so I went to a doctor in the town. With the second trip, there were a series of difficult events on the way home. I felt more and more tense driving home; when I entered the house, I was crying.

While in a counseling session with John, I made a statement about feeling burned out. In reply, John challenged me about using the term *burned out*. He said something like, "Burnout is not something you can see inside of yourself." It seemed to me he thought my using the term burnout did not fit with the rational thinking process. I thought the term was very descriptive for how I felt. After I left the session, I cried all the way home. I kept thinking John must not know how burnout feels. I was not sure whether I could or should continue on with John as my counselor. So John referred me to a Christian psychiatrist, Dr. R.

August 14, 1986

Seeing Dr. R., the psychiatrist, seemed to bring a little more light to the situation. After I told my story, he added another medicine for me to take along with the antidepressant. There is more help I need from him; please, Lord, prepare both of us for the next session.

Strain in Our Marriage

August 21, 1986

After I started taking the added medicine, I made it a week without crying. I even went on a trip with my sister, my nephew, my mother, and Kristen. By the end of the trip, I was exhausted. At first, I was mainly feeling physically tired, and then later, I also felt emotionally tired. On Sunday night, as Kathy drove Kristen and me home, I began to feel depressed when she spoke of putting a new roof on her house. I thought, "How would we put a new roof on our house if we needed one?"

When we arrived at our house, Kathy sat down to visit, talked with the children, and then stayed on to talk with me. I should have encouraged her to leave since I knew I was very tired, both physically and emotionally. My mind could not seem to take in and digest what she was sharing with me. I tried to end the conversation several times but to no avail; finally, I told Kathy we must stop talking because I needed to go bed.

I picked up a few toys, dishes, etc., then I went upstairs to find Bob lying on the bed. I sat down and started to share about the trip. I had been eager to talk with him about an incident that had occurred at my aunt's house in which Kristen had become over reactive. Bob got up to take a bath; I followed him to the bathroom to take out my contacts. After Bob got out of the bathroom, I said, "I will need some space to be alone tomorrow." Bob replied, "You shouldn't have to *rest* after taking a trip because the trip was supposed to be a means of rest for you." He was frustrated because this was the third trip I had come back from either emotionally worn-out or physically exhausted. I told Bob that his statement was hard for me to hear emotionally; tears immediately came into my eyes.

He said, "You should not have stayed downstairs with Kathy. You should have come up to be with me. Perhaps you shouldn't have gone on the trip to visit the relatives to start with knowing that the trip could possibly be tiring for you." Bob did not want to hear my pondering thoughts about my trip, relatives, etc. He wanted me to be taken up with him romantically. Bob was anticipating a romantic encounter with me, and he was disappointed.

There were other statements Bob made that night which are very hazy in my mind. "Marriage to you isn't the same!" "I hardly see you!" "You are tired!" "I am tired!"

Before we went to sleep, I told Bob I could see I had been insensitive to him by not coming upstairs earlier and being attentive to him, etc. So I asked for his forgiveness. However, I knew I could not pursue a conversation right then about those elusive statements he had made; I knew I would only cry and think very irrationally.

The next day, as I contemplated those hurtful statements, I battled despair. As soon as Bob came home, I told him that I must talk with him sometime during the evening alone. After the children went to bed, I initiated the conversation, not really knowing what I would say. Yet I knew somehow I must talk with Bob about the statements he made that were so elusive in my mind. As I initiated the topic, Bob said, "I thought everything was taken care of Sunday night." I responded, "Bob, God has given us so much grace, a car, day care for the boys, etc., and yet we still are barely hanging on!"

August 22, 1986

Oh Lord, I am tired and Bob is tired, too. Please care for him, protect him, and give him rest. Please, please help us, Father! I see myself as being the chief reason why I have a tired and worn out husband. It is hard for me to separate myself out and not feel guilt and regret. Yet, I know if the situation had been reversed and Bob had been the one to have an intense burnout, I would have done all I could to help him, just as he has for me.

God's Grace through a New Friend

Not long after this entry, I was talking with a friend, Betsy R., on the phone. She called me to see if Bob and I could help her with a special project she was doing for our minister. During our conversation, I shared with Betsy about the stress Bob and I were experiencing in our marriage. As we talked, she came up with the idea of recruiting and coordinating volunteers to come stay with our children in the evening so that Bob and I could go out on dates.

Almost every week, Bob and I went out, sometimes just for dinner, sometimes for dessert, and other times just for coffee. Occasionally, we went to a free musical program or poetry reading or art show at one of the local colleges. Being able to have *special time together* on a regular basis was one of the things that helped preserve our marriage.

Judy and Bob on a date

Judy and Bob in lecture hall at the Institutes

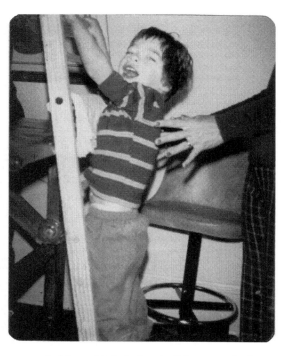

Nathan on a ladder which helps build strength for standing

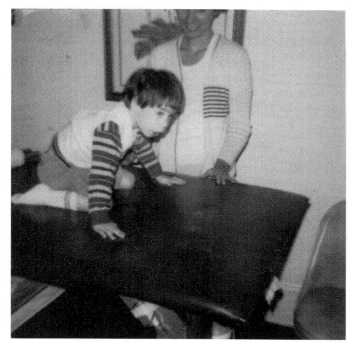

Nathan holding a modified quad position; Mom is so proud!

Mildred reading a book to Nathan as a reward

Daddy holding Nathan as they watch people rollerskating

Family snapshot in 1981

Gina is reading Nathan his favorite book about trees

Nathan enjoying talking with the girls

Gina helps Nathan exercise with the class

Cindy is leading circle time

Gena holding Nathan; Aaron and Jamie

PART THREE

Needle and Thread

CHAPTER 11

Special Education

I WENT TO RCOS (ROANOKE COUNTY OCCUPATIONAL SCHOOL). MY TEACHER THERE WAS MR. KING. I KNEW JENNIFER AND TRACY AS FRIENDS THERE.

Nathan visits with his friend Jennifer at school

Tracie gives Nathan a hug

Emotionally, it was very difficult for me to enter into the phase of placing Nathan in the public education system. I think the biggest reason it was so hard was because I viewed Nathan as very intelligent. I was deeply concerned that the special education environment would not provide sufficient intellectual stimulation for him. I had given up hope for Nathan's gross motor development, and I was focused on Nathan's mental, social, and language development.

Early in the school year, I told Nathan's teacher, Mr. King, about the intense burnout I experienced as a result of our patterning Nathan. I shared that to facilitate my recovery I was in counseling and taking an antidepressant. Also, I was spending more time doing relaxing activities while Justin was in day care.

During this same conversation, I told the story of Nathan writing numerals, words, and names at the age of four. I felt pretty relaxed in telling Mr. King what I thought Nathan could do even though I could tell that he was not sold on the idea of Nathan doing the things I said. When I finished, his response was "I will work with him and see." Yet, he said this in a way that I did not regret telling him.

Emerging Concern for Nathan's Hips

There was deep concern over Nathan's hips, which began at the Child Development Center, when Nathan's evaluation for starting school was done.

Upon doing the physical exam part of the evaluation, the attending physician said Nathan should see an orthopedic specialist about the status of his subluxed hips. That day, the nurse at the clinic worked on setting up an appointment for Nathan to see Dr. S at the Children's Rehabilitation Center (CRC) in Charlottesville, which is two hours from Roanoke.

Many of the details are a blur to me when I look back on this time. I think one reason it is not clear is because I found it extremely hard emotionally to deal with the possibility of Nathan having major surgery. I could not think about the pain he would have to go through and all the work we would need to do.

Early in the fall, when it came time for Nathan's appointment at CRC, I did not go along with Bob and Nathan. I was distancing myself from this intense situation, so I could rest and replenish my emotional reserves. I knew in the somewhat near future we would need to make a decision and I wanted to be well enough to do this.

Wendy, Nathan's PT, went with Bob and Nathan, so she could increase her knowledge on the subject of subluxed hips. She was a recent graduate of PT school, seeking to learn all she could as soon as possible. Dr. S's diagnosis was, if the hip subluxations were not corrected, then there was a high probability Nathan could have chronic pain in his hip sockets as he grew older.

Bob said he wanted a second opinion, so on that day, the CRC set up an appointment for Nathan to see a pediatric orthopedist in Richmond, Virginia. Wendy also went with Bob and Nathan to Richmond for Nathan's appointment. They left early in the morning, stopping in Charlottesville to pick up the medical records and X-rays at CRC. Then they drove on to Richmond to see the specialist. The pediatric orthopedist examined the X-rays carefully and came to the same conclusion as Dr. S—Nathan needed hip surgery in order to decrease future chronic pain. After the appointment, they had lunch with Wendy's mom and then drove back to Roanoke.

Nathan needed a new custom wheelchair; however, we could not start making the plan for a new chair until we made the decision as to whether to do the proposed surgery. Nathan's teacher Mr. King, his PT Wendy, his OT Karen, and the PT and OT from CRC all talked about how important positioning in the new chair would be. Nathan's position in his chair would affect acquiring and improving skills for working on the computer and doing self-feeding. Everyone involved seemed to think the better the status of his hips, the better positioning outcome for Nathan in his new chair.

During the fall of 1986 and the early part of the winter of 1987, I pushed the thought of the possible surgery way over, almost out of my mind, but not completely. I concentrated on doing as many relaxing, replenishing activities as possible. We left the day schedule for Justin at full day so I could have the entire day to be myself with very few demands being made on me. Often, after I dropped my car pool off at school in the mornings, I stopped for coffee at a place where I could go in and sit down. While drinking my coffee, I wrote in my prayer journal and read my Bible.

Some mornings, I got on the Blue Ridge Parkway, which runs past Roanoke. Very few cars travel this two-lane road, which goes through the scenic Blue Ridge Mountains. As I drove the forty-five-mile-an-hour speed limit, I sang hymns and prayed out loud. Frequently, I pulled over to one of the overlooks, turned the car off, and read my Bible. As I looked out on the valley below, I praised God for the beauty of His creation, and I usually took some time to write in my journal. I especially enjoyed driving on the parkway during fall when all the vibrant colors were displayed.

Over the years, writing in my prayer journals has been a way for me to release my concerns to God and a way for me to process what God is teaching me. During the first year Nathan was in public school, I made many entries about the status of our addition project. Some of the money that we earmarked to use on the addition had gone to pay for Nathan's preschool expenses and Justin's day care, so we had very limited money, time, and energy to use on the project.

The Addition

September 23, 1986

This past week, I could feel myself getting very angry with Bob for being slow moving with the addition. God, please help me to be persistent but not upset with these different aspects of the driveway and addition project. I want to be like the wise woman in Proverbs 14:1 who builds her house rather than tear it down with her own hands.

September 24, 1986

Father, as I meditate on these verses below, I am trying to piece together what my approach should be towards the driveway and addition. I believe I am doing the right thing right now, but I do sense that I become discouraged when we do not get as much done as I had hoped each day. Please, Father, enable me to be balanced concerning my approach and attitudes. The Bible seems to strongly emphasize the value of manual labor, yet at the same time the Bible seems to strongly emphasize the necessity of man's dependency on God as he works.

Proverbs 14:23
"In all labor there is profit, but mere talk leads only to poverty."
(NAS)

Psalm 127:1
"Except the Lord build the house, they labor in vain that build it, except the Lord keep the city, the watchman waketh but in vain."
(KJV)

Psalm 127:2
"It is vain for you to rise up early, to sit up late, to eat the bread of sorrows: for so he giveth his beloved sleep." (KJV)

Father, you know my heart's desire is to submit to Your will, though, sometimes it is a struggle not so much with my mind as with my emotions. It is my heart's desire to finish up soon and not have the project drag on for a long time. I feel the completion of the whole project would help us live a much more quality family life and enable us to develop more individually.

After expressing my desires and what I think our needs are, I must say to You Lord, "Do as You see fit." Give me the grace, patience, and forbearance I need to accept and deal with a no or wait a while answer You may give me. Whatever Your answer may be, please allow me to experience Your loving-kindness.

Money

Earlier in the summer of 1986, John, my counselor, said that perhaps lack of money was the root of my struggles. In light of this, I began to talk with Bob about how we could possibly increase our monthly income so that we could better take care of the needs of Nathan and our other two children. One of the suggestions I made was that Bob seriously think about getting a different job with higher pay. Since Bob had a BS degree in mechanical engineering and work experience in that field, I thought it would be good for him to think about getting an engineering position.

After we were married, Bob started in construction work because he thought it would be easier to leave a construction job than an engineering job when the time came for us to go back into full-time ministry. However, with the ramifications of Nathan's brain injury, we were no longer thinking in terms of going back into the ministry. For this reason, it seemed logical to encourage Bob to think about using his college education to help provide for our family.

When I first mentioned the idea to Bob about going back into engineering, he was not interested because he did not think he could sit at a desk all day. Also, he needed to brush up on his engineering skills. In talking we experienced, especially me, frustration as to whether money was really a part of my problem. I felt that the root cause of my emotional fragileness was probably the chemical imbalance. However, after praying about it, I thought that lack of money might play a part in this. The easier it becomes for me to get Nathan in and out of the house, the more energy I will have. In some fashion, money is needed to put in the driveway and to make the back of our house wheelchair accessible.

The topic of money became very stressful for Bob and me. Once, I even stood up and screamed, which is very out of character for me! After several intense discussions, I decided to stop talking about the idea and focused completely on praying about the subject.

October 8, 1986

In the past, it seemed Bob and I were better able to "make do" with our limited money situation. But now that we are worn out from Nathan's program and raising our three children, it is much harder to work on the addition as we keep on with our everyday lives.

October 21, 1986

Dear Father, we stand at a crossroad. Bob and I have discussed and prayed about the need for our annual income to be increased. This has been on my heart for some time and now Bob has the desire and the conviction, but, it seems like we are stuck about a job change and finishing the _____. I cannot write the word that goes in the blank. I need to realize that we are stuck–at a standstill–whatever, until you deem it right for these circumstances to change. Father, what else can I say? My emotions are haywire, but my mind and heart know the truth of the above statement.

November 23, 1986

Father, I asked You to manifest yourself in the building of our addition! I have to believe You are doing just that—in the circumstances of this tri-fold project being almost at a complete standstill. This whole idea goes against my perspective of how I think You would choose to bring glory to Yourself. But, I must believe in faith that You are in control and You are the one who deems in what ways You want to manifest Your glory.

Once again, I am meditating on my life verse Psalm 27:4 "One thing I have asked from the LORD, that I shall seek: that I may dwell in the house of the LORD all the days of my life, to behold the beauty of the LORD and to meditate in His temple." (NAS) My focus must be on knowing You, Father, not on the fruition of my dreams and personal goals. The goals are important, but the real issue is knowing You.

A Revelation Amid the Struggles

Bob sees improvement in my dealing with my emotional infirmity. I do too. I really feel, though, that I need help in better understanding my personality and how to more effectively manage it. I have been working a long time with reducing negative stressors, using the rational thinking process, and increasing activities that replenish my emotional reserves. But I have had great difficulty knowing how to manage the deep, passionate, intense emotions that run through me.

I can see a pattern with the times that I have cared deeply about the well-being of certain people, causes, and institutions. Each time there was an outpouring of prayers and nurturing energies coming forth from my heart and soul. In one way, these times have brought me into a very intimate relationship with God. Yet with the building up of these emotional outputs, at times, I have felt like my passions are trying to strangle me.

Answer to the Prayer

One day, not long after that journal entry, when I was in a counseling session, Dr. R said, "Judy, you have spiritual gifts of an emotional nature that you have not had the maturity to know how to use properly." He continued, "It is like someone being given a beautiful new car and not knowing how to drive it. The recipient gets in the car and knocks around hitting all kinds of things until she figures out how to drive the car. The driver gets some bruises and maybe some broken bones until she masters driving the car."

Over the next days, I reflected on what my counselor had said that day. I began to realize that my ability to feel compassion and my desire to nurture was far greater than my capacity to give of my emotional energies. It is as if my ability to feel compassion is like having a Cadillac heart and my ability to give is like having a Volkswagen body.

Before I had my major burnout, I had several smaller burnouts. Each time I burned out, I was trying to give to the same degree that I felt compassion for the people and situations that were heavy on my heart. This revelation was a turning point for me. From that time on to now, I have been in the process of learning that when I feel compassion in compelling situations I need to prayerfully ask myself two questions:

1. Realistically, should I give of my physical and emotional energies, at this time, to try to make a positive difference?
2. If the answer is yes, how much of my physical and emotional energies am I realistically able to give?

Joy Amid the Struggles

December 30, 1986

My Dearest Nathan,

At the RCOS Christmas party this year, God gave me a precious gift through the people who work with you at your school. As I moved through the hallways, I encountered so many people who had something wonderful to say about you!

Your music teacher, "Bart,' said to me when I went by the room to give her the Christmas present from you, "I hope you don't mind, I am in love with your son." The librarian came up to me in the hallway and asked me if I was your mother. When I said that I was, she replied, "I was thinking about sending you a card to tell you how much I enjoy working with Nathan–how special he is." Next, the nurse who worked with Paul, one of your classmates, came up to me and asked if I was your mother and she told me how much she is enjoying getting to know you, Nathan. Then one of your class aides, Winston, told me how special it was for him to work with you at school.

When people told me these special things about you, I felt like Mary pondering the things the shepherds told her. I said to God, "Thank you Father, for these comments; truly it was the best Christmas present I could possibly be given. I will treasure these affirming comments the rest of my life." Luke 2:18-19 says, "And all who heard it wondered at the things which were told them by the shepherds. But Mary treasured up all these things, pondering them in her heart."

Nathan, God gave me my second Christmas present when I was standing in line to send Christmas presents to our relatives. It was a few days before Christmas and I was doubtful that our presents would get to California before Christmas. So, I said to the person behind me, "I will be happy if my presents get to our California relatives by New Year's Day because it would still be within the Christmas holiday." The woman said back to me, "You really have up to January 6th because it is the epiphany, the day to celebrate the wise men bringing gifts to Jesus." Nathan, to think, the meaning of your name is "gift of God" and you were born on this special day. You certainly have been a special gift to our family!

Love,
Mommy

Career Change for Bob

One day after the first of the year, Bob walked from his current employer, a small construction company, to the engineering firm that was located across the street. The purpose of this walk was to ask his friend John, who had started the company, whether he had an opening for a mechanical engineer. John replied, "No, but I do have a need for an electrical engineer." Bob quickly replied, "I am willing to learn the field of electrical engineering under your supervision." So John hired him on a temporary basis. Bob was willing to take this risk and try something new because he had become fairly burned out with construction work.

Creative Outlets

Another source of joy for me was the opportunities I had for creative outlets. One of my creative outlets was my involvement with the Home Economics Advisory Committee for the school system I taught in when I was single. In the fall, at one of the meetings, the home economics supervisor asked the committee members for suggestions for possible in-service programs for the home economics teachers. I shared that I was available to present a program on either interior design or stress management. I listed the names of the different programs from which the teachers could choose. The teachers chose the following seminar: Burnout—Causes, Cure, and Prevention. I enjoyed preparing worksheets and visuals for my presentation. The day of the program, I cut roses from a friend's rose garden to take for one of my props.

In the spring, I also had a few interior design work opportunities, which included design consultations with individuals and teaching a Decorating Dynamics seminar. I was asked to come back to my mom's church to do another interior design seminar for the women's group. This time I taught on how to plan a successful color scheme. I decided to present three different color-scheme scenarios. I really enjoyed preparing for the presentation. I gathered items from my house to use. After looking at fabrics in several different decorating stores, I went back and checked out the fabric samples that I wanted to use.

In the middle of planning for the seminar, I had a very intense conversation on the phone with a former patterner. She called to let me know she had moved back to Roanoke. Also, she had recently been through a very sad divorce, and she had just lost a close friend to a tragic death. After I got off the phone, I wept.

That night when I thought about her situation, I began to cry again. I walked into the living room, sat down on the sofa, and picked up the textiles and items I was to use in my seminar. As I worked on planning the visuals for the presentation, I felt much better.

CHAPTER 12

The Big Decision

The Decision about Nathan's Hips

In June, when the time came for Nathan to return to the CRC, Wendy, Nathan's PT went again. I went for the first time. I dressed professionally and carried my clipboard folder to take notes. At CRC, Nathan's first appointment was with a developmental pediatrician, Dr. A. When she finished her examination with Nathan, I asked her if I could talk a few minutes more with her. Wendy and Bob left to take Nathan up to the X-ray department. I told Dr. A about the emotional burnout I had experienced and that I was not yet completely recovered from the burnout. I cried off and on as I talked with her.

God's Grace through Dr. A

Dr. A listened patiently; she did not look at her watch. I told her of my concern about the anesthesia aspect of the surgery: that Nathan might die or become more brain injured. I told her of my concerns about not being set up very well at home for taking care of Nathan after the surgery. For example, we needed to make our house wheelchair accessible, which would involve bringing the driveway to the back of the house, building a deck, and making a ramp.

When I finished, Dr. A so very kindly responded back to me, "Let's look at what we here at CRC can do to help you with these concerns. We can arrange for you to talk with an anesthesiologist about the possible side effects of the anesthesia. You can talk with a social worker here at the center in regard to getting your house in order."

Talking with Dr. A enabled me to be ready to go in and see the surgeon, Dr. S, after Bob, Nathan, and Wendy came back from the X-ray department. We told Dr. S that we would do the surgery; however, we were not quite ready to schedule the date. We needed to get more things set up at home in order to take care of Nathan after the surgery. It was agreed we would come back in October to set the date.

The Driveway

By early summer 1987, using a grant, we were able to put the new driveway in all the way around to the back of the house. Since we did not yet have the deck and ramp behind our house, I still was unable to bring Nathan in the house through the back. Throughout the entire summer, I continued to bring Nathan into the house by bumping the wheelchair, with him in it, up the front steps. To do this, I turned the wheelchair so Nathan faced the street, then with my back toward the front door, I pulled the chair so it bumped up each step. Therefore, at this point, having just the driveway put in was not making my life any easier.

The Loan

By this time, Bob had started his new job as an electrical engineer. With the increased income, we were now able to apply for a $10,000 home equity loan. However, the first bank we applied to denied our loan request because they thought $10,000 was insufficient to finish everything that needed to be done. We applied to a second bank, and they granted our loan request. It now looked like we might be able to finish the addition before the surgery.

At the first of the summer, we switched Justin back to half days at Young World. Each morning, I dropped Justin off at the day care center while Bob drove Nathan to Ace camp, a therapeutic day camp. It was run by the Roanoke County Parks and Recreation for children with disabilities, and Nathan attended it every summer throughout his school years.

I deeply appreciated the Ace day camp, especially since I had tried a few summers before to organize similar activities and helpers for Nathan on my own. It was great to know that each day Nathan went to camp he would have stimulating activities to do with dedicated staff to help him. The best part was, I did not have to do any of the planning or executing!

For many years, Nathan also attended Camp Easter Seal, located about one and half hours away from Roanoke. He would stay for five to ten days, and he had a one-on-one counselor. It was a great experience for Nathan to spend the night in the cabin with other campers and counselors. During the day, they had opportunities to do fun things like horseback riding, swimming, and even going up in a tethered hot air balloon. At night, they had bonfires and roasted marshmallows and hot dogs. Nathan enjoyed staying overnight at Camp Easter Seal; however, he eventually decided that he just wanted to do Ace day camp.

BOTH OF MY CAMPS WERE SO FUN FOR ME.

Downward Spiral

Summer 1987

For two weeks, while the boys were busy with their day programs, I took Kristen to advanced swimming lessons in the mornings. At noon, I picked up Justin. At 2:00 p.m., we picked up Nathan from summer camp. Then two afternoons a week, we drove downtown for OT and PT sessions. Whenever possible, I had Kristen go with me to help with loading and unloading of Justin and Nathan. Sometimes, Kristen sat in the therapy sessions so she could observe the type of work each therapist did with Nathan. I tried to expose Kristen to the world of rehabilitation because I knew in a few years she would need to start considering a possible career to pursue. I wanted her to have some ideas of what options were out there.

I always kept toys and books in the car for Justin and interior design books for me. So all I had to do was carry a few of the things into the waiting room. This way, Justin and I could occupy ourselves. One of Justin's favorite things to bring was a little brown suitcase full of Lego blocks. I loved it, as well, because no matter where we were, if Justin had his Lego set, then he was happy. By having my books, along with paper and pen, I was able to move into the beautiful world of interior design anywhere I was. In fact, one day, while the PT was moving Nathan's legs in the treatment room, I looked down at my paper and realized that I was drawing pictures of different styles of chair legs.

All during the summer, we had a lot of different problems with the station wagon. Early in the summer, when I was dropped off at Chuck's Repair Garage to pick up the station wagon, Chuck told me I would not be able to take it home yet because he was not finished with the repairs. Apparently, the problems were more extensive than he first thought. As I stood in Chuck's office, I had trouble processing what he was telling me; my brain seemed to be on overload, and I began to cry. I was unable to make the phone call to Bob, so Chuck made it for me.

The rest of the summer, as I was driving my children to and from their different places, I knew the car could die at anytime as a result of a major problem. Then the day came that the car did die. The red light came on while I was picking up Nathan at his day camp. We decided not to fix the station wagon because it was going to be very expensive to do so. This car that had been given to us had already cost us quite a lot in repairs.

Using a chunk of our equity loan, we purchased a secondhand van. As our medical bills came due, we also used the equity loan to make the payments. As I opened these bills every month, I felt increasingly discouraged. Bob felt we should not use any more money for the addition out of the loan account until we got a very tight budget in place. Once again, we were at a complete stand still with the addition project. I poured my heart out to God in my prayer journal.

July 18, 1987

Dear Father, I feel insecure as to managing my emotional reserves. My emotions have been very flaky this summer. I desire so much for more mental stimulation, looking through the papers for free seminars to attend. I desire so much to be, in a sense, moved into another world: to travel, learn new things, and go new places that are different from my everyday surroundings.

What's wrong with me? Is it wrong that I feel these desires? Do I have the attitude that if I don't get certain things or certain experiences that I cannot be happy? Sometimes I wish I didn't have these desires. Sometimes, I can't tell the difference between what is a desire and what is truly a need.

I feel my life is not balanced properly; however, it is hard for me to see what to add and what to take away. What more can I do? I am submitting myself to your will even though at times it is very hard for me to do so. I am asking the Holy Spirit to lead me and convict me.

It has been so hard, the last day or two, for me to deal with the children. The wining, crying, and demanding of Justin and Nathan this morning was overwhelming for me. I turned the radio up so that I couldn't hear the noise while I dressed. I can feel tears behind my eyes as I write even now. Please help me, Father, please help me!

August 8, 1987

Even though I don't understand the tears behind my eyes and why I feel like a pressure cooker about to blow, You do, Father. My emotions are so out of whack. Last week, I started crying at my eye doctor's office during the eye exam. This morning, when I was talking with Kristen I raised my voice then I started crying.

I need some ways to reduce the pressure so that I can make it through the rest of the day. So, I am visualizing myself fixing dinner and then slipping upstairs to eat by myself. I love to sit in my reading chair in my bedroom, looking at magazines and listening to music. This morning and last night, I was using my imagination to take myself on vacations.

Father, You know I'm worn out physically, drained emotionally and that I am back where I have been so many other times. You know how hard my being down again is on Bob. You understand Bob's frustration.

A Two-Week Respite in Chicago

Here I was back down in the deep pit of burnout. I was crying every day. In less than two months, we were to set the date for Nathan's surgery. Bob felt that I needed to get away for a break, a respite. He came up with the idea of having me fly to Chicago and having his parents fly to Roanoke. Doing this enabled me to have a two-week vacation. I was able to stay in my in-laws' house and venture out during the day to take in some of the sights and experiences of Chicago. Bob's parents were able to help take care of the children and enjoy time with Bob in the evenings.

My two weeks in Chicago were filled with lots of replenishing activities. Using the transit system, I went down to the center of the city to visit the Art Institute four different times. Each time, I spent the whole day looking at the art, going on guided gallery walks with the staff, taking in slide presentations and lectures in the institute's auditorium. Every time I visited the Art Institute, I had a late lunch either in the cafeteria or on the terrace. A special treat for me was hearing a live jazz concert on the terrace while I ate lunch next to a beautiful fountain.

One beautiful day, I spent extended time in Oak Park, touring the home and studio of Frank Lloyd Wright, followed by a walking tour. Using a tape player and headset, I was able to learn about different houses and a church that Mr. Wright had designed. Then I ate lunch outside at a quaint, little café. I loved looking around at the vibrant green grass and colorful flowers.

My sister-in-law, Phyllis, treated me to lunch several different times at a wide variety of restaurants. Before and after our lunches, we enjoyed checking out interesting shops. Also, a family friend, Dorothy, took me to a Polish festival where we watched polka dancing and ate wonderful food.

September 3, 1987

I'm sitting here at a counter in a coffee shop in the Palmer House building after spending the day at the Art Institute for the fourth time. Every day here in Chicago has been wonderful; yet, for the last few days, tears have been coming to my eyes. When I leave, I'm going right back into some of the same demands I had before I left.

Some demands will be different. Kristen and Nathan will be in school. I won't have to pick Nathan up everyday like I did after camp. He will come home on the school bus. Justin will hopefully be toilet-trained.

But Father, I'm afraid. I am afraid of going through spiritual and emotional struggles over the unfinished addition/yard/house project. I'm fearful that the strain I feel at church will drain me of the limited emotional reserves I do have. I'm scared of not being ready for Nathan's surgery. I'm frightened that I won't be able to stay on a tight budget. Please take these fears away from me or show me how to deal with them. Psalm 34:4 "I sought the Lord, and he answered me, and he delivered me from all my fears."

Last night, I cried a lot while I talked to Bob on the phone. I shared some of my fears with him. I told Bob I felt I really needed to take a leave of absence from our church in order to visit other churches. We discussed my desire to particularly check out a large church downtown. After I got off the phone, I watched the epic saga War and Peace on television and had a very cathartic cry.

CHAPTER 13

Cocooning

Arrival Home

On the way home from the airport, Bob began to fill me in on the status of our household. He had been able to get the children settled into their school schedules. Bob had made the car pool arrangements for Kristen and checked on Nathan's bus schedule. I was so happy to find out Bob had already completed all the "getting ready for school" tasks while I was gone. Another treat for me was the discovery that Justin was now completely toilet trained! This was a relief because Bob and I had been working for months with him on this endeavor. However, the final piece of news Bob shared with me was somewhat alarming.

Bob informed me of an accident that had happened while I was gone. Justin got in the van by himself and disengaged the gearshift. The van rolled down the driveway, over the bank, and into the support wall Bob had only three-fourth-finished building. Miraculously, Justin was fine! Praise God! But the two-by-four pieces of lumber Bob had used to build the support wall next to the driveway were knocked out of line. Now he would not be able to finish building the wall until he took the two-by-fours apart and redid the layering. (It turned out to be years later when we finally completed this unfinished project. Justin was actually a teenager by this time, and so he helped Bob do the repairs and assemble the rest of the wall. However, weeds had grown up all around, and so they had to hack them down before they could get even started.)

The best surprise was revealed when Bob and I drove up in the driveway; I was thrilled to see he and his dad had built the deck and the ramp on the back of our house! Now when I got Nathan off the school bus in the afternoon, I could push the wheelchair around to the back of the house on our new driveway, then up the ramp on to the deck and into the house. I no longer had to bump him up the front steps. Being able to use the ramp would help me conserve physical and emotional energy.

Coping Strategies

Nathan needed a new wheelchair, but we could not have him fitted for one until after the surgery. So until then, we needed to use a standard fold-up wheelchair for Nathan's mobility. In order to keep him stabilized in this chair, we used several pillows and Velcro belts. Whenever we took Nathan anywhere in the van, we still had to lift him out of his chair, put him into the van, and then put his wheelchair in separately. Then later, we had to take his wheelchair out, lift him out of the van, and put him back in the wheelchair. This process was very draining for me. For this reason, I was very eager to get a hydraulic lift and have it attached to the van, so it would be much easier for us to transport Nathan to and from places.

Another struggle for me was every afternoon when I had to push Nathan through the unfinished addition at the back of the house. Seeing the plywood walls and the cluttered mess of construction equipment all around was very depressing. As a coping strategy, I tried to imagine I had blinders on, similar to a horse, which enabled me to look straight ahead, not around at the room, as I walked through the unfinished addition.

Simplifying My Life

During the early weeks of being back home, I prayed extensively as to how I should use my time and energy. I did not want to lose the emotional reserves I had built up while in Chicago. I wrote in my journal,

September 23, 1987

Father, I have blocked so many things out of my life so I will have fewer demands made upon me. I feel in a way like I have placed myself in a type of cocoon so I can have time to think, pray, and evaluate my activities. I am doing this, in order, to conserve my emotional reserves for Nathan's surgery. Taking a sabbatical from my church is part of this.

I'm afraid to expend very much emotional and physical energy. I don't know if afraid is the right word; perhaps, the right word is cautious. Yet, at the same time, there is a strong sense within me of waiting on You.

I really don't know for sure what activities I should place in my life. I would like to do something in Interior Design; but, I don't know for sure what form it should take or if it would even be wise for me now. Also, I would love to have the loose ends brought together concerning our house, addition and yard before the surgery; but, I don't really expect it to be. I hesitate to become involved in the tri-fold project; in a sense, it has been a thorn in my flesh for quite some time.

Interior Design Studies

I did not do any interior design seminars or consultations; instead, I did very low key activities related to interior design. In the mornings, right after I dropped Justin off at Young World, I frequently stopped at a nearby restaurant to drink coffee and work on my Bible study. After I finished my coffee, I sometimes went next door to a paint store. As I walked through the door, the manager always gave me a warm hello and some kind of pleasant comment like, "Sure is beautiful weather we are having." This was all the interaction with people I needed. After our verbal exchange, I headed to the wallpaper section of the store, selected books off the shelf; then I sat down at the table.

As I thumbed through the pages, I soaked in the beauty of each design pattern. If there was texture on the page, I rubbed my fingers over the pattern. Throughout most of the books, there were intermittent pictures of beautifully decorated rooms. I loved to study the elements and principles of design used in the decor of each room. Sometimes, I checked out one or two of the wallpaper books to look over at home.

Many days, before picking up Justin, I stopped at the library located around the corner from Young World. I looked for interior design books to check out. If there was enough time, I sat down and studied through my books, making note of sections I wanted to spend more time on later.

Country Drives

Each day, Monday through Friday, I picked up Justin at noon. On pretty days, we often drove a few miles up the road to an old country store nestled against the foot of a beautiful mountain range. Next to the store was a creek and a picnic table. Some days, we bought a hot dog and a drink in the store; then we went outside to the table to eat. Other days, I packed lunch for us. As we sat there eating our lunch, we enjoyed the warm rays of the sunshine and the sound of the creek water rippling over the rocks.

After lunch, we drove down a different country lane that followed the creek. Our destination was a farm that had a zebra, donkey, and an ostrich. This was always our turnaround point. Our journey also took us by a horse farm and equestrian center. As we continued to make our way home, we cut down another country lane, which we knew had a llama farm.

On our "drive in the country" days, we arrived home around 2:00 p.m. Justin went down for a nap, and I rested until it was time for Kristen and Nathan to come home. In the late afternoon, I usually washed a load of dirty clothes while I cooked supper. At night, I enjoyed sitting in the reading chair, upstairs, in my bedroom. While listening to relaxing music, I looked through magazines, interior design books, and wallpaper samples. I would also use this time to fold the clean laundry.

Home Economics Week

During the time before Nathan's surgery, most of my creative outlets were quiet and low-key, not very visible to the people around me. But I had one very visible creative outlet—my position as the chairman of the Home Economics Advisory Committee. For each meeting, I wore a suit and carried a notebook, which held the past minutes, the agenda, etc.

In the fall, our committee was discussing ways we could help promote the home economics programs in the area schools. The ultimate goal was to increase the overall enrollment in these programs. During the discussion, I reported that an area home economist suggested we have a special week to emphasize our programs. The other committee members liked this idea, so we proposed it to the teachers. They liked it as well, so all together, we planned the first "Home Economics Week". We decided to have it take place in January. We needed to have the emphasis early in the semester before the students began to sign up for their classes for the next year. I thought I would only be able to help with the planning because Nathan's surgery was scheduled for January.

However, after Christmas, Bob and I rescheduled Nathan's surgery date for March 3rd so we would have more time to have Nathan's blood drawn. There had been complications with our first attempt; the technicians were unable to get the needle into Nathan's vein in order to draw blood. This meant we had to schedule another trip to University of Virginia Hospital to draw more blood.

As a result of the surgery date change, I was able to be directly involved in the Home Economics Week activities. Since I was chairman of the advisory committee, I was asked to attend the school board meeting for the reading of the proclamation. I wore my red wool suit and white blouse. I was asked to stand during the reading, declaring the first ever Home Economics Week. Bob went with me to the school board meeting. Then after the proclamation, we went to a gourmet French restaurant to celebrate my fortieth birthday. The atmosphere of the restaurant was beautiful and the food was delicious.

The next day, I was interviewed on the noon TV news about Home Economics Week. When the news show was over, the newscaster said she wanted to do a special feature on the importance of home economics education. So the following day, she and her crew shot the feature in the classroom of one of the area high schools, and it was shown on the evening news that night. I was very pleased with how the news feature turned out and so were the teachers.

Another day during the week, I gave a short presentation to the secondary school guidance counselors about the benefits of students taking home economics courses. Throughout the week, I attended several of the special events the teachers had planned at their schools for this special week. One school had a health and wellness festival in the school lobby. This allowed home economics to be brought out of the classroom and more to the forefront. Through this entire experience, I discovered how much I love to help promote things that I am passionate about.

Right now, while writing about all the different things I did for Home Economics Week, I am amazed I could do these "out in front" type of activities while the surgery issues were all around me. Not only was I able to do these activities, but also I enjoyed doing them. They truly were creative outlets. Also, I was getting to use my educational background in a very creative way.

In a sense, it was as if I was in a "protective bubble." Almost no one in that sphere knew Nathan was about to have major hip surgery, and it was very unlikely anyone would ask me what church I attended. These two areas of my life were very sensitive for me. In certain situations, upon hearing the words *surgery* or *church*, I could feel tears forming in my eyes.

Bible Study

Throughout the school year, I had only one regular activity in my schedule while the children were away during the day. It was a women's Bible study at the church where Kristen's school was located. On the morning of the study, I drove the car pool to school and Bob drove Justin to Young World.

The book being used for the Bible study was *Women in the Life of Jesus* by Jill Briscoe. I enjoyed going to the study, but there was a part of me that was concerned someone might ask me what church I attended. Finally, it happened; one day, as I was walking to class, the woman walking next to me asked, "What church do you attend?" With tears rolling down my cheeks, I said, "I am unable to answer that question right now."

The morning the lesson was on sick women in the life of Jesus, I had to leave the room because I was crying. One of the women, Kim, saw I was upset, so she came out into the hallway to check on me. I'm not sure what I told Kim as to why the topic was upsetting me, but I do remember she sent me a very nice note the following week.

The next week, when the study group broke into small prayer groups, the leader of my group asked us to write our prayer requests on index cards and pass them to her. I wanted to ask the women to pray for my emotional healing and for the healing of Nathan's hips, but I was unable to be specific. Instead, I wrote on the card, "Please pray for God's healing for two people in my family who have significant health problems." However, right before Nathan had his hip surgery, I was emotionally able to talk alone with the leader of my small group about the specifics of my general prayer requests.

The morning that our lesson was on spiritual women in the life of Jesus was a special day because the lesson had a tremendous positive effect on my life. The lesson was taken from John 12. In Bethany, Jesus was visiting with friends. Martha was serving dinner, and Lazarus was seated at the table next to Jesus, who was reclining. In John 12:3, "Mary therefore took a pound of very costly, genuine spikenard ointment and anointed the feet of Jesus and wiped his feet with hair, and the house was filled with the fragrance of the ointment." In the lesson, we were asked the following question: "What would you offer as your costly perfume?" The question stimulated me to write the following in my journal:

November 15, 1987

Father, during the past summer, I became acutely aware that you did not want us to make headway with our addition. After we were granted the equity loan, we needed to use a significant amount of it to buy a van and to pay off our medical bills. The loan was the last ray of hope I had for finishing the addition before the surgery. With that ray of hope disappearing, it has been very difficult for me to cope with the disappointment.

I asked You to manifest Your power and glory through the remodeling of the house when we bought it. And I asked You to manifest Your power and Your glory through the building of our addition. I am very aware as I think back about these prayer requests that our house is Your house and our addition project is Your addition project.

At first, when things came to a standstill on our addition, it seemed to me, in a way, You did not love me as much as You had in the past. Humanly speaking, it did not make sense to me that a messy, partial-sided addition and torn-up, junky yard would bring glory to You. I was thinking more in terms of what people would think as they drove by our house. Now, I realize You want to show me, not the people driving by on our street, Your glory and power by giving me the grace to live with the tri-fold project being at a complete standstill.

What does one do with dreams and goals that are at a standstill; yet, the dreams remain passionately a part of one's life? In a sense, the dreams are burned into one's soul. Father, this is a very important question for me and perhaps for other people too. Attached to my dreams, there are a lot of deep emotions that can be aroused in me to the point my emotional reserves begin to be depleted.

Oh Lord, I now have something to do with my unfulfilled dreams, desires, and goals. I can offer them up, symbolically, to You as an expensive perfume to anoint the feet of Jesus. As I do this, may a sweet, sweet aroma fill my house and go with me as I go about my daily tasks of taking care of Nathan, driving in the carpool, cleaning house, and doing laundry.

Because I am an aesthetic person this is a very appealing concept to me. Truly, for me be able to do this, Your power and Your glory is being manifested in my life for me to see and for others to see. The process of doing this I feel will be a means of conserving my emotional reserves.

My woodwork is chipped, my walls are dirty, my floors are shabby, and our addition is not finished and is filled with stuff and more stuff. My backyard is overgrown and spotted with junk. Yet, I am experiencing a soft, sweet victory.

Father, when there is something we should do to facilitate further development of the addition project please nudge us into whatever it is. But, until then, I have something to do with my dreams, offering them up to You. You are enabling me to do what it is written about in 2 Peter 1:6 (TLB) "Learn to put aside your own desires so that you will become patient and godly, gladly letting God have His way with you."

The Elders Pray

One Sunday afternoon, not long before Nathan's surgery date, I asked Bob to call our pastor and tell him I would like the elders to come and pray for Nathan and me. I had been thinking about this for several weeks, and that day, after having my devotions, I thought, "Now is the time!"

When the elders arrived, we all sat in the living room. Bob sat beside me on the sofa. We shared with the elders that I wanted them to pray for the healing of Nathan's hips, his upcoming surgery, and for the healing of my emotional infirmity. I was concerned about having sufficient emotional energy to handle the surgery. Since I wanted to explain as much as I could about my emotional infirmity, I began, at the beginning of the story, with my praying to have twins.

I shared about the painful happenings of Seth's death, Nathan's diagnosis of brain injury, and my burnout. As well, I explained about how these difficult events took place while our church was going through such a trying time. It was as if my personal crises interwove with the difficult situations that were happening in our church.

It was very difficult for me to talk with the elders about these things. Frequently, I had to stop, put my head on my hands, and weep. Each time I stopped, the elders waited silently for me to begin again. When I got to the end, I said, "Right now, I don't see how I can realistically be an active part of our church fellowship unless my emotional infirmity is completely healed."

CHAPTER 14

First Surgery

I HAD MY FIRST HIP SURGERY ON MARCH 3, 1988. I WAS NINE YEARS OLD. I CAME HOME WITH A BIG WHITE CAST. IT COVERED BOTH OF MY LEGS AND MY HIPS.

In a way, it is hard for me to believe Bob and I have already been to Charlottesville for Nathan's surgery after so many months of preparation. As I look back to the surgery day, I am amazed, thrilled, and very thankful to God that I had such a high degree of emotional stability. There were points, all along the way, when tears would mount up behind my eyes for a few moments and then disappear—the day before the surgery, the day of the surgery, and the days that followed in the hospital and in the Children's Rehabilitation Center's inpatient clinic.

The first time I felt a significant emotional uneasiness was the day before the surgery, when I realized I had a misconception about the care Nathan would be given by the nurses. I thought there would be a nurse or a child development person staying right with Nathan by his bedside or his reclining wheelchair during the times Bob or I would not be by his bedside. I began to realize my misconception when Kathy, a nurse, talked with us the day before the surgery about Nathan's cast. A few hours later, we went upstairs to meet Nathan's attending nurse and to see the room Nathan would go to after his surgery. I asked her about the amount of attention that would be given to him by the CRC staff.

The attending nurse and I were standing just outside the door of the room Nathan would be in when he returned from surgery. Inside the room were a six-year-old girl with cerebral palsy, who had surgery that day, and her mother beside her bed. I had just learned a few minutes earlier Abigail's mother was staying with her day and night. As the nurse and I were talking, I told her I was not planning on spending the nights with Nathan while he was recuperating from surgery. I began to cry, so I asked the nurse if there was somewhere we could talk more privately because I did not want Abigail's mother to hear me talk and cry.

The nurse found a small room for us; we sat down and I began to explain to her why I felt I should not stay, night and day, continuously with Nathan. I briefly told her about the major burnout I had five years before and the effect it had on my life. I explained how I had decided, months before the surgery date, not to stay by Nathan's bed day and night. Bob was to stay by his bed the first night or so. Then he would drive back to Roanoke, work a few days, and return the day Nathan was discharged. I was to stay every night at the Ronald McDonald House.

I knew I would get little, if any, sleep if I was on a cot next to Nathan's bed. Bob very easily returns to sleep, but I do not. I felt staying with Nathan night and day would quickly deplete my emotional reserves, then I might suffer a mini burnout. If this happened, I would not be able to function well enough to take care of Nathan during the day. The nurse was very understanding, and I felt much better after talking to her.

The second time I felt as if I might lose my emotional stability was the next day, the day of Nathan's surgery. Bob and I took Nathan into the pre-op/post-op room, where Abigail was staying. We were to wait in this room until the time came to go over to the main hospital in the van.

Very soon after we entered the room, I noticed Abigail was not in her bed, and I did not see Abigail's mother, Ann. I turned to the nurse standing next to me and asked, "Where is Abigail?" The nurse responded, "Abigail became ill during the night and returned to the main hospital." I asked what the problem was, and to my horror, the nurse told me Abigail stopped breathing during the night! I asked if there was a respirator in the CRC building, and she told me there was not. I, then, explained to her we had friends who had a child who became brain injured after having open-heart surgery because there was not a respirator nearby when she stopped breathing. The nurse said she was going to talk with Lisa, the pediatric nurse practitioner, about our concern. When she returned, Lisa told us to talk with Dr. S about having Nathan stay the first night or two in the main hospital after the surgery.

Not long after this discussion, Bob and I were riding in the van next to Nathan, who was lying straight out on his back on a stretcher. We were headed to the main hospital. I had a tremendous number of items I was taking along with me: my coat, bedroom slippers, tote bag filled with snack food, a couple of canned drinks, books to read, my interior design notebook, my Bible, my Bible study workbook. We had packed up Nathan's suitcase before we left, so we would have his clothes, books, etc., for spending the night in the hospital. It was difficult for me to get all this stuff on and off of the van.

I was not sure how long Nathan's surgery would last, and I wanted plenty of projects to work on while I waited. I decided months before the surgery date that I did not want to sit in the waiting room thinking about Nathan being "cut on" during the surgery process. I brought my slippers along in case my feet became tired.

When we arrived at the main hospital, the staff immediately placed Nathan on a gurney. Then they took him to a pediatric pre-op waiting room used just for children coming over from CRC. We followed along behind Nathan, and I even put some of my bags on the end of his gurney. On the way, we saw Dr. S in the hallway. I told him we would like for Nathan to stay in the hospital for the first night or two so he could be monitored closely, just in case he needed a respirator. He agreed!

Later that day, still lying on the same gurney, Nathan was transported to another pre-op area. The anesthesiologist came in and talked to us about what he would be doing. Then he gave Nathan an injection of a sedative that made him feel woozy. We talked with Nathan or read to him the entire time until he was taken out to go to the operating room.

At different points throughout the day, I sat down and leaned my head against the wall. Then I closed my eyes and silently quoted 2 Timothy 1:7, "For God has not given us a spirit of fear, but of power, love and sound mind," in rhythm with my breathing. Doing this helped me keep my focus on trusting Nathan into God's care.

After Surgery

When Nathan was rolled into the room, after his surgery, he was very sick, vomiting from the anesthesia. As I look back on how sick Nathan was, I am so aware of the special strength God gave me to stand by his bedside. While Nathan was recovering, I put wet washcloths on his forehead to cool him and help provide comfort.

The second day after the surgery, Nathan was transferred back to CRC. For a few days, Nathan was given morphine for the pain; it was administrated through the IV hook-up. When the morphine started to wear off, Nathan cried intensely. When this happened, I usually left the room while Bob waited with Nathan for the next injection of morphine. I could not bear to see Nathan in pain, so I immediately walked down the hall and through the exit door to take a break.

Each time, I walked over to two little shops in a very small strip mall. I breathed in the springtime air and enjoyed viewing the flowers. Perusing the interior design shop and the gift/stationary shop, I was moved into a world of beauty. There was a little café between the shops where I stopped to get a cup of coffee to take back with me to Nathan's room. By the time I got back, Nathan usually was asleep as a result of the morphine injection. Then while Bob took a break, I sat next to Nathan. I kept a stack of interior decorating books and magazines beside Nathan's stack of books. While Nathan slept, I read, studied, and took notes. This process moved me into the beautiful world of interior design.

As Nathan began to awaken, I stroked his forehead until he went back to sleep. When the medication wore off and I no longer was able to get him to sleep by stroking his forehead, it was time for Bob to take over. I am so glad that most of the time I was not in the room when Nathan suffered the most. Nathan did not recover as fast as we anticipated; therefore, Bob made no mention of going back to Roanoke. Each night, Bob slept by Nathan's bedside, and we continued to take turns during the day sitting beside him.

Back to School

After his recuperation at home, Nathan went to school in a reclining wheelchair we had rented before the surgery. Nathan needed this special chair because he could not bend at the waist. His legs were spread apart, and the cast covered both of his legs completely and came up to just above his waist. He wore sweatpants with a large drawstring waist so we could get the pants to go over the cast. We showed Nathan's teachers and aides how to care for Nathan while he was in the spica cast.

During this time, I was so thankful for Mr. King, Nathan's teacher, Wendy, his PT, and Marty and Diane, his classroom aides. God used them to help us get through the difficult days of making medical decisions, going through the surgery, and then the care afterward. Things moved along fairly smoothly for the six weeks Nathan had his cast on. But the closer we came to the date of Nathan's return to CRC to have the cast taken off, the more I felt an emotional heaviness.

April 5, 1988

Last week, I had a very intense emotional heaviness hanging over me. This week I feel much better; but, there is a slight weariness I feel. I'm not quite sure why I do.

Part of what may be bothering me is the fact that for months I have been preparing for Nathan's surgery; therefore, I have laid aside many of my usual concerns like the finishing of the addition/yard project and dealing with my church relationship status. Instead, I have been concentrating on resting and replenishing my emotional reserves, in order, to be better able to deal with the added stressors of the surgery.

Soon, Nathan's cast will come off and the event I have been resting up for will have culminated. Father, will I be bothered again by the addition/yard project being at a standstill? What am I to do about my church relationship status?

Return to My Church

After Nathan's cast came off, I decided to go back to our church. Not because I really felt comfortable about going back, but because I wanted to be with my family. Although I attended the services, I was not able to emotionally handle actually sitting in the sanctuary, so we sat in the overflow area.

Wheelchair Clinic

May 24, 1988

Now that Nathan's hip surgery and rehab was behind us, it was time for us to get into serious planning for Nathan's new wheelchair. We were entering new territory; this was to be Nathan's first customized wheelchair. There were also other students in Nathan's class who needed new wheelchairs. Mr. King helped organize a wheelchair-evaluation clinic to take place in the school library after school hours. Those participating were Dr. K, various therapists, teaching staff, vendor representatives, and the parents of each student. Each student's chair was to be custom designed according to his or her individual needs. The parts needed for the chair design would be ordered from various companies, then put together by the vendor.

Desire for Van Lift

May 25, 1988

Father, You know I have been talking with Bob about the need for a hydraulic lift for our van. Bob does not think we can buy one right now; he feels we need to make sure we get our medical expenses all paid off, first.

If it is Your timing for us to add a hydraulic lift to our van, then make your leading very evident to us. It is very interesting that there is a second-hand lift we can get for $500. If this is not the time for us to get a lift, please make this known to us and give me the grace to deal with the disappointment.

The subject matter of the hydraulic lift is a very sensitive area for me. During the wheelchair clinic yesterday, this subject came up, along with statements concerning Nathan's surgery, which I did not understand. Between the two parts of the evaluation, I slipped out of the room so I could be by myself to cry and regroup.

I so desire to have the easiest and safest way to load and transport Nathan this coming summer. Last summer was very hard for me. I don't want to have to deal with the difficulties of lifting Nathan again!

June 28, 1988

We have our hydraulic lift now! Father, thank You we were able to receive a grant to cover the cost of purchasing and installing the second-hand lift that we found out about a few months ago. The total cost was less than $1,000.

Thank You for looking out for the details of the lift so marvelously. I am so appreciative the passenger seat, in the front, did not have to be placed all the way up, in order, to accommodate the attachment of the lift. Instead, we can have that seat all the way back, giving us plenty of legroom. Also, I thank You that we can still have both of our bench seats in the back of the van.

What a difference using the lift made yesterday as we did some sightseeing after Nathan's appointment at CRC. The weather was lovely. We had such a nice lunch at historic Michie Tavern, a good time at the Thomas Jefferson Museum, and a wonderful visit at Ash Lawn-Highland, the home of James Monroe. During the afternoon, our whole family was in and out of the van at least three different times. Having the lift made it so much easier!

CHAPTER 15

Second Surgery

June 28, 1988

My heart is heavy though, Father, as I think about what Dr. S told us during our appointment. Nathan's right hip is now severely out of the socket, so, he is recommending a Kiriostomy, which is a surgery to correct this. I am distraught by the possibility of going through another major surgery with Nathan. The thought of all the pain he would have to endure is so very depressing.

The surgery, the stay in the hospital, the six weeks with the cast, then another hospital stay when the pins are taken out, and all the factors that surround this process present tremendous demands and pressures for Bob and me. But, most of all, though, Father, it is the thought of Nathan being in so much pain again that is so very hard for me at this time. In the midst of this decision, I will give thanks to You. I say this out of obedience to Your Word, not because I am happy about this decision we need to make.

Prayer for Healing

June 29, 1988

Father, I am asking You to heal Nathan's hips and legs totally without another surgery. Please, You who are all powerful, move the ball of Nathan's right femur underneath his right hip socket. Keep the left femur securely under the left socket. You, O Lord, can do these things if You choose to do so. My heart (and whole being) cries out to You to do this for Nathan and for us as a family.

I anticipate the work of Your healing hand in the next few months. If this healing does not come about, I must accept Your choice in the matter. Thy will be done!! If we are to do the hip surgery, enable Bob and I to evaluate our past surgery experience and make the necessary changes so the whole process will go smoother for Nathan, Bob and me.

Preparations

The month of July was very busy for us. I often had to call Donna, our nurse coordinator at the CRC. She helped me schedule appointments for us to come to Charlottesville and have Nathan's blood drawn for the upcoming surgery. I was so thankful for Donna! She was easy to talk with and truly seemed interested in our lives. I appreciated how she always took a few minutes to chat, like the time she asked about how Nathan enjoyed his camp experience.

Not only did I have to set up the appointments for Nathan, but also I had to make arrangements for Kristen and Justin. Which families could they stay with in Roanoke? I was praying for all this to be used in a positive way in their lives.

Difficulties

July 27, 1988

Father, two difficult situations came up last night.

1. *Finding out the electrical damage we have in our house—the outlets, TV, VCR, radio, etc. because of lightning striking the house during the storm yesterday afternoon.*
2. *Bob's report to me that John is disappointed in the speed of his electrical engineering work. Bob is to increase his speed and keep up his accuracy as well on each project.*

The latter of the two situations is especially complex since we have Nathan's surgery scheduled for September 22nd. Father, enable me to explain this complex situation to Kristen today or in the next few days. Manifest Yourself to Kristen, Bob, and me as we look to you to guide us. Thank You, Lord, for how I am presently responding to these two situations. Please continue to help us as we deal with the upcoming surgery.

Temporary Strategy

Bob and John agreed that during the next two months, his work would be closely monitored to see if there are improvements. If his work does not improve sufficiently, Bob will need to look for another job. Then John will hire someone else to do the electrical design work. Bob told John he was willing to help train the new person, if at all possible.

Pleasant Brooks and Meadows

August 9, 1988

Please encourage me spiritually today, Father as I read Your Word. Thank You for being at work in the lives of my children as we prepare for Nathan's second big hip surgery.

Psalm 16:5-6 (TLB) "The Lord himself is my inheritance, my prize. He is my food and my drink, my highest joy! He guards all that is mine. He sees that I am given pleasant brooks and meadows as my share! What a wonderful inheritance!"

Father, as I read the above verses, a very special memory is coming back to my mind: the day I stood on a mountain in Highland County looking down at a beautiful valley below with its creeks, green pastures, and grazing sheep. Highland County is called the Switzerland of Virginia. This stimulates me to think of other pleasant memories in my life.

Pleasant Brook and Meadows that God has given me:

1. *The beautiful way God prepared Bob and me for each other and the way He brought us together and nurtured our relationship*
2. *The birth experience of each of our children*
3. *The sweet relationships I have with each of my children thus far*
4. *My trip to Chicago last summer—I enjoyed all the rich aesthetic/intellectual stimulating experiences I had there. I especially appreciated my four days at the Chicago Art Institute, my day at the Frank Lloyd Wright House with a tour of the area, and the wonderful times with Phyllis, Wayne and their family. Recently, my reflections of my two weeks in Chicago have been very refreshing to me.*
   The list goes on and on.

Father, I feel compelled to write down what I think You are telling me right now in regards to our house/addition/yard projects still being on hold.

"Judy, when you become concerned about the house related projects just stop and ask Me to make you and Bob aware of when and how you should make a move concerning these projects. Don't boggle your mind right now with making plans for how you can finish the house projects.

Take the following approach, Judy. When you notice the trashcans in the back yard, when you notice the overgrown brush in the back, when you notice the junk piled up in the addition, when you notice the worn out carpet in the entrance hall, etc., stop and close your eyes, picture the sweet faces of your children, and remember the way I brought Bob into your life. Think on any one of the pleasant brooks and meadows I have given you. And I have given you many, Judy. Ponder these blessings. Smile. Praise Me and thank Me. I will give you grace through this process, Judy. I will give you grace."

All through the summer, I had been praying for God's sustaining grace. With news of Bob's job insecurity coming on the heels of Nathan's need for another hip surgery, I needed an extra measure of grace. God did this through Psalm 16:5-6 as I wrote and reviewed many different lists of people and experiences that are my meadows and brooks. This added grace carried me into and through the next surgery.

Surgery No. 2

September 20, 1988

Father, tomorrow we leave for Charlottesville. Please continue to give us wisdom, strength, and peace of mind. Be with Dr. S. and any other doctors who will be in on the surgery. Please, please fix Nathan's hip completely this time if it be Your will. Enable Nathan to be calm during the surgery preliminaries. Please make the recovery go well for Nathan and enable him to have less pain than he had with the first surgery.

UVA Hospital Family Waiting Room

September 22, 1988

God answered our prayers by enabling Nathan to be very calm yesterday and today before the surgery. He only had a few times he was anxious. This meant a lot because I was very concerned about how he would respond to the waiting time before the surgery since he knew the type of pain he had after his first surgery.

God gave Bob and me insight into how to do some things differently this time to make the process go smoother. Early this morning, we took Nathan over to the main hospital straight from the Ronald McDonald House in our van. This worked much better than before when we started at the rehab center and then traveled to the main hospital in the hospital van. Instead of having Nathan on a gurney to travel through the halls, he stayed in his wheelchair until the last minute. The injection of a sedative to make him feel woozy was given to him while he was still in his wheelchair. This helped make the experience less traumatic for all of us.

Right now, I am set up at a table, just like I was for the first surgery, with my books and paper in front of me. The last time, I did not feel like thinking much about the surgery or about the impact of the day. I did a short Bible study, then I began reading a book on managing stressors. I basically kept my thoughts focused on what I was studying in the book. I wanted to take notes to benefit me in managing my stress points and also to use, someday, in the stress management classes I hope to teach.

However, today I feel more like writing about what is going on around me right now. What I see is as follows:

Billie, the hospital's family representative in the family waiting room, is wonderful. I love her personality. She was here in March when we had Nathan's first surgery. Billie's peppy, stable personality makes the waiting so much easier. It was great to talk with her for a short while. Billie is tall, strong in character, energetic, has gray hair, and is simply dressed. Her husband was an Episcopalian minister, and she has raised five children. Billie had a minister father, grandfather, and great-grandfather. As of yet, none of her children are ministers although one seems to be thinking about it.

As I look around the waiting room, some people are reading books, some women are doing handiwork, and some people are just sitting. One man is turning his keys over and over in his hands. An attractive older woman is knitting an Afghan. Two women are sitting next to each other talking. One lady was writing letters earlier.

Before the last surgery, I was determined to have a lot of projects to work on while I waited here. Bob and I had thought we might be waiting eight or more hours, so I brought several books to study. Today, I have several books also to study. For the past four years, especially since I prepared to teach my first interior design class, I have loved to study books and take notes particularly on the subjects of interior design and stress management.

Across from where I am sitting is a large mural with a frame going around it. The picture in the mural is of a fall, woodsy scene with a country road and country plank fence. The golden tones remind me of how the fall trees look when the sun shines on their orange, red, and yellow leaves. The mural has a calming effect on me. It reminds me of my many wonderful rides on the Blue Ridge Parkway. Also, the fall foliage mural reminds me of the pleasant brooks and meadows God has given me as my share that is spoken of in Psalm 16:5-6. How wonderful to sit here and be reminded of pleasant memories of the past.

I am realizing that the way a hospital family waiting room is designed and decorated is very important for the physical and emotional comfort of the people waiting to hear about their loved ones who are in surgery. As well, I am seeing that the personality and attitude of the family representative also has a strong influence. I am so thankful for Billie's calm yet joyful presence.

In the Hospital after Surgery

September 23, 1988

Father, I praise and thank You for bringing Nathan safely through the surgery. This is not something Bob and I take for granted. I'm so glad this is behind us. Thank You, too, Nathan is not as sick as he was after his last surgery. It seems the tube down his throat to his stomach, which drains out the junk, helped him not be as sick from the anesthesia. Also, he does not seem to be having as much pain from the surgery itself as he did last time.

At Home

October 2, 1988

Thank you, Lord, for the healing process of the sore on Nathan's back and that he was feeling spunky last night. He was talking and crowing like a rooster. This is the first time since the surgery he has been this animated!

Father, I feel some of my old concerns will start to mount up inside of me when Nathan's cast is taken off. I don't think too much about these concerns now because I am very focused on taking care of Nathan while he has his cast on and then going back to the hospital for one more surgery. This surgery will be very short, about fifteen minutes long. While Nathan is under the anesthesia, his cast will be taken off and the pins taken out of his hips.

CHAPTER 16

Reflections

After Surgery No. 3

November 30, 1988

Bob and I are so thankful we are now on the other side of all three of Nathan's hip surgeries. In my mind, the surgeries posed life-and-death situations. I was concerned about having sufficient emotional reserves to deal with any possible complications from these surgeries.

Actually, this last surgery ended up being the hardest for me even though it was only fifteen minutes long. This time, there was another couple and their child in the anesthesia waiting room with us. However, during the last two surgeries, we had been alone in the waiting room. This couple had an urgent concern that there was not sufficient blood drawn ahead of time for their son's surgery. Due to the length of the surgery, there was a possibility he might have to get a blood transfusion from an unknown donor. I empathized greatly with this couple's situation. I felt like Bob and I were the ones facing the risk of a possible transference of disease into our child from someone else's blood.

During the first two surgeries, Nathan had received an injection of a sedative, while in the waiting room, to help him fall asleep almost immediately. However, this time, when our anesthesiologist came into the room, he did *not* give Nathan this sedative. Consequently, Nathan cried very hard as he was being wheeled down the hallway to surgery. Bob walked along beside him, but all I could do was lean my head over in the corner of the hallway with my back turned away from all the people. As I heard Nathan crying out, I wept; I felt like my heart was breaking into pieces.

Special Families

During the hospital stay, I was drawn to record my observations of some of the other children and their parents. At the Ronald McDonald House, I met David and Helen who are from Ireland. Their young daughter, Grace, was at the hospital to have several different surgical procedures done to help correct her birth defects. Grace had a rare genetic syndrome that caused a deformity in her lips and hands.

One day, while sitting around the kitchen table, David showed me the scrapbook he was making for Grace. This was very special to see. The scrapbook contained pictures and newspaper clippings pertaining to the fundraising activities of their community back in Ireland. David explained how many people did a wide variety of activities to raise money for Grace's trip and surgeries. In the scrapbook, there was a picture of a man sitting in a bathtub being pushed down the street for a fundraiser.

In the hospital room with Nathan was a boy named Jeremy with a rare genetic bone disorder, which causes his bones to break very easily. I had several nice chats with Jeremy's mother, Kathy. Her stress level stays rather high, all the time, because of the nature of Jeremy's condition. She never knows when Jeremy will hit something or fall and break one or more of his bones.

The last night, I picked up a book from the RM House library. When I went to bed, I read this short story written by a woman from Lynchburg, Virginia. She had actually been a guest at the RM House while her Down syndrome baby was in the hospital. I cried as I read the details about his short life and death. I felt as if I could reach out and hold the hand of this very special mother.

Wheelchair Redesign

Once we were back from Charlottesville, we focused once again on Nathan's wheelchair. This time, we were redesigning portions of the chair. The lumbar roll that was built into the back of the wheelchair had been an ongoing problem. The back of the chair had been reconstructed once already to put the lumbar roll in a different place. Eventually, the lumbar roll was completely taken out, and a separate one was made which could be secured by Velcro onto the back. The vendor put the Velcro in several different places so that we could try moving the lumbar roll around and see what would be the most comfortable for Nathan. Working on all these adjustments to the wheelchair was very taxing for Bob and me.

Nathan's Intellectual Development

Amid the struggles of going through surgeries and obtaining equipment for Nathan, there was the joy of seeing Nathan's intellectual development while he was at Roanoke County Occupational School. We were so grateful to the Lord for this blessing amid the hardships. One of the ways I expressed my excitement was by writing a letter to Nathan at the end of the school year.

June 10, 1989

Dear Nathan,

Your speech therapist, Cheryl, saw your potential to learn reading skills. She connected you with a reading teacher, Paulette, who worked with you one-on-one regularly at school. Nathan, it was very special the first time you came home from school with a lesson from your reading teacher. Paulette sent a note along with the lesson telling us to have you read the sentences to us. As I listened to you read the sentences, tears of joy mounted up behind my eyes. It was so very special to hear you read, to see you do something I knew you could do, but others would have difficulty believing unless they saw more tangible proof.

Another special event happened as well. Daddy had just bought a bottle of "Sesame Street" shampoo for you and Justin. When Daddy was bathing you and Justin, you became very upset when he began to shampoo your hair. Somehow, Daddy finally understood you wanted your very own bottle of Sesame Street shampoo.

Daddy told you, in a few hours, he would buy you your own shampoo. Since we had Joel's birthday party to attend, Daddy said a stop at Revco Drug Store could be made on the way. After Daddy bought the shampoo and got back in the van, you, of course, wanted to hold the shampoo bottle on your lap.

As we drove to Kathy's house, you asked us to spell the word shampoo. I'm not sure how you communicated that to us, but somehow, we knew that was what you wanted us to do. Perhaps you started with "S" and then we knew. You looked at the letters of the word shampoo while we spelled it for you. By the time we reached Aunt Kathy's house, you could spell shampoo all by yourself. At Joel's party, we asked you to spell shampoo for everyone there. After doing this, you started asking us how to spell all kinds of words.

Nathan, you are talking more, learning to read words out loud, learning to spell, and counting out loud. All this progress is a part of my dreams for you. I am very proud of you!

Love,
Mommy

My Personal Development

During this time, I also experienced growth and reflection related to my personal development. This was really important because it helped to balance out the intensity of working with Nathan on his development. I also gained more insight into my abilities and strengths through these endeavors.

April 12, 1988

For a while now, I have had the thought of working part time with an established interior designer. If I am to do this, Father, lead me to the best situation. Is there a place where I could feel comfortable, learn a lot, and replenish my emotional reserves at the same time?

At this time though, Lord, I find it very difficult to give myself full permission to move onward with my teaching and design work. In a way, I guess I am saying to myself, "Do I have the right to promote my skills when my house and yard do not show my knowledge and my expertise?" In a sense, I feel like I would be a hypocrite: saying one thing and yet doing another. This discrepancy affects my confidence in moving forward as an interior decorator.

Right now, I cannot say to myself, "Well, Judy, you are doing the best you can with what you have" because I am not very motivated, at this time, to clean and paint my walls and woodwork. This is primarily because when I paint the chipped areas it is not long until there are a lot more chips made by the wheelchair and toys.

Another complicating factor is to complete these house projects we are going to need more money and/or materials and labor. If I had a fairly good paying part-time job, I could help make the money to complete these projects. Part of me thinks, maybe, it would be better to work at something unrelated to interior design. However, I would love to add to my work experience in the design field.

Yet, I do not want to turn my love for interior design into a negative stressor. The fields of art, interior design, and horticulture have been my creative outlets, sources of great joy and relaxation. I want my work related endeavors in the field of interior design to, also, be a source of joy and relaxation and not a source of negative stress for me.

Through heading the Home Economics Advisory Committee to promote Home Economics education, I have gained skills in marketing. Perhaps, I can use these skills to someday further my career as an interior decorator and a seminar speaker.

Possible Ministry Direction

December 1, 1988

Father, over the past few years, I have come to see that my spiritual gifts lie strongly in the area of encouragement and exhortation. Isaiah 61:1 says, "The Spirit of the Lord God is upon me, because the Lord has anointed me to bring good news to the afflicted. He has sent me to bind up the brokenhearted." As I read and reread this verse, Father, my heart yearns to bring good news to the afflicted and to be a part of binding up the emotional wounds of the brokenhearted. I feel You are preparing me to do this.

There are many people who are dealing with very intense situations in their lives; perhaps, it may be middle age couples dealing with rebellious children and, simultaneously, dealing with aging parents who are ill. I think dealing with a parent who has Alzheimer's disease is an extremely difficult situation. Long-term intense situations, whatever they may be, are hard for most people.

Lord, You have been teaching me much through the story of the Good Samaritan in Luke 10:30–35. "Jesus replied and said, 'A certain man was going down from Jerusalem to Jericho; and he fell among robbers and they stripped him and beat him, and went off leaving him half dead. And by chance a certain priest was going down on that road, and when he saw him, he passed by on the other side. And likewise a Levite also, when he came to the place and saw him, passed by on the other side. But a certain Samaritan who was on a journey, came upon him; and when he saw him, he felt compassion, and came to him, and bandaged up his wounds, pouring oil and wine on them; and he put him on his own beast, and brought him to an inn, and took care of him. And the next day he took out two denarii and gave the innkeeper and said, 'Take care of him, and whatever more you spend, when I return, I will repay you.'"

Many people lie on the road of life, emotionally wounded and exhausted, just as the man in this story lay physically wounded. As Christians, we need to be sensitive and aware of those around us who are hurting and be ready to show them compassion. However, helping the needy can be a huge task. Even the Samaritan man enlisted the help of another person in caring for the injured man. I want to show compassion to people who are emotionally injured or hurt, but I cannot perform the entire role of the Good Samaritan by myself. In the past, there were times I have felt compelled to do as much as I possibly could to help. However, when I tried to help a hurting person to the degree that I felt compassion, I often became emotionally depleted.

Because I easily burn out, I believe my ministry needs to be more from somewhat of an emotional distance. It would not be wise for me to become, too, involved in the complex details of the lives the hurting people I desire to help. Instead, I can direct them to Christians who have the personality and gifting to handle the more complicated aspects.

When faced with a person in need, I must remind myself that the degree of compassion I feel usually exceeds the ability I have to give. I need to remember how I easily burn out if I try to walk along beside the person, who I want to encourage and help, on an ongoing basis.

I need to ask myself . . .

1. *Does God want me to be a part of the healing process of this hurting person?*
2. *If the answer is yes, then how much of my time and energies am I to wisely invest in helping this person?*

I want to have objective compassion. Over the years, I have learned about the importance of this. I describe it as the ability to show concern for someone who is in need, while maintaining an impartial view of the overall situation. Keeping this balance is not easy because after a person starts helping someone in crisis, then they often become quite personally invested. The subsequent emotional attachment tends to cloud a person's judgment. Maintaining objective compassion requires great effort and intentionality. Taking time to do a personal evaluation on a regular basis is necessary. If this is not done, the "helper" is in danger of burning out.

Utilizing the seminar setting is one way I can more easily have objective compassion as I seek to help hurting people. It allows me to point people in a direction and share encouragement without having to be personally involved in each of their lives. In this setting, I am able to ask questions and listen. Also, I can get others involved by asking the participants for their input. I really enjoy this type of group interaction for teaching and learning.

PART FOUR

Mending Heartache

CHAPTER 17

New Dreams

New Dreams:

January 6, 1989

My Dearest Nathan,

Today is your birthday. You are now ten years old. I have high hopes and dreams for you. I dream of seeing you someday in your new room sitting in front of a special computer system writing stories. I dream of you, one day, driving to your room in a motorized chair. Also, I envision a large deck or patio where you can drive around and enjoy the fresh air and view beautiful flowers, trees and perhaps a fountain. It would be marvelous to have flowers blooming three seasons of the year.

I dream of you living a very quality, semi-independent life, having friends over, going places, and giving of your talents to others. I look forward to what God will do in and through your life. You have a bright future ahead!

Love,
Mom

Conversation with God

January 6, 1989

Oh Heavenly Father, sometimes I think it would be so much easier for me not to have these hopes and dreams. It is difficult for me to know how to handle them. To accomplish the goals, the dreams, we need money and/or resources and skills donated, which at this point in time we do not have. Having these high and lofty dreams and not having the resources to accomplish them has been, at times, a source of discouragement, despair, and depression for me.

In fact, the juxtaposition of my dreams for Nathan contrasted with the disarray of the unfinished addition and yard has been a thorn in my flesh. The past four and half years have been filled with intense struggles for me:

- *First, I asked You to manifest Your power and glory through supplying the resources to build the addition; then, Bob and I did not feel the emotional and spiritual freedom to accept the full offers of help we received. We did have a peace about accepting enough money to purchase the special shower stall unit.*
- *I knew it was not Your timing to move along with the building of the addition; yet, I did not understand how an incomplete project and messy yard could bring glory to You. I have had many discussions with You about this while sitting in the car in front of our house.*
- *I felt like You had forgotten me and didn't care about my concerns, as I continued to bump Nathan up the front stairs in his wheelchair.*
- *The visual picture of my incomplete house and yard rubbed against my aesthetic nature and was an irritation to me like hearing the sound of chalk squeak across a chalkboard.*
- *I verbally gave my desires and dreams over to You, yet the struggle continues for me.*
- *I wrote out on paper my desires for finishing the addition and yard projects and for having family vacations. Then I put the papers in an envelope and put the envelope on my bedroom closet shelf. I viewed this as an act of giving my desires and dreams over to You; yet, the struggle continues for me.*
- *Bob was able to change jobs so that our family income could be raised; but, then we were denied an equity loan at the first bank where we applied.*
- *Then we were approved for a loan at another bank; but, we needed to use a big chunk of the money to get a van and then to pay for medical expenses.*
- *When I saw we could not take any more money out of the loan account, I realized receiving the loan was not going to accomplish the goal of finishing the addition and yard before Nathan's hip surgery.*

- *I came to the point where I knew of no other human effort we could make to complete the project; I realized You had more to teach me through the project being at a complete standstill.*
- *As I faced Nathan's first big hip surgery, I received grace to deal with the incomplete project by symbolically offering it up to You, Father, as an expensive perfumed oil to anoint the feet of Jesus.*
- *During Nathan's second big hip surgery, I received an extra measure of grace to deal with the incomplete project still being at a standstill by reviewing the many pleasant memories You have given me.*

I had hoped, after the surgeries, I could help raise part of the needed money for finishing our addition through my interior design work; but, I had doubts about this direction. At this point in time, I cannot give myself permission to pursue my Interior Design career ideas.

Writing a Book

Birth of a New Dream:

January 9, 1989

I have recently come to the point I can give myself permission to write a book about my journey with Nathan. I feel an affirmation from You, Father, I am to write my story. Perhaps the selling of the book will provide the money for completing the addition/yard project. I realize though, Father, You may choose to provide the money or resources some other way than by the selling of my book. But, I will have something wonderful to work on while I wait.

I really consider writing this book more important than my work as an interior decorator. Yet, I have a strong desire to do both. But, if I knew I only had one year to live, I would choose to write my book.

In fact, in the last few days, I have already begun to write. Writing this book has now become my primary focus other than my responsibilities of being Bob's wife, raising our children and managing our home. I want my book to be a spiritual legacy to leave my children and someday their children, telling them about my love for You and about Your healing hand in my life.

By writing and publishing a book, I will be able to share my story of emotional healing with many more people. It could be my book would be one of the many resources that You desire to use to point hurting people to Jesus Christ, the One who heals the brokenhearted and revives the crushed in spirit.

However, I don't think I have reached the place in my life, yet: the point of recovery, which warrants the conclusion of the book. Perhaps, I am close to the end, but then again I may not be. As I ponder about my book, I'm asking myself what I consider to be the victorious ending of my story. I don't even know if this is exactly how I want to phrase the question. I don't think the real victory is to be found in the completion of the addition.

Is the victory for me to be more emotionally healthy and when I am not, to be able to pull back, pray and analyze what is behind my emotional unevenness? Then, give thanks to You, Father, in the midst of the tears and the sadness I feel? Is part of the victory, also, being able to make wise choices based on gauging my physical and emotional reserves?

I love to write in my journals! The process of writing about my life, my passions, my dreams, my goals, my hurts, my joys, and my disappointments brings me great joy. I write for long periods of time without stopping to even figure out where I am going. Father, thank You so much for showing me Your grace through giving me a new dream. I am writing my book while I wait for You to work out my concerns.

April 11, 1989

As I have said several other times in my journal, the vision of writing and publishing my book is enabling me to cope with my unfinished house, addition and yard. When I lose sight of the vision of the book, I find it hard to cope with my house. So even though I find it a little hard, right now, to visualize my book actually being finished and published, I will keep writing as a means of expressing my thoughts and my prayers to You, Father. Also, it is a means of recording the steps You lead me to take for the continued healing of my emotional infirmities.

My Dreams for Bob:

January 17, 1989

Last night, Bob and I went to a Chinese restaurant for a dinner date to celebrate my birthday. During dinner, I shared with Bob some of the things I hope to do in the days of my life You allow me to live . . . from traveling to painting pictures. When I finished sharing, Bob stated he did not have any ambitions outside of making it from one day to the next.

Oh Father, Bob has so little extra emotional and physical energies at this point in time. It would be wonderful for Bob to have the time and place to have creative outlets that replenish his emotional reserves. Perhaps, when we finish the addition he will have a place to do this.

I would love for Bob to, once again, be in a teaching ministry. Bob is greatly gifted by You as a teacher of the Word. Recently, I read a newsletter from an old friend of Bob's, Russ, who is a part of a Christian organization which helps local churches. When I looked at the picture of Russ teaching a seminar, I thanked You for uniquely designing him as Your servant and for the ministry You are carrying out through him. Oh Father, how nice it would be for Bob to be in a teaching ministry: perhaps, in a home Bible study or in a church.

Please, Father, I ask you to place us in the church situation which would be best for each member of our family. I really think I need a church change in order to maintain and build up my emotional reserves so I can better face the crises of the future which are bound to come.

Replenishing Emotional Reserves

In the past, when I have talked with my counselors about my concern of not having sufficient emotional reserves to deal with future crisis situations, it seemed to me that they did not completely understand. However, I do believe this is a legitimate concern. Somehow, Proverbs 31:17, 25 ties in with this concern. "She girds herself with strength, and makes her arms strong . . . strength and dignity are her clothing and she smiles at the future." Because the virtuous woman took action to build up and maintain her strength, she was able to smile at the future. *Girds* is an action word.

For years, I would make gains in building up my emotional reserves and then a series of demands would rapidly decrease my supply. I needed an extra measure of emotional strength, in order, to meet the diverse demands of Nathan's surgery. God led me to take extraordinary measures. Before Nathan's surgeries, I took action to greatly build up my emotional strength. My action included drastically reducing the number of demands on me and greatly increasing the opportunities for me to be replenished. As a result of taking this action, I was able to go through four hospital stays with Nathan, three of which included surgeries, all taking place in less than one year.

I thank the Lord for giving me this plan of action. Bob and I both felt this was the direction for us to go. God enabled me to be able to give myself permission to focus the majority of my time doing relaxing, replenishing activities. Also, He gave me the grace to carry out this plan by giving me Bob as my husband, who gave me the time and support I needed to do these activities.

The Birth of a Dream:

After Nathan's first hip surgery, a seminar began to crystallize in my mind based on what I had learned. The opportunity for me to teach this seminar came very soon. I had been attending the PMS support group at the Center for Women's Health. One night, after one of the meetings, the facilitator, Julie, asked what future programs the group would like to have. I volunteered to present a program on Creative Outlets—Replenishing of Emotional Reserves. Julie liked my outline for the seminar, and so we set up a date for the near future.

March 15, 1988

I'm very excited about presenting my seminar on Creative Outlets to the PMS support group at the Center for Women's Health. This opportunity may open doors for more opportunities.

Lord, please guide my thinking and my preparation as I work on this presentation. Help me to organize my thoughts clearly and to develop interesting means of teaching the concepts and getting feedback from the group. I want to inspire the women to add one or more creative outlets to their lives. It is so wonderful to have such a happy subject matter to develop; I love talking about creative outlets.

The Presentation

The night of the seminar, I wore my red wool suit with a white frilly blouse. I set up a demonstration table on which I put several potted plants and two pitchers of water. During my talk, I used these as illustrations: The plants represented the various demands of life and the water signified a person's emotional reserves. As I talked about the using up of emotional reserves, I poured water out of the pitcher into the potted plants. While I did this, I asked the women to name different demands frequently placed on their lives that deplete them of energy. Then as I poured water from the second pitcher back into the first one, I defined a creative outlet as an enjoyable activity that replenishes our emotional reserves so that we can more effectively live our lives.

Next, I asked the women to remember different activities that have helped them replenish their emotional reserves in the past. Then I gave the women a corresponding worksheet to help them better understand these concepts. The sheet encouraged them to think through how they personally expend their emotional reserves and practical ways they can refill their water pitchers.

I shared with the participants that the most replenishing activities are those that are opposite in nature of how we spend the majority of our time. For example, during the years Bob and I patterned Nathan, I was not drawn to creative outlets that involved gathering supplies, such as sewing projects or craft projects. This was because, in order to carry out Nathan's program, I was constantly gathering supplies to make his word cards, picture cards, and homemade books.

Also, I was not interested in activities where I would have to talk a lot with people because I interacted with people every day while carrying out Nathan's patterning program. However, I was drawn to aesthetic activities I could passively enjoy, such as an art show or a musical program. When people were a part of these activities, I desired only to have light conversations about happy things. As I went to these particular functions, I could, in a sense, feel the emotional reserves being poured back into my soul. It was like water soaking into the dry ground.

One year, I received some money on my birthday and purchased a season ticket to our local ballet. It was so much fun to look forward to each ballet performance. Also, I really enjoyed reflecting on the beauty of each individual ballet; it felt like a complete escape from my everyday routine.

Through my interior design studies, I realized the importance of balancing dominance and contrast. Just as it is a key concept in beautifully decorating a room, balance is integral to a person living a joyful life. Too much dominance in a room—such as using only one color, one texture, or one pattern—is boring. Too much contrast in a room is confusing like having many diverse colors, textures, or patterns. Most of the time, the dominance of our lives is our work activities and the contrast of our lives is our creative outlets. However, before the first hip surgery, I needed the dominance of my life to be my creative outlets and the contrast of my life to be my work activities so I could build up a high amount of emotional reserves.

I used several different tools to help the women in the class understand how to best select possible activities that would have a replenishing effect for them. I made a flannel board presentation to illustrate the principles. Also, I designed an activity worksheet and a handout.

Many of the concepts in this seminar came from insights I received from the Bible. Water is a very important image throughout all of scripture; it represents life and vitality.

Psalm 22:14 says, "I am poured out like water, and all my bones are out of joint. My heart is like wax. It is melted within me. My strength is dried up like a potsherd . . ." From my personal experience, I have discovered this is what burnout feels like.

Isaiah 58:11 says, "And the Lord will continually guide you, and satisfy your desire in scorched places, and give strength to your bones, and you will be like a watered garden, and like a spring of water whose waters do not fail." As I took time to do activities I enjoyed, the Lord used these to help give strength to my bones and to pour water back into my soul.

CHAPTER 18

Motherhood

The Joy of Motherhood Returns

Taking action to increase my emotional reserves really helped me to be able to get through Nathan's surgeries. As well, I found that another benefit of having replenished my emotional reserves was the joy of my motherhood returning. This is clearly evidenced in my journal writings.

December 15, 1988

It seems as I write in my journals, thinking of the many special times you have given me in the past has brought me much joy. The happy times of my life are rising above the sad times. Yesterday, I realized I felt much more like my pre-burnout self. I was laughing with Justin and singing a lot of my "kitchen opera" as I worked in the kitchen.

I really enjoy my three children. I can see how having a higher level of emotional reserves is enabling me to sing and laugh again. Oh Father, this is vital to my relationship with my children.

I feel maintaining my emotional reserves is of utmost importance to my spiritual vitality as well. Then together, my emotional and spiritual vitality are key to how I relate to my children. I, in a sense, help show them who You are and so does Bob. I want my children to have a happy mother who radiates the joy of a close relationship with You, lives a balanced life, and who enjoys being the woman You created her to be. This is a very special gift I can give my children.

I have come such a long way, Father, with my emotional healing. I am so very thankful for the state of wellbeing You have brought about in my life. I feel I must very prayerfully manage the emotional reserves You have restored to me.

Communicating with My Children

January 18, 1989

Oh Father, I hope and pray my children do not feel they have been or are the cause of my times of crying and sadness. Oh, how I don't want them to feel this way. Over the years when I have felt emotionally overwhelmed, I have tried to consistently tell my children they are not the cause of my tears; rather, I am tired and don't feel well and so I need to rest.

When I was a child, I tended to connect myself to the moods of the people close to me if they appeared not to feel well. Looking back now, I believe I subconsciously thought I might have done something to upset them. Even during times when I knew I did not do anything, I still felt a responsibility to lift their spirits.

I realize now that I have carried this tendency into my adult life and sometimes it is a source of negative stress for me. I began to notice I was frequently feeling very emotionally drained after being with people. I observed that when I left my house my emotional reserves were built up to some degree, but when I came home I was down to almost empty. If the people around me seemed stressed or sad, then I felt stressed and sad. Not only has this realization come slowly, but also my ability to change my incorrect thinking has come slowly. I am still in the process.

As a child, I didn't think about the fact that there are a lot of reasons why a person might not feel well such as fatigue, low blood sugar, a headache, PMS, or being upset with someone other than me. Now as an adult, I can remind myself of these possibilities. When needed I can ask:

"You seem not to feel well. Is anything wrong?"

"Are we okay?"

"Is there anything we need to talk about?"

As well, I can always remove myself from the situation if I continue to feel uncomfortable. If needed, I can choose not to put myself in certain types of situations. I have choices; I don't have to be a victim.

With my own children, I can keep reassuring them I love them unconditionally and they are not the cause of my times of crying and sadness. I can continue the habit of asking them for their forgiveness when I speak unkindly to them and keep hugging them often throughout the day.

As I have in the past, on the days I experience fatigue, I can go upstairs when Bob comes home from work. Father, thank You that Bob has an even temperament and that he carries on with the children in such a beautiful way when I need to rest.

I can continue to pray for my children, pouring out my heart to You as I write in my journals.

Praying for My Children

April 9, 1988

You have chosen to bring my healing in a slow progressive way instead of instantaneously or even in one year's time. It has been a little over five years now since I bottomed out with burnout and the healing process is still taking place.

Father, in spite of my emotional struggles, please, please use me to lead my children to know You and love You. I'm especially concerned about Justin because I'm not spending as much time teaching spiritual truths to him. Help me to do this more and give Justin a desire to listen.

August 8, 1988

Father, thank You for my wonderful husband and my three sweet, affectionate children. Please enable me to nurture each child spiritually, physically, mentally, and emotionally. Thank You for the other people You bring into their lives to help with this nurturing process.

December 5, 1988

Father, throughout the day whisper in ears of my children, "I love you; I uniquely created you; you need Jesus." Encourage my children through their teachers. Thank you Father, for all the wonderful teachers you have given my children.

Priorities

I recently read a letter in "Dear Abby," written from a father who regrets he did not spend more time with his children. Also, I listened to a talk about fatherhood on the *Focus on the Family* radio program. After pondering these things, I feel more encouraged about the time and energy we have spent and continue to spend on our children. Bob will not have regrets after our children are grown that he did not spend enough time with them.

Because of our love for God and our desire to raise our children to glorify Him, we have placed their well-being above the completion of the addition/yard project. As well, we have also placed my well-being before the project. Improving houses and yards are a temporary investment, but investing in one's family can have an impact for eternity.

Ministering to My Children

April 10, 2000

As I looked over these past entries, I realized it was more important to Bob and me to keep Kristen in a Christian school environment than to use the tuition money to finish the addition. In fact, this thought never occurred to us. Knowing that Kristen had understanding Christian teachers to help be a safety net for her was a great comfort to me during my burned-out years. Also, it was important we use day care for Justin so I could rest and he could play with other children. If we had used the day care money instead for the addition, I may not have recovered enough from burnout to do Nathan's surgeries and, more importantly, to nurture our children.

Kristen

Kristen was thirteen when I began to feel more like my pre-burnout self. Often, when Kristen came home from school, she needed to talk with me about her day. Sometimes, we sat at the kitchen counter for several hours as I listened to Kristen pour out her heart about the difficulties she was having with some of her girlfriend relationships. At times, I made a few comments. Often I prayed with her. We also had many talks about the dynamics of guy/girl relationships. I shared with her biblical principles that had been helpful to me when I was single.

Kristen was on an emotional roller coaster, going up and down because of the fluctuation of hormones. For example, one day, when I went to pick Kristen up from basketball practice, she started crying after she got in the car. When I asked her what was wrong, she said, "Please, don't come up to the gym entrance in the Pinto ever again. I don't want my friends to see me get in this car. I can't believe Dad bought a Ford Pinto and a rust color one to beat it all!" When Kristen finished venting, I said, "I am so sorry the car is a source of emotional pain for you, but we will not be able to get another car right now. I will speak to Dad about being sure to get your input next time we buy a car."

Nathan

Nathan was ten years old when I started to feel more like my old self. We had made it through three surgeries! He was making progress in school and reading and spelling out loud.

January 23, 1989

> *The other night, Nathan was unhappy and I went in to talk with him. While I lay next to Nathan, he said to me, "I can't walk; why can't I walk?" Tears mounted up in my eyes when he asked me this question. I tried to explain to him what happened to cause his brain injury. Then I moved into talking about all the things he can do such as talk, read, spell, write with a computer, sing, and make people happy.*

At another time, Nathan said to me, "I can't put my pants on. Why can't I put my pants on?" Using a children's book that had a diagram of the brain, I explained about the different parts and how they control various aspects of our bodily functions. I went on to tell him about how his brain injury had affected many parts of his brain and so this is why his body cannot do many of the things that other people can do.

Throughout the year, Nathan continued to ask these kinds of questions. Once it was "Why can't I comb my hair?" Another day it was "Why can't I put on my shoes?" I realized that he was grieving over each aspect of his disability. This was further confirmed when, several times during this period, he made several unusual requests to go to his bedroom. Then, when he was alone in his room, he would cry.

One day, when Nathan came home toward the end of the school year, he said, "Some children walk some. Why can't I?" This question was stimulated by the fact that one boy in his class sometimes was in a wheelchair and sometimes used a walker to help him walk. I tried to explain to Nathan that the motor part of this little boy's brain was not hurt as much as his.

Finally, I told Nathan about how, as Christians, the Bible assures us of the hope of heaven and the gift of new bodies. I explained that with these new bodies in heaven, we would be able to do everything. He replied by going through every question he had asked during the school year. Nathan asked about being able to walk, putting on his socks and pants, combing his hair, etc. Then he mentioned something that I had not heard him express before; he asked me, "Will I be able to help Dad like Justin does?" With tears in my eyes, I said, "Yes." Nathan responded by saying that he wanted to go to heaven now. So I explained that God has certain things for us to do while we are here on earth and so our lives here are very important as well.

Justin

Justin was about five years old when I was feeling like my pre-burnout self. In the evenings, I would read to Justin and Nathan out of the *Little House on the Prairie* series. Also, I read to them out of EB White books and *Hardy Boys* books. This meant so much to me because I really did not want the boys to leave early childhood without my reading these to them.

A few years later, when Justin was new in the third grade, he began to struggle with anxiety. For example, one morning, he would not walk out the door to get in the car with Kristen. So I told my car pool partner to go on with Kristen, and I would bring Justin to school later. When Justin and I pulled up in front of the school, he would not get out of the car. I drove around with Justin hoping he would eventually be able to tell me what was wrong. I first drove him by one of the first apartments I lived in that was near the school. Next, I took him by the other two apartments I had lived in when I was single.

The whole time, I was praying that Justin would become more relaxed and be able to tell me what was wrong. I drove him by the apartment my sister lived in the first year she was married. Then, I decided we would go across the street to the VA Medical Center and see if Bob was in his office. While Bob talked to Justin, I went down the hall to get a cup of tea. I was praying intensely that Justin would be able to verbalize to Bob what was wrong. When I got back to the office, Bob said he had not been able to find out what was bothering Justin.

The next day, I was driving the car pool. When we reached the school, Justin would not get out of the car. So I drove across the street to the parking lot of a strip mall. I said to Justin, "Sweetheart, what is bothering you?" Once again, Justin was unable to verbalize. My concern was that perhaps someone or something had scared him. I held Justin's hand and prayed with him. Then we drove back across the street to the school.

I asked the principal to talk with us. Justin did get out of the car and we went in to talk with Mr. Brown, but he was still not able to verbalize what was bothering him. After Mr. Brown prayed, I looked at Justin and said, "Justin, you need to go to your class now. Mr. Brown will walk over with you and I will be leaving." As we parted ways, I had tears in my eyes. It was very difficult for me to do this, but God gave me the grace to do it.

Several years later, Justin told me that hearing Mr. Brown pray for him was such an encouragement to him during that difficult time of his life. To this day, Justin does not know exactly what triggered his struggle with separation anxiety. However, he learned to trust God with his fears.

CHAPTER 19

Emotional Wounds

How Healed Am I?

January 18, 1989

    Today is my birthday; I am 41 years old and I feel I have been given a new lease on life. I am excited about the writing of my book. I am excited about what You are doing in my life and what You might do through my life in the future. Thank You, Father, for the restoration and spiritual vitality which You have brought me thus far. I give You much praise and adoration for this precious gift. I feel like the psalmist in Psalm 40:2-3 when he says, "He brought me up out of the pit of destruction, out of the miry clay, and He set my feet upon a rock making my footsteps firm. And He put a new song in my mouth, a song of praise to our God."

    I don't know exactly how to view myself. Is my emotional capacity half full or three-fourths full? Father, please show me the answer to this question. A few years ago, I felt as if I was dying emotionally and perhaps even physically because intense stress can apparently bring illnesses, which can take one's life. At least now, I don't feel as if I am barely hanging on anymore. For years, I would go in and out of periods of tremendous emotional and physical fatigue. It seemed I spent a lot of time down in the pit of destruction and the miry clay.

    Father, I am no longer in the pit. But, when I hear about a sick baby or a baby who has died I feel deep emotional pain. I thought that when I had recovered from burnout I would not feel this kind of distress. I really identify with the prophet in Jeremiah 16:18-20 when he cries out, "Why has my pain been perpetual and my wound incurable, refusing to be healed? Therefore, thus says the Lord, 'If you return, then I will restore you . . ."

Lord, I am returning to You again and asking You to restore me. Please show me the next step You want me to take. Do I still have unresolved or unprocessed grief? Perhaps, I need to go back and, in a sense, relive the pregnancy and stillbirth of Seth in order for the emotional healing to take place. According to my earlier research about traumatic events, as long as the memory of Seth's stillbirth remains unprocessed, it can be triggered causing the pain to come back as if it happened yesterday.

Further Healing

I have discovered that the healing of my emotional wounds involves being an intentional, active participant. Since I have several emotional wounds, I need to first prioritize the sequence in which I will work through them. In Psalm 34:18, God states, "He is near the broken hearted and saves those who are crushed in spirit." As I look back, I believe God first addressed saving me from being crushed in spirit (being burned out.) He did this by strengthening me through His Word and allowing me many opportunities to do creative outlets. As well, He made His presence very near as I remained brokenhearted. Now God is beginning to help me tackle the healing of my brokenheartedness. He is in the process of bringing me to a safe place to do this.

The Tapestry of Life

All people have a blend of temperament traits and past experiences that affect the way they live and respond to life's situations. The blending of my temperament traits enables me to love deeply, commit firmly, and give abundantly to those I love. As a result of this blend, I am also more vulnerable to developing certain emotional wounds. Each wound that takes place is like a slashing in the fabric of my life.

As these emotional wounds are cleaned, stitched, and healing begins to take place, indentations or raised places develop in the fabric of my life, producing beautiful texture. Some of my wounds are not completely healed; therefore, it is as if they are very loosely stitched together, such as the pain I have in regard to Seth's death. For example, when I hear about a baby who is extremely sick or a baby who has died, it is as if this loosely stitched cut in the fabric of my life is being briefly pulled apart. After the crying spell, the cut goes back to the original state. My hope is, as I work through the grieving process, my wound will not be so sensitive.

March 28, 1989

Father, I believe You are the One who is drawing the thread in and out of the fabric of my life to bring about the healing of my emotional wounds as I follow the steps You show me to take. Psalm 147:3 is very encouraging to me, "He heals the brokenhearted and binds up their wounds." With a physical wound, it is important to clean it with hydrogen peroxide to keep infection out. Infection in an emotional wound could be caused by bitterness or malice that is allowed to linger. Ephesians 4:31 instructs us, "Let all bitterness and wrath and anger and clamor and slander be put away from you, along with all malice."

As I look down at the fabric of my life and I see the emotional wound I have in regards to my relationship with my church, I ask You through the power of the Holy Spirit to convict me of any wrongful attitudes and/or bitterness. Like Psalm 26:2 expresses, "Examine me, O Lord, and try me; test my mind and my heart." So far, I don't seem to see any bitterness, but show me if there is. In fact, one reason I am staying so pulled back at church, perhaps, is to avoid situations in which I might struggle with bitterness. In a sense, I am trying to prevent an infection in an open wound. Is this an accurate appraisal of my situation? Is this the approach You feel is best for me to take at this time, Father? Show me otherwise if You want me to see this another way.

Please help me to explain this concept to Bob, Father. Where can I go for more information about emotional wounds and healing? Lead me to more verses in the Bible. Have me hear helpful information on the radio and on the TV. Lead me to books and magazines that have articles on this subject matter.

April 6, 1989

Bob is talking with the elders of the church about what would be best for me and our family: whether to stay or to go to another church. If we stay, I will lay aside working on the emotional wound I have in regard to Seth's death. I will come back to it later, when the church area of my life is more resolved. This is because I do not have enough energy to deal with both of these issues at the same time.

In order to continue working through the grief of Seth's death, I will go to the SHARE Support Group for people who have lost babies due to miscarriage, stillbirth, or early infant death. I may also reconstruct Seth's funeral service. If I come into some money, I may even have his little casket moved here to a Roanoke cemetery. I want this journey to be special, to be sweet amid the tears of sorrow.

A Week Later

Bob, along with the elder board of our church, have made a decision. They think it best for our family to go to another church on a trial basis. So in spring of 1989, our family started visiting a new church. It was the one I had frequently visited before Nathan's first hip surgery. Once we made this choice and the change was in place, I felt so much better.

Remembering Seth

Now I had the emotional space to go back and review the stillbirth of Seth and allow myself to face the unresolved grief. I began to write extensively in my journals about Seth. As I wrote in my journals, I prayed God would use this process to bring about more healing regarding the emotional wound I had due to Seth's death.

I wanted a way to validate how I prayed for twins, God granted my request, I gave birth to twins, one died, and how He has a purpose for each of my twin sons. In a sense, the partial quote I found recently in our local newspaper expresses how I feel about Seth: "A chance to make an impact and a chance to develop an identity." Even though Seth only lived for seven months in my womb, I want to develop an identity for him and find a way to use his short life to make a positive impact in our society. The day I was writing in my journal about my concerns for Nathan's education, God began to give me more insight about where I was emotionally.

Feeling Betrayed

May 27, 1989

Recently, Mr. King, Nathan's teacher, told me there is a possibility Nathan might be eligible to be in a different class next year. He thinks the class would be a good opportunity for Nathan. Father, You see all the factors involved in choosing the right educational setting for Nathan. You know whether it should be continuing at RCOS, the possible new multi-disabled class at Herman L Horn Elementary, or some other elementary school. Because You are all knowing, You know what the potential advantages and disadvantages are for each educational option for Nathan.

Because Your wisdom is perfect, You know which educational environment would be best for him.

Somehow, Father there is a fear I have inside of me that You will not do what is best for Nathan. Does this stem back to my pregnancy and the delivery of my twins? I prayed specifically and intensely for the well-being of my babies while they were in my womb. I also prayed for the quality of their lives after they were to be born. Every concern that came to mind during the pregnancy I tried to write in my journal. When a concern returned, I reread the recording I had made in my journal and said to myself, "This concern is given over to God."

All of a sudden, right now as I am writing, Father, I realize perhaps I have felt betrayed by You. The process of writing down my concerns for my babies, Father, was not just a spiritual encounter for me, but a deep emotional encounter with You and with my babies. I became intensely bonded with my two little babies.

When I found out I was carrying twins during the first sonogram, I felt like everything was going to be okay because You, God, had so awesomely answered my prayers in regards to my desire to have twins. Since I was thinking this way, I had not thought through ahead of time on what to do if anything went wrong with the delivery. However, ten years ago, I do not remember seeing anything in the media or in print about the grieving process involved in losing a baby. So, perhaps I still would not have realized the need for holding my dead baby.

CHAPTER 20

New Beginnings

New School

AFTER RCOS, I WENT TO MOUNTAIN VIEW ELEMENTARY
SCHOOL. MR. KING WAS MY TEACHER AGAIN.

Over the summer, the new multi-disabled class was formed, and it was
located at Mountain View Elementary School. Mr. King came from RCOS to
be the teacher. Diane also came from RCOS to be one of the classroom aides.
Nancy and Shirley were new aides for the classroom.

Mr. King asked me to volunteer once a week in the classroom. Each week,
I worked with a few students in language arts and math. I loved being in the
school; it was such a happy place to be. Walking down the halls, seeing the
smiling faces of the students and the teachers was a lift for me each week.
The principal, Tom, and assistant principal, Judy, were upbeat, gracious, and
enthusiastic.

After I finished my morning session of tutoring, I stayed for lunch. I
went through the cafeteria line, stopped a few minutes at Nathan's table, and
then headed on to the teachers' lounge where I relaxed for several minutes.
Sometimes, I looked through some of my books I thought might help me in
my journey with grieving Seth's death.

In the afternoon, I went back down to the classroom and worked with
Nathan on the computer. I wanted to become more familiar with the computer
system Nathan used at school because Bob and I were hoping to soon obtain
the same kind of system to use at home. At the end of the day, I loaded Nathan
up in the van and drove across to pick up Justin at his school. I also volunteered

at Justin's school on a rotational basis, doing organizational tasks at different locations within the school. As I moved about the building, I enjoyed watching the children doing various developmental activities.

In the spring, I helped organize the big yard sale for Justin's school, which was one of their main fundraisers. It was lots of fun to interact with the other mothers as we priced the items. The day of the yard sale, I was a bagger at the checkout table. I wanted this job because I had been a bagger at a yard sale fundraiser a few years before at Kristen's school. I so enjoyed seeing the different items people bought that I wanted to have this same role again. During this time, our addition project was at a complete standstill.

Mr. King's class at Mountain View; Nathan is behind Mr. King

October 15, 1989

I almost ignore I have a house, except to do the laundry and prepare and serve meals for my family. I stay out of the house a lot reading the paper, doing my Bible study, writing in my journals, and volunteering at Justin and Nathan's schools. The volunteer work I do for the schools is very enjoyable. Truly, it is a creative outlet for me which replenishes my emotional reserves.

New Church

OUR FAMILY HAS A NEW CHURCH. MY BROTHER AND I ARE EACH IN A CHILDREN'S CHOIR.

In the fall, we joined our new church and we became much more involved. On Wednesday nights, each of the boys enjoyed going to their children's choir groups. After I dropped Nathan and Justin off at their rooms, I went upstairs to a discipleship class called MasterLife taught by Pastor Chuck, our church's minister of discipleship. The following year, Bob and I took the class together.

As I went through the two semesters of the class, it was exciting for me to study and discuss topics such as how to have a personal quiet time with God, discern God's will for our lives, share the good news of Jesus Christ with others, and disciple new believers in how to grow in their faith. By the end of the MasterLife class, another level of emotional healing had solidified for me. Now I knew my experiences with Seth's death, Nathan's brain injury, my severe burnout, and my slow recovery give me a unique platform to share the hope I have found in Jesus Christ.

Also, I became involved with one of the Women on Mission groups in our church, now called WAV. We met twice a month on Wednesday evenings to study missions, to pray for missionaries, to listen to missionary speakers, and to plan mission projects for our group to do. Being involved in this group was definitely a creative outlet for me. I so enjoyed the personalities of the women in my group and the different activities we did centered around missions. At times, we had lunch or dinner together after doing our mission projects.

Bob and I joined an adult Sunday school class with a very good Bible study and prayer time on Sunday mornings. The class also had a wide variety of fellowship gatherings, which took place in the homes of different members of the class. We had game nights, theme dinners, cookouts, and ladies luncheons, etc. Participating in these gatherings provided another creative outlet for me.

Remembering Seth

Once we were comfortably settled in our new church, I felt strong enough to open the door, even further, to process my grief in regard to Seth's death. To help me do this, I went to the SHARE Support Group, which met once a month at a nearby medical center. Bob accompanied me to give me encouragement.

Being in the room with the other parents who had lost babies through miscarriage, stillbirth, or early infancy death was so special for me. It was a privilege to hear their stories and to share our story. Participating in the group enabled the frozen grief inside my soul to thaw. As I listened to each person's story, the tears flowed and flowed from my soul. I did not try to hold them back at all.

After each meeting, I looked through the different books in the support group library collection. I usually selected one or two books to take home and read. As I read the stories about other couples who had lost babies, tears often rolled down my cheeks. At times, my sporadic tears turned into heavy weeping. I took notes from sections of the books that meant a lot to me. Later, I read and reread my notes. In conjunction with reading, I wrote, for hours at a time, in my journal about Seth. This process nurtured a desire within me to do a special project for our local Crisis Pregnancy Center in memory of Seth. It was not long until I took action on following through with this desire.

Living Memorial

February 17, 1990

This week, I went to the Crisis Pregnancy Center and talked with the director, Ruth, about my memorial fund idea. I shared my desire for a living memorial for Seth, not just a tombstone. I told her I wanted to do something that would actually make a positive change in our society. I discussed with Ruth how I felt there were other Christian couples who would like to do something of this nature in memory of their babies as well. I thought perhaps wall plaques could be put up at the CPC with the names of the babies who were being remembered by the donations given to the center.

Ruth listened warmly, and she liked the basic idea. However, she did not know whether it would work functionally for the center. She told me she would present my idea to the board and see what they thought about it. Before I left, Ruth told me she would contact me and let me know the result.

I was surprised by how painful it was for me to tell Ruth my story—how I had prayed for twins and how God awesomely answered my prayer request. Then how one baby died and the other was born brain injured. It was particularly heart wrenching to tell her I did not get to see Seth and I was not even at the funeral service for him. I conveyed to Ruth my need to recognize the significance of Seth's short life in my womb.

A New Direction

When I heard from Ruth about my memorial project proposal, she told me the board did not feel the time was right to do it. I told Ruth I needed a project to do in memory of Seth in the near future with a small amount of money. She called me later with possibilities; one suggestion Ruth made was buying parenting videos. The CPC wanted to help their clients gain skills in how to take care of their babies after they delivered. I loved this idea!

So Ruth sent me a list of videos with descriptions. As I studied and prayed over which three videos to buy, I realized that as I did this, I was using the nurturing energies part of my dream. For the women who would choose to give birth and also rear their babies, the videos would help them know better how to nurture their newborns.

Healing Writings

Poem I wrote:

May 1, 1990

"My Son Seth"

I pray to God for the courage
To walk into the pain.
As I walk into and through the pain
It will lessen and somehow will become
Like a sweet smelling rose to me
As I remember my beloved Seth.

Letter from Seth to Mommy:

May 29, 1990

Dearest Mommy,

I want to wish you a happy Mother's Day and to tell you I love you.
Oh Mommy, I know how badly you feel that you did not see me and hold me when I was born. I want you to know Mommy I forgive you for not getting to know me then. You see, Mommy, if you had, you would not have this great need to celebrate my short life that I lived in your womb. And if you did not have this great need, how would my brothers, Nathan and Justin, and my sister Kristen come to know me?

Mommy, I am so glad you and Daddy talk about me a lot nowadays. I'm so glad you have so many special projects planned in my memory. Oh, Mommy, I do want to help you preserve the lives of other babies—that will be my ministry. Just think, Mommy, if you had held me and grieved over my death, you might not be doing all that you are doing now.

Mommy, truly all things work together for good to those who love God and have been called of Him just as God says in Romans 8:28. "All things" includes the regrets you have of not seeing me and holding me.

Love, Your Son,
Seth

Recycling Raw Materials

While perusing a yard sale on a Saturday, I bought a paperback book, *Shifting Gears* by Nena and George O'Neill. As I thumbed through the book, I came across a section titled "Nothing Is Wasted." As I read and reread this section, it gave me encouragement, hope, and even a new way of viewing things.

I began to see my life in comparison to a house that was being built. The pillars holding up the roof were my dreams. The foundation of my house (my life) was the Word of God, the Bible. Each pillar (dream) was thoroughly prayed for during the young adult years of my life. Then the winds of life began to blow hard on my structure, similar to hurricane winds blowing against house built near Atlantic Coast. Just like a coastline cottage, the roof had blown off the structure of my life and the pillars progressively hit the ground and broke into pieces. The book I was reading encouraged me to take the pieces of my broken dreams and build something new and different, something with great purpose. However, I would build on the same foundation, the Word of God.

Gaining this new vision gave me great hope that my pain could turn into joy as I began the journey of rebuilding my life. With excitement, I prayerfully set about with this process, which has facilitated me sorting through my old dreams to reach the usable raw materials. Also, going to the SHARE Support Group meetings, reading books, and writing in my journals have helped me progressively identify the raw materials of Seth's part of my broken dream of raising twins. At this point in time, I see the parts to be recycled as follows:

1. My nurturing energies
2. My unmet expectations in prayer
3. My tears of grief

4. My regret of not seeing Seth
5. The meaning of Seth's name

My Nurturing Energies

When I selected the three parenting videos for the CPC, I was able to recycle some of my nurturing energies. This was the first part of the raw materials I was able to reuse. I knew I could look to God to show me how to use each piece of my broken dream to make something new and different.

My Unmet Expectations in Prayer

For years, it has been difficult for me to think back on the sixty-seven prayer requests I recorded regarding my twins during my pregnancy. To remember the no's listed in the answer column has been very painful for me. Then one day, during my devotional time, I came across Revelation 5:8, which says, "When He had taken the book, the four living creatures and the twenty-four elders fell down before the Lamb, each one holding a harp and golden bowls full of incense, which are the prayers of the saints."

As I meditated on this verse, I began to see God had another way for me to view the no answers to my prayers. Instead of focusing on the disappointment, I could now visualize all my prayers as incense in a golden bowl to be offered up in worship to God. This new perspective of my prayers being offered to the Lord as worship has helped me reframe how I felt about the answers that had been no.

My Tears of Grief

Another day, during my devotional time, I came across Psalm 56:8, which says, "You have taken account of my wanderings; put my tears in Your bottle . . ." As I read this verse, I was convicted that I had been wandering when I pushed myself beyond what I am designed to do. So I asked the Lord to forgive me for not being a good steward of my body and energies. The second half of the verse encouraged me that my tears were not in vain. In fact, after reading the article below, I realized God had actually used my tears to help save my life.

Emotional tears are chemically different from irritant tears, containing 20 percent higher concentration in the form of three chemicals known to be related to stress . . . It is Frey's theory that weeping is the body's way of excreting substances produced by the body in response to stress. ("Dear Abby," Saturday, October 31, 1987, *Roanoke Times* and *Word News*)

Psalm 56:8 also helped me visualize God using my bottle of tears in ways that will bless and encourage other people. I knew, in the days to come, God would show me how to recycle my regret of not seeing Seth. As well, I looked forward to using the meaning of Seth's name—the appointed—in significant ways.

CHAPTER 21

Challenges and Miracles

Second Year at Mountain View

The second year Nathan was at Mountain View, I felt like working part-time so I could help with Justin and Kristen's educational expenses. After praying and talking with Bob, I decided to do telecatalog work instead of interior design work. I got the idea after several of my friends started working at a local call center and enjoyed it. Yet the field of art and interior design continued to be creative outlets for me.

In the beginning of my telecatalog work, I was a seasonal employee. At a later time, I became a permanent part-time employee. I worked there over a span of five years. One of the features I liked about my telecatalog work was the fact that I took only one call at a time. When I finished one call, I waited for the next. During the busy times, the calls came one right after another from people all over the United States. Taking one call at a time enabled me to completely focus on the person I was helping. I enjoyed striving to give each customer good service with warmth and enthusiasm.

My Volunteer Work

I continued to volunteer in Nathan's classroom once a week. My assignment was different from the previous one. Mr. King asked me to type some stories onto a computer disk. They were from a textbook that Nathan and another student, Jennifer, were using to practice reading. I did this typing work in the computer lab. After I finished each story, I printed them out in large print so Jennifer could better see the words. Then I laminated the pages of each story and put them into a booklet form. Doing this enabled Jennifer to more easily read the stories. It was a joy for me to help Jennifer in this way; at the same time, I became more comfortable with using the computer system.

Bob and I continued to go to the SHARE support group meetings whenever possible. However, Kristen's basketball games and various school meetings prohibited us from going every month. I felt it was important we keep going until I could tell my story without weeping.

Equipment Needs

During this time, I did not write as much in my journal about Seth because I was focused very intensely on Nathan's equipment needs. I was working very hard on getting Nathan a toilet chair like the one he used at school. Our insurance company had denied our first request, so we resubmitted the request along with letters of justification from Nathan's physician and occupational therapist.

Also, I spent hours and hours researching and praying about how we might get a computer system for Nathan like the one he used at school. When I made the following entry in my journal, I had just found out we would not be getting a local grant to buy the computer system.

October 11, 1990

Father, I am exhausted from thinking about possible ways to get the money for Nathan's computer. I so hoped to get it sometime around Christmas or the first of the year. I still cannot find Nathan's bankbook; plus, Bob thinks there is only about $500 in the account, not a $1000. I have run out of ideas which could enable us to get the money soon.

The only option I see is to work through Children's Rehabilitation Center and it might take quite some time to get the computer this way. Now, it looks like that will be the route to go unless You show us otherwise. I can start getting the names and addresses of our former patterners, other friends, and relatives to give to the social workers at CRC. They will write a fundraiser letter expressing Nathan's need for a special computer system. Then the social workers will send the letter out to the names of the people we give to them. The donations will be sent to CRC and placed in a special account set up by the social workers. When the fund reaches the amount needed, the social workers will purchase the computer system for Nathan.

Besides the computer system, I guess the other issues on my mind are finishing the room and special bathroom for Nathan and obtaining the toilet chair. Are these really needs for Nathan? If they are, Father, You have said in Phil. 4:19 that You shall supply all our needs according to Your glory in Christ Jesus. I don't know how to cope with my thoughts and my feelings except to say, Father, that evidently You don't view the room, bath, toilet chair, and computer system as needs for Nathan right now or You would have already provided them.

It seems to me, Father, Nathan needs all that technology has to offer him so that he can develop his intellect, communication skills, and spiritual gifts. Do you want Nathan to develop to the fullest of his potential? If the answer is yes, then I know You will supply the technology that he needs at the right time.

Help from My Class

After I made this entry in my journal, I shared our situation with the MasterLife class I was a part of at church. With tears in my eyes, I asked the class to pray that God would provide Nathan with a computer system like the one he was using at school. The people in my class had become like family to me, and so I felt comfortable being vulnerable with them.

Not long after this, one of the class members called me and said she wanted to help. Anne had an idea of doing a letter-writing campaign nominating Nathan to be the one to win a computer as part of a radio station contest. She actually carried out this plan of entering Nathan in the contest. Bob and I were deeply touched by this effort, but Nathan did not win.

December 31, 1990

Yesterday morning in the church service when our pastor asked us to think of one thing to trust God for in the next year, I immediately looked over at Nathan and I thought of his need for a computer and a unicorn board (a large keyboard).

I am not sure now what steps to take, humanly speaking, other than approaching the CRC to raise the money to get the computer for Nathan. The social workers already have the list of names. I look to You, Father, to show me another direction to go in if You desire for me to go another way.

God Provides

After the Christmas holiday, Anne and several class members decided to form a committee to work on getting the computer system Nathan needed. Their plan was to work with the CRC to help raise the necessary money. Anne called someone she knew in North Carolina who worked in a computer business to see if he could get a good price on the equipment we needed. To her surprise, this businessman said he wanted to buy the entire computer system for Nathan! Anne then went to Nathan's school to talk with his teacher

Mr. King. He gave Anne a complete list of everything Nathan needed and where to order the components.

MY FIRST COMPUTER WAS BROUGHT TO ME ON A JET. I WAS WAITING AT THE AIRPORT FOR IT.

After all the pieces had come into the businessman's office, he had one of his employees bring the entire computer system up to Roanoke from North Carolina on his company jet. Bob, Nathan, and Mr. King went to the airport together to accept the gift. Our friend Wayne came over to our house and helped Bob put together the computer system.

One of the pieces was the unicorn board, a flat lapboard that had large alphabet keys on it. Another piece was the thick, hard plastic cover that had 1.5 inch holes. These openings were over each of the keys on the extra large keyboard. In order to access the characters, Nathan needed to get his fingers into the appropriate hole and then push. Nathan's first typing project was sending a thank-you letter to his benefactor.

God used Anne in a very special way to enable Nathan to get his own computer for use at home. After years of trying to work on how to get the adaptive equipment, we were weary. Anne, in a sense, picked up the ball and carried it to the finish line.

As well, we received more good news. Our appeal for our insurance company to pay for the toilet chair for Nathan was granted. Our family rejoiced!

More Challenges

After these two victories, we began to experience an onslaught of medical and educational needs regarding Nathan, all of which needed prompt attention. When we took Nathan for his orthopedic clinic visit at CRC, the doctor told us that Nathan's left hip had now moved 60 percent out of the socket. Dr. S recommended that a surgical procedure be done to lengthen the hamstrings on both of Nathan's legs. This procedure would hopefully prevent the left hip from moving any farther out of the socket and prevent the right socket from developing the same problem.

At the time of this diagnosis, Nathan was outgrowing his current wheelchair and we were in the beginning stage of working on the plans for the next wheelchair, which was hopefully to be motorized. We were excited about this possibility because it would give Nathan the opportunity to have some independence. Nathan's PT, Wendy, said she wanted Nathan to have a motorized wheelchair evaluation done at CRC after his hamstring surgery bandages were taken off.

Richard, Nathan's teacher, was concerned about Nathan's current inability to stay focused on his schoolwork. Since there might be a possibility of seizure activity, he recommended we schedule a neurological examination for Nathan. So Bob and I made an appointment with a neurologist.

Also, due to his spasticity, Nathan had great difficulty getting his fingers into the hole over the keys he wanted to strike on the unicorn board. Plans were made to have an OT work with Nathan in regard to this situation. This would be done while he was at CRC for his hamstring-lengthening surgery.

For some time, Bob and I had known we also needed to schedule a urology surgery for Nathan. We were planning on a late summer date for this particular surgery. It was overwhelming to have all this going on within such a short amount of time.

Then, right before we took Nathan to Charlottesville for his orthopedic surgery, Bob's bosses told him his total number of working hours per week would be significantly reduced. The recession of the late '80s was now hitting Roanoke. Bob was also told that he, along with some other engineers, might be laid off in the near future. During this intense time, I temporarily put on hold my efforts to process my grief in regard to Seth's death. Even so, God still brought more insight and healing to me.

Unexpected Help with Grieving

Something very interesting happened to me while Nathan was having his pre-op exam for his hamstring surgery. The day before the surgery, Bob and I were sitting in the examination room with the attending nurse. While waiting for the doctor to come in and finish the exam, we chatted.

I shared with the nurse that Nathan was a twin, his brother Seth was stillborn, and I had not seen Seth because he was taken out of the delivery room while I was unconscious. Therefore, I did not process the grief early on. Instead, I focused on helping Nathan, who was in distress. Now I was, in a sense, going back to process the grief. In response, the nurse shared with me about a woman she knew who delivered twins; one baby died while the other baby lived. On the first birthday of the living twin, the mother was still so grief-stricken over her baby who died; she could not enjoy the birthday celebration of her living twin. In a sense, she was somewhat ignoring her living child as she grieved for her baby who died.

The story for me was reversed. I was so focused on helping my living son, Nathan, that I, in a sense, ignored my dead son, Seth. The nurse also reminded me that I had a lot going on in my life when I gave birth to my twins since

Kristen was not quite three years old at the time. This affirmation meant so very much to me.

Rehabilitation

Throughout Nathan's stay at CRC, an occupational therapist diligently worked on making pointer-hand splints for Nathan to wear while he typed on the unicorn keyboard. The splints did help Nathan with his typing, but because of his spasticity, he still had difficulty getting his arm in position to hit the center of the hole over each key.

After the bandages were taken off Nathan's legs, the therapists did the motorized wheelchair evaluation with him. They tried out a variety of hand controls (stick, knob, etc.) for Nathan to use for driving his wheelchair. When I saw Nathan drive himself through the doorway, I felt the same way I did when I saw Nathan crawl for the first time and the way I felt when I saw Justin take his first steps!

Very Distressing News

May 31, 1991

It has finally come—Bob's final notice—he has 30 days before his job ends. Oh Father, I am having a hard time with this. In particular, I am concerned about the insurance coverage and the fact that Nathan needs a motorized wheelchair and a urology surgery. Can we get these needs taken care of while we are still on our current insurance policy?

During the next 30 days, can Bob get a good hold on job hunting and still work enough to pay our bills? Please help me. I'm having a hard time talking to Bob about all of these matters. Father, if it pleases You, would You provide "the job" for Bob this month. With the way the job market is now, this will take a miracle. BUT MIRACLES ARE WHAT YOU ARE ABLE TO DO!

Career Preparation

Before the final notice came, Bob had already been preparing himself to look for another job. He had been through career testing and counseling. He knew he wanted an engineering position that did not require him to sit at a desk all day—perhaps something more along the line of a field engineer. Bob has the mind of an engineer and also a personality that enjoys interacting with people and being on the move.

A professional résumé writer had already helped Bob write his résumé. The finished product was beautiful. So we were not totally unprepared for this layoff, but we had no money in savings. Furthermore, we were getting ready to do Nathan's urology surgery, and we were in the middle of both his neurology testing and the wheelchair proposal.

June 13, 1991

Oh Father, I feel like I am moving into the eye of the storm. Please minister to me, and give me the ability to take care of my children today. I do not feel like I can talk with anyone today about major decisions or maybe even little decisions. Tears are behind my eyes almost continuously.

There are so many areas of our life that will be affected if Bob does not have a job. Oh Father, hold on to me and hold me up. Hold me. Hold me. I need you. I need you. Enable me to be nice to my boys today. Enable me to be patient especially with Nathan.

A Clue

The day Bob and I took Nathan to the hospital for an EEG, I stayed behind in the lobby for a few minutes. After I bought coffee and a newspaper, I headed upstairs. In the elevator, there was a man standing next to me, and I noticed he was wearing a badge that indicated he was a hospital engineer. My mind immediately started to think about this type of engineering work as a possibility for Bob.

I shared this idea with Bob. That same day, he checked by a central human resource center for several medical facilities in our area to see if there was an opening in engineering. After finding out there was one, he immediately filled out an application. Later, he received a letter saying the position had already been filled.

Meanwhile, Bob and I searched the classified ads section of the local newspaper for engineer positions at medical centers. He sent out a résumé with a cover letter to each one that was within a one-hour driving distance. As well, he pursued any job we saw listed for which his skills might be appropriate.

Potential Lead

June 19, 1991

Today, I received a phone call from a friend, Tommi. Being a single mom, she wanted to interact with Bob about a problem she was having with her house. Tommi asked about Bob's job hunting. I told her about the hospital position Bob applied for at Lynchburg General Hospital. The word *hospital* triggered Tommi to suggest that Bob check at the VA Medical Center because she had noticed new construction going on there.

When I got off the phone with Tommi, I called Bob and told him about her suggestion of checking at the VA. Bob made some phone calls and found out there was, indeed, an opening for a mechanical engineering position. The position had been advertised in the newspaper, but we probably missed seeing the ad. This was because it ran at the time when we were going through Nathan's surgery and rehabilitation.

The VA Medical Center was still taking applications for the position, but the closing time was very near. Bob quickly filled out an application. To our delight, he was called to come in for an interview on Wednesday.

June 26, 1991

Father, be with Bob in a very special way during the job interview today. Proverbs 21:1 says, "The king's heart is like channels of water in the hand of the Lord. He turns it where ever He wishes." (NAS) If it is Your will for Bob to have this job, please work in the hearts and minds of the people doing the hiring. Enable them to want Bob to be in the position or in some other comparable position. If Bob is not offered the job, I will assume it was not Your will for him to have this particular job.

Good News

June 28, 1991

Oh Father, how I praise and thank You for what You have done for Bob and for our family by bringing the phone call yesterday: Bob was selected for the mechanical engineering position at the VA Medical Center. I am in awe of the timing . . .

God's Faithfulness

Bob started work at the VA Medical Center the following Monday. Bob never even had one day of being out of work! It was obvious to Bob and me and to our children that God had moved in a marvelous, miraculous way to provide this job. The next month, Nathan had his urology surgery here in Roanoke, and it went well. This seemed to be the end of the era of surgeries for him.

Chapter 22

Coming to Terms

The Middle School Years

MY DAD HAS A NEW JOB. I HAVE A NEW SCHOOL, JAMES MADISON MIDDLE SCHOOL. MY TEACHER IS MRS. HAMBRICK. I LIKE HER. MANIGAULT AND FLORA ARE INTRUCTIONAL ASSISTANTS IN MY CLASS.

The first time I remember seeing Mrs. Hambrick, she was standing behind a student who was becoming frustrated at the computer. She gently encouraged her to relax her arms by raising them and moving them around. Hambrick, as Nathan likes to call her, is a cute blonde with a wonderful smile and a kind of Doris Day persona. Over the five years Nathan had Mrs. Hambrick as a teacher, I enjoyed seeing her work with Nathan and the other students with the same kind of gentleness I saw on that first day.

I did not volunteer weekly at Madison Middle School, but I did volunteer to help with the overnight field trips. Mrs. Hambrick led the parents in doing bake sales to raise money for the trips, and I assisted with those as well. The students were able to go on some really memorable excursions:

1. Colonial Williamsburg and Bush Gardens Amusement Park
2. Virginia Beach and Kings Dominion Amusement Park
3. Camping trip at park one and half hours away from Roanoke

I HAVE A NEW WHEELCHAIR. IT IS MOTORIZED.

Not long after Nathan started at his new school, his motorized wheelchair arrived. In the days that followed, Nathan experienced extreme problems adjusting to sitting in his new chair. Therefore, he was unable to focus on learning how to drive his wheelchair. Nathan's physical therapy assistant, Beth, was helping us evaluate what the cause could be for his discomfort. All three of us came to conclusion that Nathan's discomfort was probably caused by the very firm planar cushion in the seat of the chair. Nathan was unable to tolerate the firmness of this type of cushion. The longest he could last in the chair was one hour.

We had a secondhand Jay cushion given to us by a couple when their son passed away. So we took the firm planar cushion out of the chair and put the Jay gel-pack cushion in it, instead. This made a big difference in the length of time Nathan was able to comfortably sit in his wheelchair. Now Nathan could focus on learning to drive his new motorized chair up and down the halls of his new school.

A Jay gel-pack cushion is what our local therapist recommended originally. But since the prescription for the wheelchair was from the doctor at CRC, we went with the seat recommendations of our therapists at CRC. Making the decision was difficult for Bob and me since we respected the experience of each therapist.

Coming to Terms with My Regret

Once Nathan was more comfortable in his wheelchair, I had the emotional space I needed to return to writing about Seth in my journal.

February 26, 1992

Father, please lead and guide me as I continue the grieving process for my dear sweet baby, Seth. The day, after the SHARE support group meeting last week, I was frightened to think about the pain that lies latent in my soul. In certain situations, the pain springs forth like an erupting volcano.

About 2 years ago, I realized I needed to see Seth's casket. Also, I seriously thought about moving Seth's casket and tombstone to a cemetery here in Roanoke. But I am unsure about pursuing that direction right now because our economy is in a recession. As well, there is a need to finish the addition, which takes priority.

I spent most of last Thursday and Friday reading my books on stillbirth and reading the Bible, but now I need to focus on Kristen and Justin's birthday or I will not be ready to celebrate with them. Oh Father, it seems I must snatch time here and there to work on grieving about Seth's death and celebrating his short life in my womb.

Nathan is getting situated with his new wheelchair. Bob has a new job, and basketball season is almost over for Kristen. There seems to be time and emotional space for me to begin to open up the emotional wound even more.

Last Thursday night, at the SHARE meeting, it was very good for me to listen to the stories people shared about their babies dying. When the couple from Henry County told about their twin boys being born early, living a short while and then both dying, I leaned my head over on Bob's lap and sobbed. Several of the couples had pictures of their babies who had died. It was good for me to look at these pictures.

February 29, 1992

Father, once again I find myself snatching time here and there to do my grieving work in regards to Seth's death. Earlier in the month, I wrote this in my prayer journal . . .

Lord, be with me because I am afraid to make the journey of grieving over Seth's death. I think the biggest part of my grief has been in a sense frozen in time. Going to the SHARE support group meetings has enabled me to grieve. Hearing the stories of the other parents melts my frozen grief like warm summer days melt a frozen ice cube.

Oh Lord, how long will it take to process the grief? What all will I need to do to let this intense amount of grief come all the way out of my soul? I can have confidence that You know all the steps I need to take.

One of the hardest aspects of facing Seth's death is I did not ask the nurses to bring Seth back into the delivery room. I wish so much I had followed up my initial question, "Where is my other baby?" with the statement, "Bring him back in here right now!" But I cannot go back in time and change this.

While I am writing today on this subject, tears are mounting up in my eyes and slowly moving down my cheeks. I know some people might think that I am wasting my time on the "I should have" and the "I wish I had" statements that we can make about our past. But I feel I must face my regrets honestly.

I find a lot of comfort in 2 Samuel 12:23 when David's responds after he is told his baby son has died. He says, "But now he has died, why should I fast? Can I bring him back again? I shall go to him, but he will not return to me." David was a man after Your heart; so, I find encouragement from his words. He was looking toward heaven where he believed he would see his son again. This gives me great hope that even though I did not get to hold Seth here on this earth, I will hold him one day in heaven.

March 11, 1992

Bob and I went to the SHARE support group last Thursday night. It is the first time we have been able to go two months in a row. On the way to the meeting, I wondered if I would cry as much as I had the month before.

Normally, each person or couple that feels comfortable sharing with the group tells their individual story of how their baby died. However, the nature of this meeting was different in that Becky asked each person or couple how things had been going since the last meeting. So this time, I did not cry as much when other people were talking since they weren't directly telling the stories of their babies dying. However, when it came my turn to talk, I cried as much as I had the month before.

I explained to the group that I had frozen grief that melts some at different times. During the meetings, I have a lot of thawing that takes place. I wonder how much frozen grief I still have left inside of me.

When I tell my story in the SHARE group, the emotional pain comes back as if I am actually reliving the events. The book *Empty Cradle, Broken Heart* is very helpful because there are stories somewhat similar to mine. It encourages me when I read about other women's experiences. They have the same kinds of questions and feelings I have about not seeing Seth; they feel cheated, in a way, by the doctor and the hospital system at the time.

March 22, 1992

I told Bob yesterday that reading the stories of others who have had a baby die helps to give me healing. I particularly like to read stories where people have regrets about different aspects of what happened to them. When I shared with him I was not sure why that was the case, he gave me some verses to read.

I Corinthians 10:13 "No temptation has overtaken you but such as is common to man; and God is faithful, who will not allow you to be tempted beyond what you are able, but with the temptation will provide the way of escape also, so that you will be able to endure it." This verse reminds me that the temptations I have are the same temptations many people experience. It helps me to know that I am not alone in my struggle with regret.

I find the journey of my emotional healing in regards to Seth's death to be very interesting. I am still not sure whether I need to have Seth's grave dug up so that I can see and touch the casket in order to facilitate maximum healing. I have continued to put this idea off because it would take a chunk of money to do this. And I do not feel good about spending the money, right now, when we have so many needs that require our finances such as finishing the addition.

At this point, though, I can continue with my readings, my being a part of the SHARE support group, and doing my projects that are in Seth's memory. Next year, I would love for our whole family to go to the SHARE memorial service. Soon, I want all of us to go to the cemetery where Daddy and Seth are buried. Maybe a Sunday afternoon would be a good time to go.

Of course, there is my writing, too. Much healing seems to come through my writing and the rereading of my writings. The window of emotional space I had to write about Seth did not stay open very long.

Distressing News

When we took Nathan to CRC for his six-month orthopedic checkup, Dr. S told us that Nathan's left hip was now completely out of the socket and that he recommended the Kiriostomy be done. This was the same procedure that had been performed on the right hip in the fall of 1988. Then he said, "I will not be able to do the surgery because I am leaving to assume a position at a Shriner's Hospital on the West Coast." However, he referred us to another surgeon who he felt would be capable of doing this particular procedure.

March 19, 1992

Dear Father, please be with me today as I feel a fluctuation in my emotions. I am excited for Nathan to be driving his very own chair; yet, I feel very apprehensive about doing another hip surgery. Will I feel this mixture of emotions until we decide what to do about Nathan's hip?

Oh God, You who are all powerful, would You please move Nathan's hip back into the socket so we would not even need to do the surgery at all? Please, oh please, would You consider doing this for Nathan. I praise You and thank You for what You will do or not do.

March 23, 1992

I really do not want to put Nathan at risk of the possible side effects of another surgery. I do not want Nathan to go through all the intense pain again. Just to think about the possibility of another hip surgery brings tears to my eyes!

Be with me as I am with my family this afternoon. After I cook dinner, I think it might be better for me to spend time upstairs while they eat. I feel as if I will either fuss at the children or cry during dinner. Also, I probably need to exercise tonight to release some of the emotions built up inside of me.

Please help me not to be overwhelmed by looking at the whole picture of where we are going with Nathan; it is too much for me. I wish the addition could finish itself on its own. Bob is so unmotivated and our money is still tight. There is so much stuff in our unfinished addition! What am I to do with all this stuff?

April 2, 1992

We are leaning toward getting a second opinion regarding Nathan's hips, perhaps in Richmond where we went once before for a consultation. Oh Father, lead and guide us as to what direction we should pursue. Should we, also, get a third opinion here in Roanoke? How do we deal with the doctors having access to the x-rays?

It is going to take a lot of time, prayer, and energy to research and talk with different professionals in regards to this proposed surgery. We have to make a decision about the proposed surgery before we can address Nathan's current wheelchair needs. I would like to get some dates on the calendar for getting additional medical opinions.

God's Grace through a Friend

Later, I had a very encouraging visit with my friend, Jean. It was so good to talk with her and just to have someone listen. While we were chatting, she suggested I request copies of the X-rays. This way, we could take the X-rays with us to our appointments with different doctors. This was a great suggestion!

So at the beginning of the summer, we took Nathan to Richmond for a second opinion, along with our copies of the X-rays. For a third opinion, we took Nathan to an orthopedic doctor here in Roanoke. He told us that if Nathan had another surgery, the scar tissue buildup could possibly cause Nathan pain in the future. Since preventing pain was the main reason for us to do another big surgery, we decided *not* to do the surgery. It was a difficult decision, but we had come to terms with it.

A New Seating System

Fall 1992

With the surgery decision finally behind us, we turned our attention to Nathan's current wheelchair needs. The secondhand Jay cushion was wearing thin. This was causing some discomfort as well as not providing enough support.

CRC referred Nathan to a rehabilitation engineer, John, there in Charlottesville. In the fall of 1992, John made a customized seat for Nathan's wheelchair using a new computerized system. We took Kristen with us so she could increase her knowledge of the rehabilitation world.

John also made changes on the back cushion of the wheelchair so it would better accommodate Nathan's spine. I was very impressed with John's kind and gracious demeanor and also with his high degree of expertise.

It was marvelous watching the different disciplines interact together to make recommendations: Amy (PT), Joan (OT), Erick (wheelchair specialist), and John (rehabilitation engineer). There is nothing I can think of that compares with seeing them at work except, maybe, a symphony orchestra or perhaps a better analogy is a chamber music group. Each professional made their suggestions through the lens of their individual expertise yet was in great harmony with the team as a whole. Their goal was to design the best seating system possible for Nathan.

Remembering Seth

After Nathan was settled with the new seating system, I was once again able to invest time and energy in further processing my grief in regard to Seth's death.

February 24, 1993

As I read the stories in "Ended Beginnings" by Claudia Panuthos, I am developing a bond with the various women who have lost babies. It does not matter what the reason is for their loss: miscarriage, stillbirth, SIDS, abortion or giving up for adoption; I feel connected to them. I am realizing that this is a special bond I could not possibly have unless I had personally experienced losing a baby. I love the bond I have with these women. However, I am not sure right now, Father, how I am supposed to use this special bond. But I know in time You will show me.

My Regret Recycled

This book gave me some pivotal insights into my grieving process. I now recognize that I had not been strong enough to ask the nurses to bring Seth back to me. I have come to grips with the fact that there is no way I can go back and change the past. However, I can take the regret I feel and recycle it by using it to do something good. For example, the Crisis Pregnancy Center sponsored a support group for women who are experiencing post-abortion traumatic stress disorder. As a project, I purchased the books for the women in this group to use. This was a great way for me to recycle my regret of not seeing and holding my precious Seth. It was amazing how much this simple action helped in my grieving process!

PART FIVE

Piece by Piece

CHAPTER 23

Opportunities

MY BROTHER JUSTIN PLAYS SOCCER. I LIKE GOING TO HIS GAMES.

New Opportunities for Justin

Not only did I have the necessary energies to deal with the regret of not seeing Seth, but I was able to also offer a new experience to Justin through him playing on a soccer team. This was very important to me because I had an increasing desire to expose him to organized sports before he left childhood. I was so thankful the Lord allowed me to have enough energy to help Justin do this.

Bob and I purposely waited to do this until Kristen finished playing women's basketball. Many of our friends had all their children in organized sports simultaneously at various times during the year. It took a tremendous amount of time, energy, and coordination for them to attend their children's games. Sometimes, the mom went to one game while the dad went to another game and the grandparents still to another. I knew I did not have the stamina to keep up with this kind of pace.

Just as Kristen entered basketball by going to a summer sports camp, Justin entered soccer by going to a summer sports camp. For the first few years, Justin played soccer, both outdoor and indoor, with the city recreation department. Then he started playing soccer for his school.

Part of me, at one time, felt badly about not introducing Justin to a variety of sports at an earlier age. But it all worked out just fine because Justin loved playing soccer, and he did not have time to play another sport because of his involvement in the school symphonic band. Justin started playing the trombone in the sixth grade and played all the way through until his graduation from high school.

As for Kristen, when, in middle school, she decided all on her own that she wanted to go to basketball camp. However, with Justin, I chose to encourage him to go to soccer camp and to sign up for a recreational soccer team. It helped that Justin had a friend going to the same camp and playing in the same league.

The flip was true for the introduction of musical instruments to Kristen and Justin. I coaxed Kristen to take piano lessons when she was eight years old, and she wanted to quit after two years. On the other hand, Justin wanted trombone lessons without any coaxing from me.

A Long Time Dream Comes True:

IN THE FALL OF 1993, DAD AND JUSTIN FINISHED MY ROOM.

In November, we celebrated the finishing of our downstairs addition by hosting a dinner party for Kristen's senior class. Finally, nine years plus after starting our addition, we were able to put the furniture in the downstairs room and start using it. For the dinner party, we set up card tables all throughout our house, even upstairs in Kristen's bedroom and the study. It was such fun to have young people laughing and talking all around us. Our entire family enjoyed this special event. After this, we did a lot of other entertaining using our new additional space. We had groups over from church for wedding showers, baby showers, and potluck dinners.

A Question

During a conversation with my friend Crystal, she asked me how we were able to get the ball rolling again on the addition after such a long standstill. After some contemplation, I shared the following story: During the summer of 1989, Bob's older brother, Wayne, called to tell us he was coming to Roanoke on a business trip. When Wayne said he wanted to visit us while he was in town, I experienced an intense mood swing.

I was upset that Wayne's upcoming visit was disturbing my comfortable cocoon of complacency in regard to the house. Once again, I was very aware of its flaws. I hurled myself into a spring cleaning mode trying to make the most of the main part of our house: painting walls, washing windows and curtains, etc.

While Wayne was visiting us, Bob took him around the house and showed him the status of the upstairs and downstairs parts of the addition. Sometime later, Wayne called Bob and told him that he and the other siblings, Lois and Ray, wanted to each give us a gift of money to help us get the addition project going again.

Much later, I began to reread through my prayer journals. After reading one particular entry, I realized that Wayne's visit and the subsequent gifts were a specific answer to my prayers. Six months before Wayne's visit, I made the following entry in my prayer journal:

January 4, 1989

Father, if you want us to make a move concerning the completion of the house/ addition/yard project please show us what You want us to do. Or drop something out of the sky on us if You so choose, an anonymous gift, whatever. In the past, I have believed that You can work in mighty ways, unexpected ways. Renew this belief in me. If You so choose, Father, would you do a little or big work in the near future in regards to our addition? This would be such a spiritual encouragement to me.

Because I have prayed the above, I will know any work brought about on the project will be from You. Manifest Your presence and Your love for me through Your answer. I greatly anticipate Your next move!

Rebooting the Project

Even though the gifts of money, along with refinancing our house at a lower interest rate, did get us working again on the addition, we were unable to stay focused continuously on the project. The following year was filled with intense situations such as Nathan's last two surgeries, the designing and refining of Nathan's new wheelchair, Bob's job change, and the process of deciding whether to do another hip surgery.

Since Kristen only had a few more years at home before she went away to college, we decided to finish the upstairs part of the addition first. So in the fall of 1992, Kristen moved into her new bedroom. She now had plenty of room to research colleges, to have girlfriends over to visit, and to work on craft projects.

After Kristen's room was finished, we focused on the downstairs addition. Since we no longer needed space for extensive therapy for Nathan, we decided to make the room into a combination family room/bedroom. We divided the room into different areas or centers—a computer center, a game center, and a conversational center—which turned into Nathan's bedroom at night.

Justin helped Bob finish the addition. Doing this enabled Justin to learn a lot about construction work. It is funny to think that Justin was a baby when we started the addition project, and years later, he was a part of bringing the project to completion.

New Endeavors

Once the entire addition was completed, we had the time and the energy to get involved as a family in some new projects. We ended up focusing, as a family, on politics and short-term missions. Our motivation in both areas was to make a positive impact in our society for the glory of God.

Political Campaigns

In the fall of 1993, it was our dear friends, Sam and Cathy, asking for our help in a political campaign that drew our family into the political world. Sam and Cathy shared with us that they felt, next to sharing the Gospel and helping Christians grow in their faith, helping elect good political leaders has the most profound positive effect on our society. I could see they viewed their volunteer work in a way as a calling. They were deeply concerned about issues affecting the sanctity of human life and the well-being of the American family. These were the very same reasons our family entered into the political world. For me, though, every act of volunteer work has also been a way for me to celebrate the importance of Seth's short life in my womb.

We stayed actively involved for several years. Sometimes, we did more work; sometimes we did less, depending on which candidate it was and how much time and energy we had. Some of the activities our family did in the 1990s were as follows:

- Made phone calls
- Put up signs
- Passed out literature
- Helped address and stuff envelopes for mailings
- Went to rallies
- Worked in campaign offices alongside of other volunteers

Sometimes, we even worked on the mailings in our family room by setting up an assembly line. This way, each person in our family helped get the work done. It was a lot of fun to work on these activities together; also, it was a way for us to work toward making a difference.

Also, by addressing, stuffing, and putting in the mail a large amount of invitations to political fundraisers, Bob and I were able to attend quite a few of the events for free or half price. This way, we were able to participate in lovely luncheons, dinners, and receptions and often heard nationally known speakers. Attending these events provided enjoyable creative outlet experiences for me.

During our years of volunteering, we met many young men and women who worked on the campaigns. Through our interactions with these delightful young people, who were working hard to elect our candidates, we had opportunities to share about the hope that we had found in Christ. We invited several of the young people to church and to dinner.

Through our campaigning together as a family, we helped elect Governor George Allen, who signed the Parental Notification Bill; Governor Jim Gilmore, who signed the Partial-Birth Abortion Ban Bill; Attorney General Mark Early, who strove to protect these laws and other laws that are important for building strong families. We have also helped to reelect our beloved Congressman Bob Goodlatte, who votes in a manner that is consistent with our family's values.

As well, we gave money to the Crisis Pregnancy Center in honor of several of our Commonwealth officials who helped bring these two bills into legislature. Beautiful certificates were mailed to the officials from the CPC stating that we had given gifts of money in their honor. The CPC sent us copies of these certificates, which I placed in a very special chest.

The chest is handmade with a hinged lid. In the lid is a heart-shaped cutout lined with a small piece of an old quilt. Over the years, I have used this chest to hold items that are reminders to me of the importance of Seth's short life in my womb. Examples of these memorabilia are my journal writings, programs from CPC events, and programs from the SHARE support group memorial services.

Short-Term Missions

In the summer of 1996, it was the WAV short-term mission trip that launched our family into short-term mission work. Our destination was a primarily African American church in New Jersey. Our purpose was to accomplish a construction project; help conduct Vacation Bible School.

Each woman who went on the mission trip took her children. Two of us took our husbands, Suzanne and me. During the day, Bob and Justin worked, along with Eddie and his son, Jamie, to put vinyl eaves on the church building. Nathan supervised while sitting under the shade of a tree.

Inside the church building, the women on our team conducted a morning-time Bible school for the children in the church and the surrounding neighborhood. The children of the team members went to the respective class for their age. I was a gopher and did errands for the teachers.

In the late afternoon, our whole team ate dinner at the church, which was prepared by the women of the church. At night, Bob and I led a Bible class for the women of the church. Also, another woman, Laura, taught a class for teenagers.

Each night, Bob taught about a Bible character using an interactive style during the first hour. Then after our snack break, Justin and I taught the craft, which was making decorative flowerpots. This proved to be an ideal project.

The first night, we all applied the base coat of paint to the pots. The second night, Justin and I demonstrated different techniques of applying paint glazes. Then the women decorated their own flowerpots using a wide variety of colors. The third night, we applied a protective coat of clear polyurethane. The fourth night, we planted flowers in the pot. I brought potting soil and different colors of geraniums.

After we finished potting our plants, I presented a shortened version of my creative outlet seminar. I explained the importance of replenishing one's emotional reserves and how it is similar to plants needing frequent watering in order to grow. I shared that maintaining a joyful, balanced life enables one to be a healthier vessel for continuing to serve the Lord.

The fifth and final night, the entire Bible school came together for a closing program. Each class gave a presentation, a summary of what they had studied during the week. When it was time for our class to present, I had the women stand with their flowerpot in hand. No two pots were alike. I said, "Just as each woman had uniquely created her own flowerpot, each woman had been uniquely created by God." I shared a little about each woman, and I spoke words of appreciation as to how each woman served in the church and how each had been an encouragement to us.

The week was wonderful. The only thing that might have made the trip better would have been to have Kristen with us. She had a summer job and felt she could not lose a week of work. After this trip, I began to yearn for our entire family to have an opportunity to minister together, all five of us.

More Teaching Opportunities

Through the Center for Women's Health, I had several opportunities to teach and facilitate women's groups. Julie, the nurse who was responsible for the PMS support group, asked me to be the new peer facilitator for the group, which met once a month. She also asked me to present my creative outlet seminar for a second time to the PMS support group and for the first time to the Menopause support group.

In the fall of 1993, I developed a new seminar called Relaxing Your Home. I was then able to present it to the PMS support group. The idea for this seminar first came into my mind when I was staying with Nathan after his second big hip surgery.

In the presentation, I combined some of the principles of stress management with some of the concepts of interior design. My purpose was to stimulate each woman to design her home in ways that encourage the building of happy memories and facilitate the personal development of each family member. An example is creating a place to play games and work puzzles or for family members to work on hobbies. To assist the women in designing comfortable, attractive, and functional spaces, I created worksheets and handouts.

As well, for three years while Nathan was at Madison, Bob and I taught the discipleship class, MasterLife, together. We each had taken this class after going to our new church and had the desire to facilitate others being able to benefit from the teachings.

Bob and I being able to minister together was very special for both of us. We were blending our individual gifts to co-lead the group. Each Wednesday night, the tables were placed in a rectangular shape. Bob and I sat at the head of the table. We remained seated unless we needed to use the blackboard, which was directly behind us. Due to the seating arrangement, Bob and I were able to see each person's face, which is very important to us both. We both like to ask questions that encourage class participation.

Another opportunity came while I was attending the Smokey Mountain Women's retreat. The leader of the conference, Vel, asked me to give a short talk about how God had been at work in my life during the past year. She wanted me to do this in the hour before dinner to lead off a time of sharing. Earlier that day, while walking around in an antique store looking at quilts hanging from the rafters, I had an epiphany for the theme of my talk and, eventually, for this book.

The following year, I was able to build on this theme. I received a phone call from a woman named Jerry, who was co-leader of the women's group for her church. She had received my name as a possible speaker from her daughter who worked for the Center for Women's Health.

I agreed to come and speak to her women's group. I titled my presentation "Broken Dreams, Beautiful Quilts", and I took lots of quilts and items made from quilted materials to display behind me. I spoke for about fifteen minutes on different ways to decorate their homes using quilts. Then I began to explain how my life is like a beautiful quilt that is being made from the recycling of my broken dreams.

Overnight Women's Retreat

Over the next year, I had several opportunities to present and therefore refine this seminar presentation; one of which was at an overnight retreat. Jerry passed my name along to one of her co-workers, Martha, who was looking for a speaker for an overnight women's weekend retreat. Martha called me, and during our phone conversation, she invited me to come to the next retreat-planning committee meeting.

At the committee meeting, I shared some possible topics I could present, and we decided that the theme for the conference would be Balancing Life's Ups and Downs. Over the summer, we met again to continue the planning. At that meeting, I was encouraged to see that even more women were there representing their various churches in the denominational district.

The overnight retreat took place at a conference center on the top of a mountain in early fall. The color of the leaves was spectacular. The weather was what I consider to be perfect fall weather, with a slight crisp feel in the air. On Friday night, I opened with an introduction from Ecclesiastes 3, particularly verse 7, which says that there is "a time to tear and a time to mend . . ." Then I moved into presenting my talk, Broken Dreams, Beautiful Quilts. At the end of my talk, I passed out worksheets I had designed to help the women identify parts of their own broken dreams and possible ways to recycle these parts in a positive way. Then on Saturday, I presented my creative outlet seminar using various visuals and worksheets, which I had prepared ahead of time. The worksheets were designed to help each women determine the demands being made on her emotional reserves and ways to replenish and conserve her emotional reserves.

CHAPTER 24

Staying Busy

WHEN MY SISTER, KRISTEN, WENT AWAY TO COLLEGE,
MY MOM AND I MISSED HER BIG TIME.

Fall 1994

A month and a half before my overnight women's retreat speaking
engagement, Kristen started college in the eastern part of Tennessee. This was
a very difficult time for both Nathan and me because we missed Kristen so
very much.

One day, after our family returned home from taking Kristen to college, I
went into her bedroom to get a belt for the outfit I was wearing. When I saw her
bed all made up and her closet doors closed, I fell down on her bed and wept.
She hardly ever made her bed or closed her closet doors. Therefore, seeing her
room being so neat and tidy was a painful reminder that she was gone.

That same day, I heard about a tragic event that occurred here in the
Roanoke Valley. A young mother I had gotten to know at Justin's first school
was murdered along with her two daughters and her husband, and then their
house was set on fire. Between finding out about this tragedy and dealing with
Kristen being away at college, I felt very sad.

However, making the visuals and handouts for the fall retreat helped soften
the intensity of missing Kristen. Also, I really enjoyed picking out the outfits
and jewelry I would wear for the conference sessions. All this activity gave me
something positive and fun to do.

I was still working four days a week at the telecatalog center, which also
helped me keep busy. Most days when I arrived home from work, I immediately

sat down at the kitchen counter and wrote Kristen a short letter, then put it out for the letter carrier to pick up. Midafternoons initially were very hard for me emotionally because I was used to Kristen pulling up in front of our house with Justin around 3:45 p.m. Typically, when she came inside, we sat down together and talked at the kitchen counter. Writing Kristen at this time of day helped me cope.

Each time Kristen came home from college, it was so hard for me when it was time for her to leave. I felt the grief all over again. Yet as the year progressed, the grief lessened each time she left to go back to college.

I KEEP GROWING AND GROWING. EVERY FEW YEARS, I NEED TO HAVE A NEW SEATING SYSTEM FOR MY CHAIR OR A WHOLE NEW WHEELCHAIR.

During the fall of 1994, it was time to make changes to Nathan's wheelchair because of an increase in his body growth. The frame, which was adjustable, was expanded to accommodate Nathan's growth. A new Jay gel-pack cushion was selected for the seat of Nathan's wheelchair and a new back cushion was made also.

Unfortunately, in the following days, Nathan experienced great discomfort in the seating system in his chair. Hoping to get some insight into this situation, Beth, Nathan's physical therapy assistant, set up an early-morning appointment at the school. She invited the wheelchair technician to meet with the three of us to talk about Nathan's chair. The morning came that we were supposed to meet at the school. Beth arrived. Bob and I arrived. However, the technician did not arrive! I felt very frustrated that he did not show up. Later, though, we found out there had been a communication mix-up. I said to Beth, "I don't understand why we have so many difficulties when we work on wheelchairs. Before every wheelchair endeavor, I pray and I ask others to pray and we still have these problems."

As I drove to work, I thought about what I said to Beth and I felt badly. I was concerned that what I said perhaps sounded like I was putting God in a bad light. I shared my concern with a co-worker, Elaine, as we walked from our cars into the center. She said, "You are a perplexed Christian. It is not that uncommon." My talk with Elaine was encouraging just as all our other talks in the past had been for me.

The mystery of what was causing Nathan's discomfort was solved when we took him for his orthopedic checkup here in town. Our main concern was to address the discomfort Nathan was having in his chair. As we talked with the doctor, it came up in discussion that when the new seating system was installed, a small wedge had been placed under the Jay cushion to level out Nathan's pelvis. After hearing this, the physician suggested taking the wedge out. Once the wedge was removed, Nathan was able to sit comfortably in his chair for longer periods of time. This scenario reminded me of the children's story about the Princess and the Pea. Now Nathan could concentrate on learning to drive his wheelchair.

Resigning from My Job

In the spring of 1995, right before the school year ended, I resigned from my telecatalog consultant position. I had enjoyed the work up until the extra demand was added that I was to greatly reduce the length of my talk time with the customers. This was becoming a growing emphasis through out the entire call center. The process of reducing the length of my talk time was requiring a greater and greater expenditure of my emotional reserves. During the school year, I had already used a significant amount of my reserves working on the new seating system for Nathan's wheelchair and adjusting to Kristen being away at college. It seemed unwise to keep using so much of my energy for this particular job.

The previous summer, when I was working, Justin had stayed with our neighbor, Laurel. Justin enjoyed playing with Laurel's son, Jonathan, and we paid her a modest amount of money for keeping him. In the mornings, Justin helped me load Nathan, and then he walked down to Laurel's house. Then I drove Nathan to his day camp. Getting Nathan out of the van required me moving into the center of the van and undoing the tie-downs, then getting out of the van and bringing him down on the lift. After getting Nathan inside, I drove across town to the telecatalog center. After work, I drove back across town, picked up Justin, and then together we went to get Nathan. Justin was the one to load Nathan in the van and unload him when we got home.

I was able to carry out this schedule four days a week the previous summer because my supply of emotional reserves was great enough to meet the demand. However, now I knew that Laurel would not be able to keep Justin this summer because she was going through chemotherapy treatments for cancer. Bob and I did not want to leave Justin alone. In addition, I knew that my emotional reserve level was nowhere close to being enough to meet the same type of schedule I had the summer before. I had reached a point where I realized it was not wise for me to continue investing my diminishing reserves into my telecatalog work. So I stopped working my part-time job in order to provide the care the boys needed that summer.

MY LAST YEAR AT MADISON I HAD DORO AS MY COTA (CERTIFIED OCCUPATIONAL THERAPY ASSISTANT). SHE DESIGNED MY NEW COMPUTER SYSTEM.

Doro had a strong expertise in computers and adaptive technology. Early on, I knew God had moved in a special way when he brought Doro into our family's life so Nathan could benefit from her expertise. As she worked with Nathan, I became more and more encouraged that she would be able to design a much better computer system for him. As I watched her try different approaches, I eagerly awaited seeing what the final system design would be.

Not working freed me to devote a lot of time and energy to observing Doro work with Nathan. When I saw how well Nathan was coming along on the new system Doro designed, I immediately began to work on the process of getting him the same kind of system to use at home. I went to different stores looking at computers. Then while I observed Doro's sessions with Nathan, I asked her what she thought about my research. From my talks with her, I found out about all the extra components we needed and from where to order them. Since I had a feeling that Doro might not be back the next year, I told Bob that we needed to get moving. It was vital that we get the same system set up for Nathan at home while we still had Doro to help us. Fortunately, we had a source of money from our equity loan we could use to purchase all the components. Right before the school year ended, we executed the purchase.

Also, the Lord worked it out that Doro was able to come in the summer to help train Nathan on the new system. We were able to get extended school year services through Nathan's IEP (individualized education plan). This was great because it allowed Doro to come to our house once a week throughout the summer to work with Nathan. In order for us to be able to continue with Nathan at home on the computer, I had Justin watch along with me everything Doro did to get the system set up and to instruct him.

MY LAST YEAR AT MADISON, I WORKED AT A SHELTERED WORKSHOP TWO AFTERNOONS A WEEK.

This workshop experience was written into Nathan's ITP (individual transition plan) to help evaluate future work possibilities for him. However, because Nathan has very limited use of his arms and hands, he was unable to perform any of the tasks at the workshop. By the end of the year, everyone involved thought it would be better for Nathan to focus on improving his computer skills as a means of occupation.

Over the summer, Bob and I worked on making sure Nathan's new school would have the same kind of computer system in place he had used at Madison. Bob and I wrote a letter to the director of special education, stating Nathan's IEP required this particular computer system. Then we followed up the letter with phone calls. If we had not done this, the computer system very well may not have been in place.

CHAPTER 25

Mixed Emotions

High School Years

In the fall of 1996, Nathan started high school at Cave Spring. The principal was Dr. Martha C., who was a friend of mine. Martha and I had taught home economics together at Glenvar High School before I was married. I was very pleased she was the principal because I knew her to be a cheerful yet strong leader. Also, because of our long-time friendship, I felt comfortable talking with her and approaching her about Nathan's needs.

Ms. Anderson was Nathan's special education teacher. He was fortunate to have her as a teacher because she not only had a pleasant demeanor but she also had many years of experience helping students with all different kinds of disabilities. In fact, Ms. Anderson designed and implemented a unique community-based program as a part of her curriculum. One of the things I will always remember about her is how she saw each student as an individual and tried to place each one in the program according to their ability and interests. For example, Nathan participated in a community-based training that involved working on life's skills such as going to the mall, shopping, and maneuvering his wheelchair.

I LIKED DRIVING MY CHAIR AT THE MALL. GETTING ON AND OFF THE ELEVATOR WAS HARD, BUT I DID IT!

Working on a New Wheelchair

Once the computer system was in place for Nathan at school, I turned my attention to working on a new wheelchair for Nathan. He was outgrowing his current chair and its base could not be expanded anymore to accommodate his growth. Knowing the past challenges of designing and refining Nathan's wheelchairs, I recruited a lot of prayer support, including my weekly Wednesday-morning Bible study group and our Sunday school class at church.

It was very hard for me to get in gear to work on another wheelchair. The process is always very involved, from working on the design of the chair to the medical justification of each part of the chair for the insurance company to the fitting of the chair. As well, as a result of his spasticity and dislocated left hip, Nathan is very difficult to fit for a wheelchair.

We were so blessed to have the same PT, Sherry, who had helped us with the last changes made on Nathan's chair. Bob and I had enjoyed working with Sherry on that project. The fact that someone we already knew would be assisting us was a great comfort.

December 9, 1996

Even though, I am overwhelmed with the wheelchair proposal and very concerned about Nathan's education and future occupation, You are not overwhelmed, Father. Psalm 139:11-12 is an encouragement to me: "If I say, "Surely the darkness will overwhelm me, and the light will be night, even the darkness is not dark to Thee, and the night is as bright as the day. Darkness and light are alike to Thee."

December 12, 1996

Oh Lord, You know how weary Bob and I are from working on wheelchairs and how burned out we are with the whole process. Please give us the strength, wisdom, and patience to help develop the best seating system for Nathan. Specifically, be with us as we talk with Sherry, our PT, about the wheelchair evaluation coming up in January. Kristen is going with us, to participate in Nathan's wheelchair evaluation. I scheduled the appointment to be before she goes back to school at EKU. Bob and I value her input; plus, this will be a good experience to go alongside her education in occupational therapy.

December 13, 1996

Thank you for how well the initial discussion went with Nathan's wheelchair proposal. Oh Father, You being all-knowing, know all the factors which are of concern in regards to Nathan having the best fit and function with the new chair. Please, enable us to move in the right direction. Please be moving ahead of time to bring the needed money together. Strengthen Bob and me. Manifest Your presence through us and to us.

Inheritance

In January, we found out Bob's Aunt Emily passed away. Since she did not have children of her own, she made Bob and his three siblings heirs to her estate. Bob's older brother, Wayne, was the executor of the estate. He told each of the siblings would receive the inheritance in several installments. Using part of the first installment, we were able to take care of the deductible for the wheelchair cost.

An Expanded Dream:

February 24, 1997

Father, I have this idea of how Nathan and I can write a book together. Nathan has been writing his life story for many years using his computer system; I have been writing in my journals for many years. It recently occurred to me we could combine our writings into one book.

Family Dream:

Ever since the New Jersey trip, I had been eager for our entire family to participate together in an outreach project or trip. In Matthew 28:18-20, Jesus gave a command right before he ascended to heaven. He said, "Go and make disciples of all nations, baptizing them in the name of the Father and of the Son and of the Holy Spirit, and teaching them to obey everything I have commanded you." So as a family, we decided to use a portion of the first installment of the inheritance for this purpose.

Family Retreats

As I prayed about this, I remembered a program on *Focus on the Family* radio show that featured Joni Eareckson Tada, the founder of Joni and Friends. During the show, Joni discussed one of the newer ministries they had developed called Family Retreats. She shared statistics show families who have a disabled member have higher degrees of stress, strained relationships, and divorce.

Therefore, Joni and Friends have designed summer family retreats in order to minister to the needs of the whole family. They seek to provide a supportive environment where families can get away to relax and try new things together. Another benefit from these retreats is the opportunity to meet other families who can relate to the blessings and challenges of life with a disability. Also, these times of respite are for family members to grow in their relationship with God.

I was interested in learning more about whether our family could be involved in helping with their family retreats. The first step I took was to check with Joni and Friends about their summer camp program. I talked with a representative about our family's desire to minister together and about the possibility of our doing this through their camp ministry. She said we first needed to come as participants; only after that could we be considered as possible staff for future camps.

Joni's office sent us some information in the mail about the program and we reviewed it. However, when I talked with Kristen about this opportunity, she did not feel going to the camp as participants was the way we should use the inheritance money and neither did I. We wanted to use the money to be able to serve others.

Romania

Once a month, our church had a mission dinner; after which we heard a person or group talk about a recent mission trip they participated in. Bob and I attended one of the dinners and heard a couple speak about their recent mission opportunities in Eastern Europe. As I listened to Mac, the husband, speak of the deep spiritual hunger of the Romanians, I looked over at Bob and thought how marvelous it would be for him to go to Romania on a mission trip. Since Bob had a yearning, even before we were married, to minister in Eastern Europe, we talked all the way home about this possibility.

A few days later, I saw an article in our local newspaper about a team being formed locally to go to Romania. Bob called the contact person and found out all the slots were filled. This seemed to be a closed door.

God's Timing

April 19, 1997

It is so interesting how You, O Lord, are working. Wednesday, we heard our insurance company will pay 80 percent of the wheelchair, minus the tray. Thursday, *we received the first inheritance check for $35,000. Then, yesterday, we received in the mail one of the state publications for our denomination. As I read it, I saw a notice for a mission trip to Romania to do construction of a chapel and to conduct an outdoor Bible School.*

If it be Your will, enable Bob to hear today about the mission trip to Romania. If he is to go on this trip, please open the door of opportunity and take Bob through the door. If there is another door to open, please show us where and when we are to open the door.

May 1997

Bob signed up earlier this month for the trip to build a chapel in Romania. Afterward, the idea came to me maybe Justin could go with him on the trip. I felt this was an important opportunity because it would enable Justin to catch a glimpse of what God is doing in a country other than the United States. I hoped this trip would be a way to fan a fire within Justin to give to others who are around the world. Also, it made sense because Justin had learned some basic construction skills through helping Bob finish our addition. I thought Bob and Justin working on the Romanian chapel building project could be a bonding experience for the two of them, filled with happy memories. I mentioned my idea to Bob, and so he checked with the leader organizing the trip. Thankfully, he was able to obtain special permission for Justin to go even though he was only thirteen years old.

Kristen was planning to go on a mission trip to Guatemala with other college students for the entire month of June. She had been preparing over the past several months and had raised enough money to cover the cost of the trip. I realized there was not enough time or money this summer for us to plan a family mission trip out of the country. However, we did have enough finances to help send Bob and Justin to Romania.

Summer 1997

Nathan's new wheelchair came in around the time school let out for the summer. We loved the tilt-in-space feature on the chair. This feature allows the entire seating system to be tilted back at an angle with just the flip of a switch. The ability for his chair to change positions, in space, helped make Nathan more comfortable by relieving pressure from bony prominences like his hips and tailbone.

Our entire family took Kristen to Atlanta to fly out with her mission team to Guatemala. A month later, we went back to Atlanta to pick her up at the airport. Then we spent a few days in the area vacationing.

In preparation for Bob and Justin's mission trip to Romania, we used some of the inheritance to purchase a hydraulic lift. We needed the lift so Kristen and I could safely get Nathan in and out of the wheelchair while the guys were gone. We practiced over and over before they left until we felt comfortable using the lift to transfer Nathan by ourselves.

Bob rented a car to drive to Washington, D.C. airport so he and Justin could fly to Romania with their mission team. Each team member was responsible for bringing certain construction equipment and supplies packed in an extra suitcase. This way, they could just leave the tools there in Romania for the church to use.

While Bob and Justin were in Romania the last two weeks of July, I drove Nathan to camp each morning. Kristen helped me get him dressed and into his chair using the hydraulic lift, but she did not want to go with me to camp every morning, so I did the unloading there by myself. She did, however, go with me in the afternoons to help me bring Nathan home.

Wheelchair Stress

Almost daily, when we picked up Nathan, the staff told us they were having trouble with seating Nathan properly in his new chair. Constantly, Nathan expressed to Kristen and me that he was uncomfortable in his chair. So we took a foldout lawn chair for Nathan to lie on while he was at camp. We showed the staff how to use several Velcro belts to keep him upright in the chase lounge chair.

One evening, while Bob and Justin were gone, Kristen and I took Nathan and my mom out to eat in a restaurant. We had to leave early because Nathan started crying and I could not get him situated correctly in his chair. I felt so frazzled!

Every time I met with the therapists throughout the summer to work on the process of fine-tuning Nathan's chair, I found myself fighting back tears. One day, while I was talking with Sherry, our PT, I could not hold back the tears. The tears rolled down my cheeks; I could barely talk. As we discussed the discomfort Nathan was experiencing, I began to weep. Fortunately, no one else was around us at the time.

CHAPTER 26

Light in the Darkness

Second Year of High School

In Nathan's second year of high school, another class was formed for the students who were multi-disabled. Ms. Tinsley was the new teacher for this class. She was a young, attractive, and perky woman with dark hair and a pixie haircut. She always walked with a bounce in her step.

Nathan's Discomfort

August 28, 1997

Unfortunately, Nathan had a lot of pain and muscle spasms yesterday. Please give us wisdom in how to address making the new chair more comfortable for Nathan. I am a little concerned about talking with Sherry and the other therapists because I was weepy during the summer when talking with them.

Please help us to get Nathan better situated so we can move on to helping him improve his computer skills and his academics. You, being all-knowing, Father, know exactly what causes Nathan pain and muscle spasms and You know what we can do to help him.

God provided Janey to be Nathan's occupational therapist for the current school year. She worked faithfully in making changes to his wheelchair, which enabled Nathan to be more comfortable in his chair. God gave me an extra measure of grace through Janey. Her caring personality and compassionate demeanor made it easier for me to tell her I was having a difficult time emotionally.

Emotional Fragileness

As the school year progressed, I increasingly felt more and more emotionally fragile. During the fall, Bob was teaching a class on Wednesday nights about the Old Testament book of Nehemiah. I told him I might be interested in coming the last night of his class and sharing with his participants about how God had used my study in Nehemiah to help facilitate my recovery from burnout. Bob shared my desire with his class, but he also told them there was a possibility I might not come. The day came for Bob's last class. Throughout the afternoon, a heavy gray cloud seemed to be pressing in on me. I did not feel well enough to share, so I told Bob I would not be able to come.

Not long after this, I attended a meeting at our church where I heard the wife of one of the national leaders of our denomination speak. As I listened to her share about the Great Commission work being done across the United States, I yearned to be a part of reaching the United States for Jesus Christ. While I was listening to her talk, my heart began to beat faster and I felt prompted to try to meet her.

When she finished speaking, I went up front and waited for my turn to speak with her. I shook her hand and said, "I am Judy Rossbacher." As I began to say more, I started to cry and I could not get any more words out. So I handed her a piece of paper with my name, address, phone number, and the topics about which I was available to speak. I had reached a point in my life where I had so much I wanted to share, but there was a dark veil hanging over me, holding me back from using my gift.

Throughout the school year, I strove to increase my emotional reserves by doing the following:

1. Walking three or four times a week
2. Taking vitamin supplements
3. Doing more relaxing activities going to a vocal concert and visiting the art museum
4. Making sure I had daily time in prayer and Bible study

Yet the dark veil still hung over me. By spring, I began to think that my increased fragileness might be related to menopause. After all, I had just turned fifty years old.

One Sunday afternoon, while I was talking with Charlotte, my Bible study leader, tears began to mount in my eyes as I shared about some of Nathan's current needs. All of a sudden, my few tears turned into weeping and my head dropped over on Charlotte's shoulder. The next Sunday, I began to weep in the middle of the morning church service. I knew I had to see my doctor soon!

During my past visits, he and I had talked about menopause. After the service, I talked with Bob about the possibility of him calling my gynecologist to see if he could treat me with an antidepressant along with the supplementary hormone therapy.

Monday morning, Bob called my doctor and talked with him and set up an appointment for me. When I went into my doctor's office, it helped a lot that Bob had already briefed him about my symptoms. Throughout most of the appointment, I could get out a few words and then I needed to stop and cry. Since I had not yet stopped having menstrual periods, my doctor prescribed supplemental hormone therapy and also a low dosage of an antidepressant. Within twelve to twenty-four hours, I could tell a night-and-day difference in how I felt. As I felt better emotionally, I began to work on two new projects in addition to the book Nathan and I were writing together.

Project No. 1—Mission Trip

The first project had to do with my continued desire that all five of us go together on a family mission trip. Right after the final inheritance installment arrived, I came down the stairs on Sunday morning and made an announcement to my family. I said, "I think we should use the entire amount of the last installment to go to Eastern Europe on a mission trip!" My vision was to do mission work in either Austria or Slovakia and then vacation in the opposite country. Bob's paternal grandfather was from Austria and the three other grandparents were from Slovakia. While I had been in Chicago years ago, I wrote down the exact locations where Bob's grandparents came from in these countries; I had always hoped that we could visit these specific locations. As well, Eastern Europe was where Bob and I had desired to minister years ago.

After I shared this idea, the look on my family members' faces was one of dismay. "Do you think we have enough money to do this kind of trip?" I responded by saying, "I will do some research and find out."

The next day, I went to the AAA office to pick up travel books and maps. I talked extensively with a travel agent. He figured out roughly how much the trip would cost, including renting a special van for Nathan. He made a call and found out we could rent one with a lift in Vienna. I reported back to our family that it looked like we had enough money to do the trip.

We all started to get excited about the possibility. I went to the library and checked out books and videos about Austria and Slovakia for us to do research regarding these two countries. We looked over the maps and located the places where our ancestors had lived. I was so glad I had taken detailed notes while talking with Bob's relatives years before.

Wheels for the World

The first avenue I researched was a really special ministry called Wheels for the World, started by Joni and Friends. The organization asks communities in the United States to gather secondhand wheelchairs to donate to developing countries around the world. Before the chairs are taken overseas, they are first restored. Then volunteer teams of rehabilitation specialists and wheelchair mechanics go to countries where there is a huge need for wheelchairs and help to attain the best possible fit for each individual who receives one of the refurbished chairs. As well, each person who receives a wheelchair is given a Bible.

I called the Joni and Friends' office in California to find out if there was a possibility that our family could be a part of a Wheels for the World team. When I got off the phone, I knew this was not the direction for us to go in at this time. Their upcoming schedule did not include sending any teams to the two countries we were interested in for our mission trip. Plus, the nature of their mission opportunity was not a good fit for our entire family.

Slovakia

Then, I remembered there were partnership mission opportunities through our denomination. After I looked up the number for the state office, I called and talked with Jessica. To my delight, I found out our state, Virginia, was partnering with the country of Slovakia. One of the locations within the country, that asked for a team, had a special education school and nursing homes run by the Slovakian national branch of our denomination.

For these trips to locations in the partnering country, the state office makes all the arrangements for the teams it sends. They work out the specifics of the assignment as well as arranging for a translator, lodging, food, transportation, etc. So all the participants have to do is pay the required fees to the state office, get any necessary vaccinations, have passports in hand, and gather supplies for their assignment. However, our family would need to plan our own transportation since we needed a van with a lift.

I thought, "This might be it, our family mission trip!" I envisioned Kristen using her occupational therapy training to evaluate the needs of the children in the school and the older folks in the nursing home. I envisioned Bob and Justin making adaptive devices for Kristen to use in helping people and me using my sewing skills to help make the devices. I also could picture Nathan and me encouraging the children, their families, and the older folks in the nursing homes.

In January, when I shared my ideas with Jessica, she said we needed to let the people decide how to use us, not to have preconceived ideas of what we would do while we where there. Jessica asked us to make a list of the skills and abilities of each person in our family and e-mail it to her. She said she would forward it on to her contact in Slovakia. I prayed for the leaders in Slovakia to have wisdom from God in knowing how to best use us as a family.

Jessica also gave me the names of people who had gone on a partnership mission trip the year before to Slovakia. I called two different women from the list. I loved hearing the stories about their experiences. I even met personally with one of the women, and she showed me her pictures.

Project No. 2—Crisis Pregnancy Center

Our second family project involved doing a project in Seth's memory at the Crisis Pregnancy Center (CPC) here in Roanoke. A year ago, when we received the first installment of our inheritance, we had set aside $1,000 to do a project. The meaning of Seth's name, "the appointed," was the remaining piece of my broken dream of raising twins. I felt I needed to use his name in a positive way, and so doing a project for the CPC seemed very appropriate.

Even though the money had been set aside for a year, we did not actually move on doing a project until I felt more even emotionally. In November, the same week I talked with Jessica for the first time, I went by the Crisis Pregnancy Center to talk with the new director, Tom. I told him about our family's desire to use $1,000 to do a project in memory of Seth.

First, Tom and I discussed a scholarship fund idea I had heard about while listening to a radio program. The purpose of the fund would be to help women who come to the center and choose to carry their babies to further their education in order to be able to support themselves and their baby. Tom and I decided a one-time gift of $1,000 would not go very far to do this kind of project.

Next, I mentioned the memorial fund idea I had originally talked about with the previous director, Ruth, a few years before. Tom shared with me his dream of someday having a memorial prayer garden where people who have lost babies could come and remember them in a special way. A brick would be purchased in memory of the baby and then placed in the garden patio with the baby's name on it. I loved this idea, and I thought it would be very therapeutic for families similar to the way the Vietnam War Memorial Wall is for the Vietnam veterans and their families.

Then toward the end of our conversation, Tom shared with me about a particular desire the CPC staff and the board of directors had. At the time, the counseling rooms were painted white; they looked very bare with only office chairs and a small table for furniture. The CPC wanted to have these rooms furnished and decorated in way that would create a cozier and more relaxing atmosphere. They hoped that this would help each client feel more comfortable and at ease while meeting with the counselor. I went home and shared with my family about us helping to make this desire happen; each person loved it!

The Rooms

As I thought about this project, I realized by decorating and furnishing a counseling room at the CPC, our family could help women who are dealing with a crisis pregnancy feel safer: safer to choose life for her unborn baby, safer to raise her baby, safer to choose adoption, and safer to deal with the regret of an abortion.

We were all very thrilled when our idea for this project started to become a reality. In January, we were blessed to be able to buy two love seats and two upholstered chairs at a warehouse auction for a very good price. This meant we still had money left to buy lamps and accessories, enabling us to furnish and decorate *two* counseling rooms. Since it ended up being two rooms, we decided that one room would be dedicated in memory of Seth and the other room would be dedicated in honor of Nathan. We chose the first two rooms that were across the hall from each other. This reminded me of how Seth and Nathan nestled in my womb next to each other during my pregnancy.

During this same time, unbeknownst to us, Beverly, a friend of ours from church, was organizing two groups of women to do the painting of the two rooms. The painting project was to be done in honor of one of our church's pastors, Chuck, who was on the CPC board. Initially, Beverly had no idea that our family was the one who bought the furniture for the rooms.

She selected one paint color, a soft golden yellow, to be the base color of each room. For Seth's room, Beverly decided to do a ragging application in a lighter shade of the paint to go over the base coat. For Nathan's room, she chose a sponging application in a lighter shade to go over the base coat. To have the same base coat yet different decorative applications for each room reminded me of the fact Seth and Nathan were fraternal twins. It worked out that our family was actually able to help with applying the base coat of paint to each room along with my Women on Mission group from church. Then later, another women's mission group applied the decorative overlays to the walls in both rooms.

The first decorative item I brought into the CPC to try out was a very large basket of artificial sunflowers I had bought at one of the thrift stores that I frequent. This was very appropriate because these flowers had become very symbolic to our family. The significance started while Bob and Justin were in Romania on their mission trip; they really enjoyed viewing the many fields of sunflowers there. As they watched the heads of those tall flowers turn to follow the sun, it reminded them of the importance of keeping our eyes on the Son, Jesus Christ, throughout the day. The basket of sunflowers found its home in Nathan's room.

During the days that followed, I thoroughly enjoyed shopping for accessories, rugs, and lamps for our two counseling rooms. At lunchtime, I brought different items into the rooms to try out, getting the opinions of any staff members who were around. If an item did not work, I took it right back to the store. Throughout the entire process, I prayed for God's guidance.

Busy Months

January and February of 1998 were very busy months for me. Almost daily, I went by the CPC to try out different items in the rooms. We finished the decorating the rooms the second week in February when Bob, Justin, and I hung the window treatments in Seth's room.

Over the Valentine's weekend, we celebrated Kristen and Justin's birthday with our usual family party for their shared birthday. We decided to make the celebration be at dinnertime. So I purchased and wrapped gifts for both of them, prepared the meal and made two separate cakes, and invited friends and relatives.

On Valentine's Day, Bob and I went to visit a friend, Marilyn, who was a single mom. Her son, Alan, was one of Justin's friends. Marilyn was in a very late stage of cancer. Over a period of time, I had been collecting small items to be put in a heart-shaped basket to take to her. During the visit, I sat next to Marilyn's bed. Propped up in bed, she enjoyed looking at each item in the basket. While Marilyn and I chatted, Bob and Alan did household projects.

I enjoyed all these activities. They were ways I could minister and serve others, but they required me to give of my emotional reserves. Along with these activities, I also had been concerned about the state of matters in Washington, D.C., in particular, the impeachment hearing for President Clinton. For months, I prayed and fasted in regard to my concerns. However, I bottomed out with the intensity of prayers. I reached a point where I could not pray any more.

Crying Every Day

By the end of February, I was crying every day. I knew I needed to talk with my doctor about my medication, but there were a lot of complications with my efforts to get in touch with him. In an attempt to get some respite, I asked Bob if we could go to a bed-and-breakfast one hour away from our home. We had seen this lovely bed-and-breakfast a few years before and had hoped to go there one day in the future. Now was that "one day"! I was hopeful a change of scenery and relaxing activities would help me be replenished.

When we arrived home from our weekend trip, I was feeling much better. I was able to talk with my doctor's office about my medication and the dosage was adjusted. I began to analyze what had happened to me the week before. I saw that over the past few months, I had given of my emotional reserves far more than I realized. Also, listening to the local and national news had been very draining for me, so I stopped listening to news programs altogether.

Sunshine and Filters

In my endeavor to feel better, I began to read *Lightposts for Living: The Art of Choosing a Joyful Life*. The author is Thomas Kincaid, one of my favorite current day artists. He is commonly known as the Painter of Light because of how he accentuates light in his paintings. As I was reading Kincaid's book, I gleaned much insight into the importance of shielding one' self from too much information. Just as receiving too many sun rays is dangerous for skin, too much information or incorrect information can hurt one's state of mind and soul. Many people are aware of the importance of using sunscreen to protect their skin from developing cancer; but, I wonder how many people realize the importance of screening the amount and the kind of information they receive on daily basis.

After reading Kincaid's book, I determined to establish some kind of filter in my life to help me manage the huge amount of melancholy I have in my temperament. This is important because I have a great propensity toward feeling the pain and suffering of others, sometimes almost more than they do themselves. Now, I am learning how to choose on a daily basis what I will allow into my life, my mind, and my heart by using Philippians 4:8 as my filter: "Finally, brothers, whatever is true, whatever is noble, whatever is right, whatever is pure, whatever is lovely, whatever is admirable—if anything is excellent or praiseworthy—think about such things" (NIV).

As a practical step, I stopped listening to news programs and also stopped reading the different newsletters I had been receiving. Often when I read them my spirit would become downcast and my joy seemed to flee from me because they had detailed information about the moral decline of our country.

How to Make a Difference

March 3, 1999

Father, I passionately believe some of the essential components for a morally strong country are:

- *Biblically committed marriage*
- *Healthy family life*
- *Strong work ethic*
- *Sanctity of life*
- *And most of all–The gospel of Jesus Christ*

O Lord, how much of my emotional reserves am I to give in my efforts to make a positive difference in these areas or components? What is the best way to maximize the use of my allotted reserves? I have the conviction and passion of a crusader; but, I am not a confrontational person. I have the compassion of a social worker or a counselor; but, I do not have the stamina to walk along beside the person who needs help.

I need a way to make a positive difference, but in a manner I will not be overwhelmed emotionally and be pulled back into burnout and depression. By writing books and presenting seminars, I am able to address, in a low-key, upbeat way, each of the components which are essential for building a morally strong country. In a seminar setting, I am better able to listen to the concerns of people (mostly women) without being emotionally overwhelmed. Also, I can facilitate group discussion which encourages the participants to find and implement biblical solutions to their problems. In a seminar setting, it is much easier for me to have objective compassion.

Focal Point

In my study of interior design, I have learned that having a focal point is very important. For example, hanging a large beautiful painting over a fireplace can make a wonderful focal point in a living room. If a spotlight is placed to shine on the painting, the colors will be enhanced even more. In fact, the whole color scheme for the room can be based on the painting. As well, the sofa and chairs can be placed around the fireplace, in view of the artwork, to make an inviting conversational area. Accent pillows can even be selected to bring out some of the colors in the painting.

Just as a focal point can help in planning a well-designed room, having a focal point in one's life can help in planning and living a balanced, beautiful life. By establishing what our life's focus is, we are better able to choose what activities to be involved in and which ones to decline. Focal point could also be described as our mission in life or the passion that gives us motivation to get out of our bed every morning. It is what drives us and what we strive toward. After praying and seeking the Lord, I have determined that my personal focal point is "to encourage and inspire individuals to live a balanced, joyful life in Christ Jesus."

March 10, 1999

Today, as I study 1 Timothy 4:13-16 and 2 Timothy 1:6-7, I am inspired to write in my journal what I sense God is saying to me . . .

"Judy, until I come, give close attention to the public reading of Scripture, to exhortation and teaching. I have given you the spiritual gifts that are within you. I have gifted you in the area of exhortation—encouragement and also with a gift for teaching. As well, I have gifted you to encourage people through your hospitality.

Judy, do not neglect the spiritual gifts within you. I have shown you much over the past 20 years about the way I have gifted you. Remember what Dr. R told you when you were counseling with him years ago. He said you had been gifted with emotional type gifts; but, you did not yet have the maturity to know how to use them wisely.

Judy, you are gaining this needed maturity and I want you to focus intently on the kindling afresh of your gifts. I want you to devote the majority of your time using your gifts with:

- *The CPC project*
- *The family mission trip*
- *The book you and Nathan are writing*
- *Someday presenting seminars again*

Be absorbed in these things. Take great pains with these endeavors, but be ever mindful to lean on Me for understanding and guidance. I want you to focus, focus, focus on what I have called you to do! Persevere. Keep going. I will bring many people to myself through what you and Nathan will do. I will use you, both, to encourage many people. I will use Seth to accomplish great things just as I told you in the recovery room after the delivery of your twin sons.

Judy, I don't want you to be as concerned about what is happening in Washington, D.C. Continue taking a break from listening to the news programs. Don't use your emotional reserves on these concerns right now.

Regarding the projects I have given you to do, Judy, I will bring the people and the resources that you need, when you need them. I want you to be intent on what I have given you to work on now. Judy, remember 2 Timothy 1:7; I have not given you a spirit of fear, but of power, love, and sound mind."

Setting Goals

After I made this entry, I was able to set the target goal for having the rough draft of the book finished by my next birthday, my fifty-second. A major reason I chose this age is because it was how old my father was when he died of a massive heart attack. Another goal for me was to finish up on our CPC project. This gave me something to concentrate on while we waited to hear from Jessica about our possible mission trip to Slovakia.

Since I had not been at Seth's funeral service, I had a need to plan a dedication ceremony for our rooms at the CPC in which each member of our family could participate. I worked many hours on writing a letter to Seth and a letter to Nathan in regard to their rooms. Each room had a developed theme.

Seth's room has a seaside-cottage look with a lighthouse painting, containers of seashells, and a lighthouse birdhouse. The color scheme was pale greens and pale yellows. Nathan's room had more of an English country look with a mahogany-framed mirror, a large basket of sunflowers, and an urn of hydrangeas. The color scheme was navy blue, cherry red, and warm yellow, which are all jewel colors. I looked up Bible verses to go with the theme of each room. For Seth's room, I chose verses that pertained to God leading us from darkness out into the light. For Nathan's room, I chose verses that speak of God transforming our lives from being like "dry" deserts to being like "lush" gardens.

I had hoped to have the dedication of the CPC rooms right after I finished researching the verses; however, life was very busy. So the actual family dedication service did not take place until January 2004.

Chapter 27

A Memorial

Family Outreach Project

April 3, 1999

    Today, I was reading in the fourth chapter of Joshua from the Old Testament. As I read, I began to visualize how our family project could be similar to how the Israelites made a memorial on their way to the Promised Land. In Joshua 4:21-24, Joshua instructed the twelve men he had appointed from each tribe to gather twelve stones from Jordan to be set up at Gilgal. Joshua said to the Israelites, "In the future when your descendants ask their fathers, 'What do these stones mean?' tell them, 'Israel crossed the Jordan on dry ground.'" The stones were to be a reminder of what God did for them: Israel crossed the Jordan River on dry ground. He dried up the water of the Jordan just like He had done to the Red Sea. Joshua explained to them God did this so all the peoples of the earth may know He is mighty and He is to be revered.

    I envisioned that in the future, when our grandchildren would ask, "Why did you go to Europe the summer of 1999?" we could share about the Israelites. After telling this story, we will share that You, God, brought us through many difficult times:

- *The death of Seth*
- *The diagnosis of Nathan's brain injury*
- *My burnout and long recovery period*
- *Nathan's different surgeries*
- *Bob's job changes*

- *Nine year struggle of building the addition and acquiring needed equipment for Nathan*
- *Then, we will share that You, God, have brought us to the point of being able to minister as a family to other people.*

Father, I see the CPC project we have already done as a memorial to our belief that all human life is precious and to be highly regarded because You are the Creator of life. However, at this point in time, I am not sure whether the European trip is to be our family "memorial" project.

April 12, 1999

We have heard from Jessica that the specific area of Slovakia we were interested in has closed its requests for help. Jessica also said that the director for the denominational work for the entire country says that they are not set up in Slovakia to handle wheelchair situations like Nathan's.

I am so disappointed and sad. In a sense, I had already started to bond with the people. Now it looks like we will not be meeting them.

Austria is another country of interest, particularly because part of Bob's family heritage is from there. However, I do not know whether to pursue it at this time. Since it is not one of the countries currently partnering with Virginia, we would have to make all our own arrangements and plans. So right now, we are waiting to hear from Jessica after she contacts the denominational missionary who works in Austria. She hopes to find out from him what type of ministry possibilities there might be for us there.

When I talked with Bob, he said he did not feel we should definitely rule out going to Europe for a mission trip. But he said, "I am not as excited to go as you and Kristen are since Justin and I went to Romania last summer on a mission trip. However, I would love to have Rhonda, our neighbor from up the street, over for dinner. Since she has given me several rides to work, I want to do something nice for her in return." My response was, "Don't you want to think big for this summer?"

Since Bob did not feel we should definitely rule out a mission trip to Europe, the thought occurred to me to contact friends of mine who worked with my former ministry organization. John and Joann had contact with missionaries all over the world through their office at the national ministry headquarters. I first tried to call them. When their line was busy, I sent them an e-mail to ask about what opportunities they might be aware of in Slovakia and Austria. A few days later, the e-mail that I had sent came back to me; I did not attempt to contact them again.

April 16, 1999

Father, it seems to me the trip would be a wonderful way to end the book. The timing seems to be right for the trip. Hopefully, we will still have the money. Kristen will have finished her schooling and will not have started her job. The trip would be before Y2K (the year 2000). But, Lord, is a mission trip to Europe what You want us to do for our family project?

Other Options

April 18, 1999

Dear Father, I just don't know what to do in terms of the possible mission trip to Austria. Jessica told us the missionary in Austria sees possibilities for us. Yet, I am uncertain as to whether this is the direction to go in or whether we should go in a different direction. I spent quite a bit of time yesterday morning thinking and praying about this.

Then later that day, I went by the CPC to talk with Tom about our situation. At one time, Tom and his wife were missionaries in Spain, so I thought perhaps he might have some discerning insight. Tom said, "Make sure about the van situation, make sure the assignment is specific, and think about the doorways in regard to Nathan's chair."

Before I left, I threw out another idea to Tom: the possibility of our family spending two weeks during the summer helping build a prayer memorial garden for the CPC. We would buy the brick and supply the labor to build a patio and a wall. Tom said, "I am not ready to talk with the board yet about a prayer memorial garden project. And if we do it, I envision a lot of community involvement in this project."

After talking with Tom, I went home and looked over some of the brochures that Jessica had sent me. They gave an overview of short-term mission opportunities in the United States with our denomination. The resort ministry possibilities looked very interesting to me, particularly the Great Smokey Mountains and Virginia Beach. In the past, I had greatly enjoyed visiting both of these places. Virginia Beach even has a boardwalk! If we went there, Nathan could drive his wheelchair near the ocean.

The Smokey Mountain project involved ministering in a campground. The beauty and peacefulness of this lush green mountain range with its babbling creeks always appeals to me. However, we were not experienced in camping together. So I thought we would need to rent equipment and do some camping together before the assignment.

That night, I shared with Bob and the boys about my talk with Tom earlier that day. Also, I told them about the two resort ministry opportunities. However, they did not latch onto either of these possibilities.

In early May, I went to visit Kristen in Morganton, North Carolina, where she was doing her second internship in occupational therapy. I shared with Kristen about the conversation I had with Tom. Kristen did not lean one way or the other in terms of continuing on with the possibility of a mission trip to Austria.

May 5, 1999

Dearest Father, after talking extensively with Kristen last weekend and with Bob and the boys last night, I still don't know whether to drop the European trip altogether and pursue another direction. Yesterday, I had the thought that perhaps we could help with Mission '99, our church's local youth outreach project. When I mentioned this idea last night to Bob and the boys, during devotions, Justin said, "I don't want you all to be involved in Mission '99! I want to enjoy being with the youth group that week and have a total break from being with my family."

Lord, if You don't want us to do a mission trip or a mission project, please show me. If You do, please point us in the direction to go. I anticipate Your leading.

A Different Direction

A week later, God answered this prayer for me while I was having my devotional time.

May 13, 1999

Dearest Father, today, as I was reading Isaiah 55:13, one of my verses for the dedication of Nathan's room at the CPC, the word "memorial" jumped out at me. "Instead of the thorn bush, the cypress will come up; and instead of the nettle, the myrtle will come up; and it will be a memorial to the Lord." Father, an idea is crystallizing in my mind . . . Do you want us to transform our wilderness backyard into a beautiful garden as a memorial to You and as a place to minister to others?

During family devotions, I shared my vision with the rest of the family. I said, "If we went to Europe, the jet would take us there for the ministry opportunities. However, fixing up our yard and building a patio is comparable to our family flying to Europe; it is a vehicle to get us to the point of ministry. It will provide an actual physical location where our family can minister to people in an ongoing way instead of just two weeks." Everyone in our family liked this idea and so we all agreed that this would be our summer project: work on the backyard and build a patio.

May 15, 1999

   Father, in what order do You want us to do our yard project? Should the patio be built first? Or should we focus on the yard first? We need to take out the overgrown bushes in the backyard with a backhoe, add dirt to even out the slope, and then replant the grass.

Building the Patio

After much prayer and discussion, our family decided it would be better to build the patio first. At that time, our yard was on a slight slope and the ground was uneven. This made it difficult for people to move from the picnic table to the serving table. A patio would provide us with a flat area to grill, serve the food, eat at the picnic table, and sit around and chat. A brick patio would be a lovely, warm environment for our guests.

We already had in place a wooden privacy fence that would shield the patio from the view of the street. Also, at the end of the driveway, which curves around to the back of our house, we had a lattice fence with ivy growing up on it. Both of these structures would help our patio seem more like an outside room.

Justin and I used the garden hose to design the shape of the patio right on the grass. We decided the patio would work best on the lawn beside the addition and deck. We made the width of the patio ten feet and the length twenty feet to accommodate the picnic table, a serving area, and a sitting area. Justin designed the patio with curves on the corners in order to make it more aesthetically pleasing. Justin also had a certain type of brick paver he wanted to use. Cutting the pavers to make the curves was hard, but the curves added to the beauty and warmth of the patio.

We had one of the pavers engraved with the inscription: "Rossbacher, Memorial 1999, Joshua 4." We decided to place the engraved paver in the area of the patio where our guests step down from the deck. When we were asked about the inscription, we would say, "The engraved brick is to remind us that God brought our family through difficult times to the point where we can use our home to encourage our friends, neighbors, and relatives. God has been gracious to us just as He was to the Israelites. Since God told the Israelites to build a memorial to remind them of the fact that He brought them through the Red Sea and the Jordan River, we wanted a physical memorial to remind us of God's faithfulness to our family."

While Justin and Bob were building our patio, I shopped for outdoor decor. I went to flea markets, yard sales, and thrift stores looking for outdoor furniture, candleholders with hurricane globes, wind chimes, etc. We finished the patio in about two weeks; after which, I planted petunias, geraniums, impatiens, and ivy all around the patio. Our plan was to invite one or two families over every week or two for a cookout. Then at the end of the summer, we would have a block party and invite all our neighbors.

Summer Hospitality

Since there were many neighbors we did not yet know, I made a conscious effort while watering my flowers to watch for our neighbors to be outside. As I saw them out watering their flowers or pulling up in their driveway, I walked over and introduced myself. This usually led to a short conversation, and while we were talking, I concentrated on learning their first name. This way, the next time I saw them out in their yard, I could call out their name and say hi. Through being intentional like this throughout the whole summer, I was able to get to know most of my neighbors better.

Since Bob wanted to thank Rhonda for giving him rides to work, we decided she would be our very first guest. In fact, we had Rhonda over even before we started building the patio. We served a meal in the side yard on a wooden picnic table in the area where we planned to put the patio.

After the patio was finished, we all worked together to plan and carry out each one of our cookouts. Despite the fact that I did not do cooking projects with Justin when he was little, like I did with Kristen, he has become an excellent cook. Justin loved doing the barbequing on the grill, making special desserts, and cooking gourmet-type dishes for each of our dinners on the patio. Throughout the summer, Kristen made several of her specialty dishes for our guests. Bob swept the patio and set up all the furniture and coolers. I enjoyed deciding on the decorations and table settings to use for our outdoor entertaining. Nathan was always the greeter for each of our parties. Each person in our family thoroughly enjoyed getting to know every neighbor who came.

August 5, 1999

Dearest Father, I had thought our family outreach project would be going to Eastern Europe on a mission trip. This way, the original dream Bob and I had 25 years ago of being career missionaries would be at least partially fulfilled. Instead, You led us to build a patio, as an ongoing outreach project, right here in Roanoke, in order to minister to our friends and neighbors in our own backyard.

Lord, You impressed us as a family to go next door, up and down the street, and around the corner getting to know our neighbors. You led us to build our patio so that we could have a more permanent place to strengthen our relationships with the people in our neighborhood. We are making ourselves available to be used by You in the lives of our neighbors. Use us as You wish. Perhaps someday we can even open our home for a neighborhood Bible study.

Neighborhood Block Party

August 10, 1999

Dearest Father, please lead and guide us as we continue to meet our neighbors and as we strengthen our relationships with them. When should we invite the whole block over for a cookout?

October Potluck

Since the end of the summer and the beginning of the school year are such a busy time for people, we felt we needed to wait and have our neighborhood block party in October. We decided to do a potluck dinner. Our family would provide the meat and beverages, and we would ask people to bring a side dish or dessert to share with everyone. It turned out to be a perfect time of year to have the party because the weather was still nice enough to use the patio.

At one of my favorite thrift stores, I found some beautiful fall party invitations that were brand-new. We used these to invite our neighbors to the potluck dinner. Kristen printed the invitations using calligraphy. A few weeks before the party on a Sunday afternoon, Bob and I went door to door to deliver the invitations.

Throughout the year, I had been buying decorative fall items at thrift stores and yard sales. At the beginning of October, I got out all the fall decorations. I placed some on the front porch and the rest throughout the downstairs of the house. Also, I put out a lot of table arrangements made from dried flowers. As well, I made a large arrangement of artificial and dried fall flowers to go in a large basket, which I set in the corner of the living room on a plant stand. Outside, I arranged pumpkins and potted chrysanthemums around a bale of hay next to the front lamp post. Also, I put chrysanthemums on the patio in the back.

Fortunately, the summer before, Bob, Justin, and I had already done a lot of repair and painting work on the front porch so that we could make it into an outdoor living area. I had purchased a small bistro table and two matching chairs on sale, which we put on the front porch. Justin and I scraped and painted a bench, and then we placed it on the opposite side of the porch from the swing. In addition to that, I bought a round rattan table to put in front of the bench.

We hung grapevine garland around the edge of the porch ceiling. Then we wove lights through the grapevine. On the evening of our fall neighborhood potluck, the lights provided a warm welcome to our guests. Also, the lights woven through the lattice around the back deck helped entice our guests to move out onto the patio.

That night, our party guests were able to flow back and forth from the front porch, through the downstairs, and out onto the patio. It was a perfect fall evening with a slight crisp feel in the air. We served hot apple cider in the family room, which people drank as they went out to mingle on the patio. We used the kitchen island as the buffet table for serving the food. Some people chose to eat dinner on the patio and some decided to eat in the dining room inside the house.

Nathan's Dream:

Recently, Nathan has been talking every day about wanting to be a school bus aide after he graduates. We pointed out to him that he needs a bus aide to help him get on and off the bus. Therefore, it did not seem very possible that he, himself, could be a bus aide. This information did not faze him; in fact, Nathan seemed more determined than ever to pursue being a bus aide! Either he does not actually understand that his physical disabilities limit him from doing this type of work or he does and is in denial. This whole situation was really difficult for me, so I asked Bob if he could be the one to follow up with Nathan about it. I was relieved when Bob agreed to do this for me.

One day, when Nathan came home from school, he immediately began to talk with me about wanting to be a school bus aide. I said, "Nathan, I talked with Daddy, and we decided he will be the one to help you with your dream of wanting to be a bus aide, and I will continue to work on our book. So you need to talk with Daddy, not me." That evening, when Bob came through the door, Nathan instantly began to talk with him about his desire to be a school bus aide.

Soon after this, while my sister Kathy was having dinner with us, Nathan talked with her about his dream. Kathy ran through some of the qualifications of school bus aide and after each one she would ask him if he could do this. He answered no to each qualification. She concluded, "It does not look like you can do the job of a bus aide." Upon hearing her words, Nathan cried and cried! Bob decided to take Nathan into the family room so he could have some time to regroup.

Later in the evening, Nathan wanted to know who he needed to talk with about the job. Kathy told him it would be the department of transportation. So then, Nathan wanted to know when Bob was going to talk with them. After he asked this question, Nathan told Bob, "I want to go with you."

March 9, 2000

Today, Nathan wanted to call Bob at work to see if he had contacted the transportation office. Therefore, I dialed Bob's work number for Nathan. Bob reported he had talked with Anita, the director of transportation, and had explained the situation to her. He asked her if she would be willing to talk with Nathan. She said she was and so an appointment was set up for Nathan to meet with her.

The day before the interview with transportation, I went to our church to pursue a possible idea for Nathan. I first saw my friend Carolyn, who was on staff at the church, and told her I wanted to find out about possible opportunities for Nathan to help with children. So we went together to talk with Rosemarie, the director of the Child Development Center (CDC). They both really liked the idea of having Nathan volunteer in a classroom as long as he had a personal assistant.

That evening, I shared with Nathan that Rosemarie was interested in talking with him about volunteering at the CDC. I told him the center was excited about him being a part of their program. I encouraged him, "If things don't go the way you hope today at your interview, remember that Carolyn and Rosemarie want to talk with you."

March 16, 2000

Father, thank You for giving grace to Bob and Nathan as they talked with the director of transportation yesterday. Thank You, that Anita was kind and gracious with Nathan, even when he answered "yes" to all the job qualifications which he is unable to perform. Also, I am so glad Nathan did not cry until he was in the van after the appointment. Today, Tim, the bus driver told me Anita said talking with

Nathan about him not meeting the qualifications to be a bus aide was one of the hardest things she has ever done.

In light of this whole "bus aide" ordeal, I am particularly appreciative for the wonderful talk I had on Tuesday with Rosemarie and Carolyn and some of the staff at the CDC at our church. How wonderful it is they can see potential ways Nathan can help with the children at the Child Development Center. They seem truly interested in incorporating Nathan into the program! Please raise up a person to be Nathan's personal aide if it is Your will for us to continue in this direction.

Tim R.

Not long after Nathan's disappointing interview, an interesting thing happened. One morning, when I was putting Nathan on the bus, the driver, Tim, mentioned he was looking for a summer job. Since I had been impressed with how Tim interacted with all the special needs children, I told him about our need for someone to help Nathan. Then, I asked him if he would be interested in working for us as a personal assistant for Nathan over the summer. Tim responded that he was, and so I invited him to our house for an interview.

That very same day, Tim came over. Bob came home at lunchtime so we could interview him together. We explained the position would involve going with Nathan one day a week to the CDC and helping him do different activities on other days. We felt good about Tim, so we offered him the job for the summer, and he accepted.

Graduation

Right before Nathan graduated, his wheelchair frame was expanded to accommodate his growth and a new seating system was made. This time, Nathan was comfortable in his new seating system from the very beginning.

WHEN I GRADUATED FROM CAVE SPRING, IT WAS GOOD. EVERYONE STOOD UP FOR ME!

The night of graduation, we arrived early at the civic center so we could get Nathan situated. We brought him in the back entrance because the stage was not wheelchair accessible from the front. Then we were able to take our seats before the crowds of people filled up the auditorium. This worked out very well for me because it allowed me to be more relaxed and greatly reduced my stress level. Nathan was positioned to watch from the side of the stage as his fellow graduates walked across to receive their diplomas. Justin waited there with him. When it was Nathan's turn, Justin pushed him out to receive his diploma; Nathan received a standing ovation from the audience! His friend Jennifer also received a standing ovation as Justin pushed her out to receive her diploma.

Graduation Letter to Nathan

June 2000

My Dearest Nathan,

It is time for you to graduate from high school. As I look back on the journal entry I made on your 10th birthday, it is so special to see how many of my dreams for you God has brought to be. Your room was finally finished after a little more than nine years. To think, your brother Justin was just a baby when we began to build the addition which contains your special room and bathroom. Then years later, your brother was able to help Daddy finish the addition.

Then in the summer of 1999, Daddy and Justin built the patio next to the deck. Also, they made a ramp to connect the two together. What a joy it is to see you drive out onto the deck, down the ramp onto the patio, and then onto the driveway. The patio is especially beautiful when the flowers are in bloom all around it.

Also, God brought about your first computer system in a miraculous way through the efforts of our Christian friend, Ann, and her friend. Then God used Doro, your COTA, to design an even better computer system for you a few years later. What a joy it is to watch you sit in front of your very own computer system, in your finished room, as you type away using your red button switch.

Nathan, I see the following as some of your skills, abilities, and interests:

- *You can converse and talk with warmth.*
- *You can ask questions.*
- *You can answer questions.*
- *You can drive your wheelchair.*
- *You can keep up with schedules. You are good at reminding people in our family about their appointments.*
- *You can read and spell words.*
- *You can do basic math problems.*
- *You can write using your special computer system.*
- *You enjoy children. You have expressed a strong desire to work with children.*
- *You have expressed an interest in teaching math to children.*
- *You like to pray for babies.*

Nathan, I can visualize you one day being the author of children's books. Then you could give a type of guest lecture to children where you demonstrate how you write your books using your adaptive computer system. Nathan, I can picture you helping in a preschool classroom with your own personal assistant to help facilitate the interaction between you and the children. This experience would enable you to better write books suitable for young children.

Nathan, it is a privilege to be your mother. I greatly anticipate all God will do in and through your life in the future. May God receive all the glory!

With much love,
Momma

PART SIX

Bold Designs

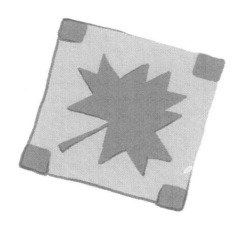

CHAPTER 28

Life after Graduation

Summer 2000

While Nathan was beginning his post-graduate life after high school, Kristen was starting her post-graduate life after college. She had recently graduated from Eastern Kentucky University and was looking for a job in her field as an occupational therapist. Initially, Kristen was focusing on jobs in other states near Virginia, but it ended up a position opened up for her here in Roanoke. To my delight, she moved into a duplex in a really beautiful neighborhood only two miles away from us. It worked out for her friend Katie to live with her in this old brick colonial. They loved the huge brick fireplace in the living room, the hardwood floors, and the spacious rooms.

That same summer, an opportunity did open up for Nathan at the Child Development Center. After the director talked to the staff about Nathan's desire to work with children, Ms. Patsy, the four-year-old classroom teacher, said she would love for him to volunteer in her room. So Nathan and I met Tim at the Family Life Center of our church to do a practice run. We checked out the logistics of how to get Nathan's wheelchair to Ms. Patsy's classroom. While we were talking in the game room of the church, Gretchan, a friend of Tim's, came in the room. Tim introduced Gretchan to Nathan and me.

Gretchan and I stood and talked for a while. She told me that, before she married, she worked for several years helping disabled children and adults. I asked Gretchan if she would think about being one of the personal assistants for Nathan. She said that although she was interested, she would not be available until school started. Later, I realized meeting Gretchan that day was a providential gift from God since after the school year began, Gretchan ended up being able to work several days a week with Nathan. She did an absolutely amazing job!

The Van Lift Breaks

During the early part of the summer, Bob flew to Chicago to visit his mom and dad. The primary purpose of the trip was for his sister, Lois, and him to relieve, Genina, the caregiver for their parents. After Bob left, I did not go to church Sunday morning. Nathan and I stayed home. I wanted to conserve my energy so I could enjoy going to church that night to hear the Mission 2000 presentation by the youth.

I thoroughly enjoyed the presentation. After the service, Justin said he would like to go out to eat with Allie, the youth pastor, and the rest of the team. I lingered to talk with different people after church. When I got outside with Nathan, everyone was gone except for our friends Dick and Nancy and the people they were talking to in front of the sanctuary. I slowly brought down the wheelchair lift in the van, then drove Nathan's chair onto the lift. However, as I started to bring the lift up, the chain broke. I quickly turned and called out to Dick, "Could you help me?"

We lifted Nathan out of the wheelchair, and Dick placed him in the front seat. He got inside the van and together we got the lift back up into the vehicle. Then I shut the doors. Dick took the wheelchair into the church and had the janitors lock it up in the coat closet.

Justin had told me which restaurant he was going to, so I drove there. I went in and told him what happened. Then I asked him to come home with me so he could carry Nathan into the house. After Justin and I got Nathan situated inside the house, we called Bob to tell him that the lift was broken. I was surprised that throughout the actual situation, I remained relatively calm; however, the next day I began feeling very fatigued and frustrated.

Monday morning, I took the van to the business that originally put the lift in for us. They had successfully made other repairs on our lift in the past, so I was hopeful they would be able to fix it again. But it was not to be; the damage was too great and the lift was too old. We needed a new lift!

Another problem was Nathan's wheelchair was still in the coat closet at church, and I did not have any way to transport it. Thankfully, I got the idea to call Ron, a friend who has a van with a lift because he has a son in a wheelchair. I asked him if he could pick up Justin in the afternoon, then go to our church and get Nathan's chair out of the closet and bring it home. He agreed, and the wheelchair was returned to our house.

Next, I contacted Tim and told him I would be unable to get Nathan to the "Duck" class at the CDC. As well, Justin and Nathan were supposed to start their volunteer work with the Therapeutic Recreation Program, but they were unable to do so because of this transportation problem. It was very disappointing to Nathan and me that he had to stay home. By Wednesday night, I was physically and emotionally exhausted. As I was talking with Bob on the phone, I began to weep. Bob said he would work on the lift situation as soon as he got back to Roanoke.

When Bob arrived home, he and Justin took the old lift out and made a wooden ramp to use to get Nathan in and out of the van. We decided to wait until school began to buy a lift; this way, we would have more time to hopefully find a used one in good condition. As soon as Justin went back to school, I would be the one to transport Nathan. Since the wooden ramp was too heavy for me to maneuver, the lift would need to be purchased and installed before school started. We prayed about this need; God provided when Bob was able to find a secondhand lift for a good price right at the end of the summer.

Ms. Patsy's Class

August 15, 2000

It has been such a blessing from the Lord that Nathan has had this wonderful opportunity of going to Ms. Patsy's classroom this past summer. Tim has been doing a great job facilitating interaction between Nathan and the children. It seems to be a good match for both Nathan and the kids.

Tim told me Miss Patsy presents a letter of the alphabet every two weeks. Toward the end of the summer, when the children were being introduced to the letter Z, a thought came to my mind. Nathan and I could write a short story in book form using the letter Z. Bob helped us work on the project; the final product was fantastic. The children loved the story!

When it was time for the new fall school year to begin, Ms. Patsy said she needed Nathan to take a few weeks off from coming to the classroom. She wanted to go through orientation with her new students and get things settled before bringing in a guest. So Nathan took a break from going to the "Duck" class.

It was also time for Tim to return to his school bus driving job. Before he left us, he suggested Nathan and I might want to write a book for each season of the year and include Nathan as the main character in each story. I thought this was a neat idea, so I worked on getting together magazine pictures to use in making these books.

Carolyn

We needed someone to take Tim's place as a personal assistant. We wanted Nathan to be able to return to Ms. Patsy's class at the CDC as soon as she was ready for him. While in an antique store near our house, I ran into a friend, Carolyn B. I asked her if she would be interested in working with Nathan. To my surprise, Carolyn immediately said yes! She was very excited to accompany Nathan to the Duck class. While we waited for Ms. Patsy's students to be ready, Carolyn came to our house and did a lot of special activities with Nathan.

However, Ms. Patsy kept delaying the start date because her new class was not ready yet. Finally, she said that because she had a few very challenging students, she did not think it was wise to have Nathan volunteer this school year. I was very disappointed when she told me this; nevertheless, the silver lining to this situation was Carolyn and Nathan ended up working on a very special writing project together. They called it the *True Adventures of Grizzy the Cat*, and they based it on funny stories of things that had happened with Carolyn's cat. Carolyn even helped Nathan to illustrate the book with some unique art techniques.

More Activities for Nathan

September 15, 2000

Oh Father, I want to plan neat activities for Nathan to do which will stimulate him. But, I will need people to assist him with these activities. I only have enough energy and time to come up with the ideas; I do not have the stamina to actually do all of them with Nathan. Just now, I am having two ideas crystallize in my mind . . .

The first idea is Nathan possibly being able to volunteer at the College of Health Sciences in the Occupational Therapy program. He could show his special wheelchair and demonstrate his driving skills as well as his computer system and typing skills. I would like to meet with the head of the OT department at the college to see what she thinks about my idea.

The other idea is to have our friend Grace help Nathan create artwork. She has done such a good job teaching art at ACE camp. Grace, originally from England, has a delightful British accent. She, also, has a very relaxing way of interacting with the kids and helping them to enjoy art activities. But, I am not sure how to get in touch with her.

Answers to Prayer

Not long after this, on a Sunday afternoon, I ran into Grace at the book section of the Vinton Goodwill store. We began to talk, and I quickly turned the conversation to my idea of her doing art projects with Nathan. I was so excited when Grace said she would love to help Nathan with this! Soon after, she started coming once a week and did creative, artsy projects that encouraged Nathan to use his hands as much as possible.

Sometime later, I discovered that our neighbor, Kim, was an occupational therapist and an instructor of an assistive technology course at the College of Health Sciences. I mentioned to her my desire for Nathan to be a "guest presenter" for the OT students. So Kim worked it out to bring her students to our house. Nathan was able to demonstrate his use of adaptive technology. He showed them how he types on his computer by hitting a big red button switch while the program scans the entire alphabet. Nathan also demonstrated driving his electric wheelchair, and I showed the students some of its special features like the tilt-in-space function.

Another day, while shopping at the Salem Goodwill, I saw an old friend, Anna. She told me her husband, Jorge, might like to work with Nathan. Ever since Nathan was in preschool, I had desired to have someone teach him a foreign language. Being from the country of Venezuela, Jorge could teach Nathan Spanish.

Jorge was excited to begin assisting Nathan in this endeavor; as well, I was thrilled. He started coming one evening a week. Jorge helped Nathan make Spanish flashcards. First, he asked Nathan to select pictures from magazines. Then Jorge cut out each picture, glued it to a piece of cardboard, and wrote the Spanish word underneath. They reviewed the flashcards during each visit. Also, Jorge made a tape with his voice saying the Spanish words to coordinate with each card. This way, other people could practice the vocabulary words with Nathan throughout the week.

Community Projects

On Fridays, I was Nathan's personal assistant, and we did volunteer work in the community. The first month, we visited different facilities that service the Roanoke Valley. By the end of month, we had decided to concentrate on helping two particular places: the Crisis Pregnancy Center and the Ronald McDonald House.

At the CPC, we decided to volunteer every few months. We decorated the bulletin boards for each season of the year. Also, we brought special snacks for the volunteers and staff each time we came. The workers there greatly appreciated these little encouragements. For Valentine's Day, I even bought red roses and put one in a vase on everyone's desk.

For the Ronald McDonald House, we decided to do seasonal social events and decorations. Nathan made door hangers to put on each guest's door that celebrated the current season. Gretchan helped him make these using rubber stamp designs. We adapted the stamps with a long handle so Nathan could help to make the door decorations. During Thanksgiving, we all went and decorated the tables with fall arrangements, which I already had. Also, we visited with the guests who were staying at the house during this holiday. At Christmas, our whole family helped plan a special musical evening. We sang Christmas carols accompanied by a friend of ours who is a pianist. As well, we brought apple cider for people to drink and Christmas cookies for them to eat.

When Bob, Nathan, and I went to the Crisis Pregnancy Center appreciation dinner for volunteers, we met Lynne, another CPC volunteer. Nathan and I enjoyed chatting with her. Originally from Namibia, which is next to South Africa, Lynne spoke with a beautiful accent. Since she did not have a full-time job, I asked her if she would be interested in working with Nathan.

A Variety of Helpers

Lynne ended up coming every week to spend time with Nathan. She helped him work on playing a keyboard, which my nephew Joel had given him. As well, she reviewed the Spanish flashcards with Nathan and also made a book about Africa with him.

Gradually, we added more personal assistants, and they each contributed something special to Nathan's life. Judy, a retired schoolteacher, has the most amazing smile, and she loved to read books with him. Amy, a high school student, often brought her dog for Nathan to enjoy. April, an occupational therapist, frequently took him for long walks in the neighborhood. Tim M., a retired teacher, loved to sing hymns and other songs with Nathan. Delores, a friend from Nathan's classroom, was able to have conversations with him as a peer. Tyler, a friend of Justin's, taught him some German and also worked on composing music with him. Gretchan, who came two times a week, was able to take him out into the community to do special projects.

So Nathan could have the experience of helping children, I arranged with a friend, Cathy, that she bring her children, Leis and Eric, once a week to our house. This way, she had a few hours to do errands, work on projects, or just be by herself. I bought all kinds of toys and educational games at thrift stores for us to use in interacting with the children.

Nathan and I wrote a book together for each season of the year. Nathan decided to put Leis and Eric in his fall storybook. The winter book included Nathan's personal assistants, Gretchan and Tim, and each of their families. Our spring book was about Nathan's secret garden. The summer book was based on our family being at the beach with Carolyn's family. We also made books about several colors, letters, and holidays.

Gretchan helped Nathan plan and give many parties including Green Day party, surprise birthday party for Grandma, Hawaiian luau, and an All Saints Day party. They made the invitations, party favors, and food and came up with games to play. As well, Kristen and Nathan planned a wedding shower for Kristen's friends Katie and Nathanael.

Guest Speaking for Nathan

Although Nathan enjoyed all these opportunities, he was still bringing up his yearning to help children in schools. I also desired Nathan to do activities with children; however, I wanted the emphasis to be on his ability not his disability. I began to think about Nathan being a guest speaker in elementary classrooms. I asked Gretchan to prepare an interview presentation with Nathan in regard to the books he had written with others and me.

Bob made a mock keyboard using poster board. Gretchan attached the red button switch to Nathan's chair. By moving her finger across the mock keyboard, she was able to simulate the process of how the special computer program scans the alphabet. Nathan would hit the red switch when her finger hit the letter he wanted use.

April 4, 2001

Dearest Father, thank You that Nathan is now having his second speaking engagement. Please be with Nathan and Gretchan in a very, very special way. Bless the children and the teachers who listen to them. Enable Gretchan to draw information out of Nathan. May Nathan's speech be as clear as possible. Lead him to use the words he needs to express his answers and his questions.

In a way, Nathan is coming alongside of the teachers and helping the children. I would love for Nathan to catch a vision for how important this role could be for him. May Nathan have a sense of satisfaction from doing this.

Bonsack Elementary

My sister, Kathy, was able to line up some guest-speaking opportunities for Nathan at her school, Bonsack Elementary. Being the school guidance counselor, Kathy accompanied Nathan and Gretchan to each classroom and stayed in the rooms to help in any way she could. She also had lunch with them in the cafeteria. Nathan enjoyed spending the entire day at Kathy's school.

The speaking engagement at Bonsack led to the children in one of the fourth-grade classes wanting to plan a surprise spring party for Nathan. The party included everything from entertainment to refreshments and gifts. The other fourth-grade class presented Nathan with a book of poems that they had written especially for him to enjoy.

Gretchan helped Nathan to compose a thank-you note for each of the fourth-grade classes. Then Nathan typed this note on his computer, and Bob made enough copies for each student to have one. It worked out that Nathan's cousin, Joel, met him at the school on field day to hand out the cards. Actually, because Joel had just graduated from college, he was able to spend some extra time with Nathan during the summer.

Garden-Style Seminars

During the time that Nathan was doing his guest speaking, a yearning began to grow in my heart to do something totally separate from Nathan. I desired to do a project or activity that expressed my uniqueness. I wanted to do something fun and creative that would help bring balance to my life.

While we were building the patio and inviting over friends and neighbors, I enjoyed finding pictures in magazines of outdoor rooms and ways to use garden-style elements indoors. This process of collecting pictures inspired me to learn more about garden-style decorating and entertaining. Soon, I began to have a desire to teach others about what I was learning.

April 6, 2001

Dearest Father, a fleeting thought went through my head this afternoon: should I ask Lisa at "Teaberry's" (a garden café and gift shop) if I could present a decorating feature at her shop? Perhaps the subject matter could be something about connecting the outdoors with the indoors. Then, I could present the feature at other places if it went well.

April 12, 2001

I talked to Lisa, on Sunday afternoon, about my idea of presenting a feature on Garden Style decorating at her store. She liked the idea. I sense this is the direction You, Father, are leading me as I develop the concept.

April 20, 2001

Wednesday afternoon, I stopped by the Gilded Lily, a store that sells cottage and garden-style items. As I was paying for a decorating book at the counter, I mentioned to the owner, Beverly, "I am going to be teaching classes on garden-style decorating." Beverly replied, "Where are you going to teach them?" I responded, "I have spoken to the owner of Teaberry's about the possibility of teaching classes at her store, and today I thought of your store's patio area." Beverly then said, "I tell you what you could do for me. I have been asked to speak at the Garden Club Council on the subject of garden-style decorating. Would you be interested in giving the talk for me since I don't enjoy speaking before groups?" I exclaimed, "I would love to do the speaking engagement!" Also, I asked her if it would be possible for me to present two different seminars at her store before I did the program for the Garden Club Council. Beverly agreed to my request, and we set up two dates to do the seminars. One topic was garden-style decorating and the other was designing outdoor rooms.

I knew when I left the store that I was headed in the right direction. It was so encouraging to think I now had three speaking opportunities! So with growing confidence, I called the contact person for the council and we confirmed the date of June 15 for the presentation.

Preparations

Before my presentations at the Gilded Lily, I made flyers to advertise each seminar. I placed them at the Gilded Lily and other strategic stores and then mailed them to friends and acquaintances. I also made worksheets and handouts for each seminar, using lime green and bright yellow paper. This worked out well because I was able to use some of the same handouts for the talk I gave later at the Garden Club Council.

May 25, 2001

Thank you so very much, Father, for the two different seminars I taught at The Gilded Lily. There were ten participants, including Beverly, at each seminar. Ten people was a good size; since, each time we had to meet inside of the store because of the weather. If there had been more people and it would have been difficult to show Beverly's items and my vintage fabrics, etc.

I know You, Father, opened the door and moved me through the door into these opportunities. Please lead me in preparing the presentation for the Garden Club Council. This may lead to other opportunities for me to speak at individual garden clubs.

In late June, I developed and presented a brand new seminar on garden-style entertaining at Berry Creek Hollow. This theme fit well with this particular store because they sell many pieces of cottage and garden-style merchandise. About twelve people attended; two of which were from the Garden Club Council. I demonstrated unique ways of how to use atypical items like vintage kitchenware and garden containers as serving pieces. For example, I showed how to use a large white enamel pot filled with ice to hold glass canters filled with different juices. Also, I put paper products and eating utensils in the various slots of a garden toolbox. As well, I put ice in a white enamel dish pan, placed several plastic containers down in it, and then filled them with various colored fresh fruit. Since it was almost fourth of July, I arranged red, white, and blue carnations in old glass soda bottles filled with water and then put the bottles in an old wooden Pepsi crate.

Fridays Just for Me

June 26, 2001

A few weeks ago, I talked with Bob about whether he could be responsible for planning Nathan's activities one day a week when school starts. Bob told me today that he has been thinking about this idea. He has asked our friends, Joy and Blaine, who recently retired from teaching school, about the possibility of Nathan coming to their house on Friday mornings, and they agreed. Also, he is talking with my mom about Nathan coming to her house on Friday afternoons.

This agreement from Bob is very encouraging to me, but I'm not sure if having only Fridays off will be enough for me. I will not know until we try it when school starts. I am planning to use Fridays to further investigate interior design opportunities. Over the past several months, I have presented garden-style decorating seminars in four home decor shops and three garden clubs; by doing this, I am building up a résumé.

Also, I have some new ideas I want to explore. Tracie, the owner of Millie Home, liked the seminar on garden-style decorating that I presented at her business. She is interested in my ideas for Friday afternoon features on cottage style as well.

Cottage-Style Decorating

September 7, 2001

It is with excitement, yet with a little apprehension, I start my Teatime Feature at Millie Home today. It will be every Friday afternoon for the month of September.

Ever since I knew Carolyn was going to let me use her silver tea set, I have felt even more confident about going in this direction. The tea set will help set the elegant ambiance I am trying to establish. During today's feature I am going to have examples of how to use vintage linens to make window treatments, wall hangings, and pillows. My idea is while the customers sip tea from beautiful china cups, each with a different pattern, they can view the decor items and pictures I have displayed.

September 14, 2001

Dearest Father, I was disappointed yesterday that my teatime features have been put on hold right now. I am to wait until Tracie calls me about resuming these Friday afternoon events. Since the 9/11 tragedy, there are not very many people coming into the store, Millie Home.

Now, I do not know what to do for my creative outlet time on Fridays. What direction do You want me to go in now? Point me in the right way at the right time. What about the Rescue Mission's Store, "Art on A Mission," inside Tanglewood Mall? The store sells vintage linens, quilts, antique furniture as well as local art work. Is this a possibility? I know the manager of the store, Fran.

"Art on a Mission" Features

November 4, 2001

I finally was able to meet with Fran, in October, and share my idea of doing different vignettes at the Art on a Mission store in the mall. Fran responded positively and said she would talk with the director of the Rescue Mission. I now have three dates on the calendar. The December theme will be using vintage textiles to enhance your holiday entertaining. Then the January focus will be decorating with quilts. Lastly, in February the subject will be using vintage textiles to make nostalgic keepsakes. I am going to make a flyer for each of these features; I will use a different color paper for each month. These flyers will serve as advertisements for me to place in various stores and as invitations to mail out to friends.

December 15, 2001

Dearest Father, thank You so much for enabling things to go smoothly for the teatime feature at Art On A Mission. The silver tea set looked beautiful on the vintage crocheted tablecloth. I served the cookies on a three-tiered plate rack. To enhance the look, I placed green crocheted pieces in between the clear plates and then used a green and red plaid tartan as a tablecloth.

Lead and guide me as I prepare the next two features for the store. Give me the ideas progressively and bless the preparation of the ideas. I so enjoy looking through the store and seeing what merchandise I can highlight. Also, I am having so much fun making decorating items at home to compliment my teaching.

My Decreasing Capacity

Over the past several months, it seems my emotional capacity to work with Nathan has gone from 50 percent to 25 percent. It has been very scary to have this happen to me. I think the hormonal changes in my body have contributed to the reduction of my emotional ability. I am wondering if it is possible that the longer I work with Nathan the smaller my capability becomes.

December 20, 2001

Father, I do not know how much longer I can coordinate Nathan's activities and opportunities for him. I don't know whether to put an approximate quantitative amount of time down on paper or not right now.

December 21, 2001

Last night, I talked with Kristen and Bob. I told them that I think I can only, at the most, coordinate Nathan's life activities for about one and a half more years. This would be until the end of the 2003 school year. In a sense, I have given my notice.

I have been meditating on James 3:17 as to the characteristics of godly wisdom. "But the wisdom from above is first pure, then peaceable, gentle, reasonable, full of mercy and good fruits, unwavering without hypocrisy." To continue, indefinitely, as I am now, coordinating Nathan's life is not a peaceable, gentle, and reasonable thing for me to do. I feel that my work with Nathan thus far has produced many good fruit; but, I know there is a point somewhere in the future when this will not be the case.

Please, Father, enable me to entrust Nathan's future to you. Prepare Nathan and me for the future opportunities You have for each of us. If You want me to work with Nathan shorter or longer, show me. Have Thine own way!!

Nathan's Increasing Desires

December 27, 2001

Father, it seems the more unique the activities I plan for Nathan, the more he wants to do. When Nathan came home from guest speaking at Grandin Court

Elementary School, he said to me, "I don't want to show my books anymore, I want to be the teacher of the class."

Since Jorge is teaching Nathan Spanish, perhaps Nathan can teach a Spanish lesson using some of the words he has learned. What other things could Nathan teach children? Should this be something he does on a regular basis? My mind keeps thinking of possible ways I can help Nathan get closer to what I think he desires.

Nathan's Dream:

Nathan continues to want more and more out of life. Recently, while crying, Nathan said, "I want my own house! I want my own apartment like Kristen!" It was so hard for me to see and hear him cry about this unfulfilled dream. Each time he brought this topic up, I told him, "Dad and I will work on helping you find a place of your own. It will need to be a special place because you will need a lot of help. Since there are not many places like this, it will take some time. Please be patient with us."

A Difficult Day

February 15, 2002

Dearest Father, here I am at a restaurant way out of the city so I will not see anyone I know. Yesterday was a bad day for me emotionally. Leis and Eric were at our house for playtime. I used a lot of energy facilitating the activities we did.

Bob came home to do lunch with Nathan and the children so I could have a short break going out in the car. As I went to the door, I said, "Bob, may I have a few extra minutes today?" He replied, "No, I have to get back soon." In the car, I began to cry and could not stop. So, I drove to Justin's school and asked him to come home so Bob could go back to work. I cried off and on all afternoon.

Please enable me to have a divine perspective on where I am, emotionally, right now. Give me your wisdom as I regroup today. I do not know if it will take another day for me to regroup or possibly longer. I will evaluate tonight as to where I am with my emotional reserves.

CHAPTER 29

Changes

Burned Out Again

February 16, 2002

Father, here I am again experiencing burnout. Oh, how I hope I have caught myself soon enough so it will not take me years to recover! I have decided I will write out lesson plans for the personal assistants ahead of time. This way I will not have to expend a lot of energy explaining the plans to them in person. Whenever possible I will have Justin meet them at the front door and give them the lesson plan. Also, I will set up guest speaking engagements only at schools which are within walking distance of our house. This way, Nathan can drive his wheelchair and Gretchan can walk beside him.

Teaching Spanish

I still had enough energy to think of a few new activities for Nathan. So I asked Lynne to go through the Spanish cards with Nathan and have him pick ten or so words he would like to teach children. Bob made a big flip chart that we placed on an easel. Then Lynne, using bright-colored markers, drew the picture of each card selected by Nathan. Underneath each drawing, she printed the corresponding Spanish word.

Since Nathan had a positive experience at Raleigh Court Elementary as a guest speaker, I arranged for Gretchan and him to return to this school. This was to be Nathan's first opportunity to teach his Spanish lesson to children. To enhance their presentation, I made costumes for them to wear. They wore ponchos, sombreros, and carried maracas. Later, Kristen arranged for Nathan to come and teach Spanish at one of the middle schools where she worked as an OT. One of her students, Geoffrey, co-taught with Nathan. They really enjoyed wearing the costumes and being the "teachers" for the other students.

High Anxiety

August 7, 2002

Dearest Father, Justin left this morning at 4 a.m. to go on his mission trip to El Salvador. I am feeling very anxious about him flying in this post 9/11 era. Last night, I was crying so hard I finally got up and went to the bathroom. I splashed cold water on my face in an attempt to gather myself. Then, because I was going to get Justin up at 3:30am, I decided to stay up and clean the bedroom rug. When I was finished, I got Justin up; I gave him breakfast; then, I kissed him goodbye and sent him out the door to catch his ride to the airport. After this, I tried to go back to sleep; but, I could not. I was still restless from thinking about Justin traveling to El Salvador.

Everyone in my family is out of town today. Justin is flying; Mama and Kathy left on a trip this morning; Bob, Kristen, and Nathan are in Chicago. I did not go with Bob and the children to visit his family because they were driving the 14 hours with as few stops as possible. I can only travel that long of a distance when we break up the trip and take a lot of rest stops. So, here I am today, at home by myself. Oh Lord, I feel so alone!

Father, please bring each member of my family back home safely. I am afraid I might not be able to handle the ramifications if anything goes wrong. Emotionally, I feel like I am sitting on a pinhead. I can only handle a very small amount of life's daily demands. If the harsh winds of life blow hard, I fear I might fall off of the pinhead and not be able to cope.

I have called my Dr.'s office and the dosage of my antidepressant has been increased. Father, should I see a counselor? If so, who? How will I manage things with Nathan this upcoming fall? Will Justin be able to do the coordinating of the people coming and going and fill in where needed?

August 15, 2002

Father, I am at a very different spot right now with my journey for emotional healing. One way that it is different is I feel like my actual emotional capacity is so very, very small. It does not seem to be as much an issue of replenishment, but more an issue of capacity. The replenishment is still necessary and it has to come more often because I can deplete my reserves very quickly. I have reached a point where

I need a larger emotional capacity. How do I accomplish this? Please show me the steps I need to take for my continued emotional healing.

Repairing Emotional Deficiencies

August 19, 2002

During the days and months that followed, I discovered several helpful books on the shelves of my favorite thrift stores. Many of the books dealt with various aspects of emotional health. As I read the books, I began to realize there are developmental stages for emotional growth just as there are for physical growth. I filled many journals with notes, reorganized the notes, made charts, and also looked up verses in the Bible which addressed those subjects. I set my focus on prayerfully repairing the deficiencies in my emotional development. As a part of this process I interacted with my counselor, Martha, *over a span of several years.* The more God enabled me to do this, the stronger I became. Since I was pulled back from Nathan's daily activities, I had more time and energy to read about and process the steps I needed to take.

Fall Features

During the month of October, I had a wonderful opportunity to do fall features, every Friday afternoon, at Berry Creek Hollow. Each week, I enjoyed going through the store and picking out which merchandise I wanted to highlight that particular Friday. At home, I picked out other decor items and textiles to add with the store merchandise. Also, I added pumpkins, gourds, and chrysanthemums to enhance the features. In these features, I focused on how to use fall decorations both inside and outside.

Expressing Concern

October 29, 2002

While visiting Kristen with Bob this afternoon, I cried as I shared my apprehensions with them for planning Nathan's future. I expressed these as my primary concerns:

- *Kristen not being here this summer to help with planning. She is going to Berlin, Germany.*
- *Justin possibly moving away to pursue his education.*
- *Bob's "day by day" type personality.*

- *My diminished emotional capacity*
- *Nathan's increased desire to have an occupation and to live away from home.*

When I finished talking, Kristen told me I have to trust Bob, Justin, and her to get "things" (day activities and residential setting) lined up for Nathan. She also told me I need to be realistic in my expectations. Father, when I think in terms of a quality residential setting, should I think in terms of different degrees of quality? My heart's desire is to have a setting fit for a "prince," but being realistic would probably mean less than this.

I am looking at Isaiah 43:18-19. "Do not call to mind the former things, or ponder things of the past. Behold, I will do something new. Now it will spring forth; will you not be aware of it? I will even make a roadway in the wilderness, rivers in the desert." I am hoping You are telling me that You are lifting me up from all the past difficulties we have had accomplishing things for Nathan. I pray, with all my heart, You will make a way through the wilderness.

Father, after years of writing the story of our journey with Nathan, I'm still wondering what the ending of the book is to be. It seems to me that the ending should be the culmination of Nathan's dreams and my dreams as to the semi-independent life he is to live. Oh Lord, how will we get from where we are now with Nathan to a quality, semi-independent life situation which will please him?

Jochebed's Bold Action

December 13, 2002

This afternoon while reading in the book of Exodus, I received much encouragement as I saw how Moses' mother, Jochebed, handled the crisis situation she faced concerning her baby son Moses.

Exodus 1:22
"Then Pharaoh commanded all his people saying, 'Every son who is born you are to cast into the Nile and every daughter you are to keep alive."

Exodus 2:1-10
"Now a man from the house of Levi went and married a daughter of Levi. And the woman conceived and bore a son; and when she saw that he was beautiful, she hid him for three months.

But when she could hide him no longer, she got him a wicker basket and covered it over with tar and pitch. Then she put the child into it, and set it among the reeds by the bank of the Nile. And his sister stood at a distance to find out what would happen to him. Then the daughter of Pharaoh came down to bathe at the Nile, with her maidens walking alongside the Nile and she saw the basket among the reeds and sent her maid, and she brought it to her. When she opened it, she saw the child, and behold, the boy was crying. And she had pity on him and said, 'This is, one of the Hebrews' children.' Then his sister said to Pharaoh's daughter, 'Shall I go and call a nurse for you from the Hebrew women, that she may nurse the child for you?' And Pharaoh's daughter said to her, 'Go ahead.' So, the girl went and called the child's mother. Then Pharaoh's daughter said to her, 'Take this child away and nurse him for me and I shall give you your wages." So, the woman took the child and nursed him . . . then the child grew and she brought him to Pharaoh's daughter and he became her son."

While reading these verses, I realized Moses's mother was, in a way, backed into a corner. She had reached a point where if she did not do something extraordinary, something bold, her baby son would be killed by being thrown into the Nile River. I find it very interesting that the rescue idea God gave her involved the Nile River, which was the source of death for other baby boys.

I pictured Jochebed preparing the basket; perhaps, she had woven the basket at an earlier time to use as a bed for her baby. Then later, in preparing for hopefully saving Moses' life, she covered it with tar and pitch. I so admire Jochebed; I identify with how she must have felt when she put him in the basket. Right before the basket was placed in the river, she must have thought, "This is the hardest thing I have had to do in my life, but I must do it to save the life of my precious baby."

I am now also, in a sense, like Jochebed, backed up into a corner. I have reached a point where, if I do not do something extraordinary, something bold, in regard to Nathan, I will "break." And if I break, this may drastically affect the quality of Nathan's life.

It is as if, for many years, I have been making the "wicker basket" to hold Nathan. And now I must cover the basket with the "tar and pitch" of prayer, situate Nathan in it with covers to keep him warm, then place him into the river of life, trusting you to guide the basket through Bob, Kristen, and Justin.

When Jochebed let Moses go, he ended up becoming a prince because he was raised by the daughter of the Pharaoh. I am praying the destination for Nathan be a life of quality activities during the day and a quality residential setting. I am praying the place will be "fit for a prince!"

Future Residential Setting for Nathan

January 2, 2003

Today the thought came to me that if the setting Kristen and Bob find is less than my heart's desire, and if Nathan likes the setting and goes there to live, I could then perhaps prayerfully look myself for the setting fit for a prince. Thinking this way, helps me cope, Father. Once Nathan is settled in the first setting he enjoys, I think I will have the emotional energy to research other settings.

Father, give me other coping "ideas." Is this a good way for me to look at things right now? Please show me, Lord, if it is not. I don't think it would be wise for me to write down yet what I think would be a residential setting fit for a prince. I do not have the emotional freedom to do so right now. May the Holy Spirit bring the points forth to You as I pray generally about this subject.

A lot of times, when I am concerned about particular situations, it helps me to go ahead and think briefly about the possible worst-case scenario and prepare mentally and spiritually for it. But I am not able to think about what the worst-case scenario could be for Nathan if things are not in place for him when Justin is no longer able to take care of the loose ends. I do not have the emotional space to think about this.

I feel like I am in a cocoon floating in between these two extremes. I am afraid to think too much about what my ideal setting would be for Nathan because I do not want to get my hopes up. But also, I am not sure if I can think about the reality of the worst-case scenario either because I am afraid I might fall into deep depression.

David Provides for Jonathan's Son

February 12, 2003

Today, I am reading about King David in 2 Samuel 9:1-13. King David wanted to give everything that had belonged to King Saul's family to an actual heir. He asked if there was anyone left in Saul's family still alive. He wanted to show kindness to them for his friend Jonathan's sake. David found out about Mephibosheth, one of Jonathan's sons, who was crippled in both feet. King David sent for Mephibosheth and told him he wanted to give him all the property that once belonged to his grandfather Saul; also, David gave him an invitation to eat with him at his table! So, Mephibosheth, who was crippled in both feet, lived in Jerusalem and always ate at the king's table.

Father, I praise You and thank You for who You are. Your attributes are awesome! I am asking once again that You do a miracle in Nathan's life. Please provide a life "fit for a prince" (very quality day activities and a very quality residential setting) for Nathan, like you did for Mephibosheth, the lame son of Jonathan and the grandson of King Saul. I am asking You to do this in a fashion which will not require months and years of research and action on the part of Bob, Kristen, Nathan, and Justin.

For this request to be answered, it will take a miracle, Father. But miracles are what You do when Your people call upon You. I am calling on You, Lord. In fact, I am pleading with You. What I have been writing comes from a mother's heart.

As a mother who loves her son so very deeply and as Your daughter, Father, I am asking You to give me the grace to accept anything that might be less than what is my heart's desire for my beloved, Nathan.

April 13, 2003

Oh Father, I still feel like I am sitting on an emotional pinhead, almost to the point I feel like I might fall off. I am crying a lot again and it is scary. Going through my 50's so far has been rather hard for me. I have been perimenapausal and now perhaps menopausal. And presently I am in limbo about Nathan's future after burning out coordinating his life since graduation. I'm not sure how to view my menopausal symptoms. I think I need to call the doctor's office and talk with them. If it is a time when I am weepy, hopefully I can just leave a message.

My doctor's office asked me to come in for an appointment. We discussed my symptoms, and so a change was made in my medicine. The very next day, I started to feel much better.

A Summer of Research

One Sunday afternoon in the summer, I asked Bob if we could drive around and look at the outside of the residential places on the list we had received from our caseworker at Blue Ridge the previous summer. Several of the places were old motels on Williamson Road that had been made into residential settings. I was not impressed with these at all! Also, there were several listings in Lynchburg. Since this city is only one hour away, we drove out there to take a look at the places on the list. As well, while in the Lynchburg area, we decided to drive around the campus of Central Virginia Training Center, a state facility for the disabled.

I was very surprised at myself for being able to work on doing this much research regarding Nathan's future. Apparently, I had just enough emotional energy on this particular day to slightly lift the veil of anxiety in order to look at the residential possibilities. Another day, sitting in the living room, I even read over the list of Christian residential settings that Lynn, one of Nathan's personal assistants, had printed for us off the Internet.

June 10, 2003

I had lunch with Carolyn B., one of Nathan's former personal assistants, at a restaurant near our house, Freddie's Sunset Bar and Grill. During our time of talking about Nathan, I shared with her that I was researching residential settings for Nathan. Carolyn mentioned a residential setting in Richmond, Virginia, the Virginia Home, that she visited as a child.

June 28, 2003

Once again, I am meditating on what I consider to be my life verse, Psalm 27:4 "One thing I have asked from the LORD, that I shall seek: that I may dwell in the house of the LORD all the days of my life, to behold the beauty of the LORD and to meditate in His temple."

Father, as I move in the world of beauty and get to know You better, as I behold Your beauty and as I meditate on who You are, Your attributes, and Your ways, will You lead us to the place for Nathan? I want beauty to be a big part of where Nathan is to live. Specifically, I want him to have a courtyard with flowers, trees, and a fountain.

July 6, 2003

Father, continue to lead and guide in regards to the places I should research in terms of possible residential sites for Nathan. So far, I am doing fine emotionally with the research I have done. Please show me though when I am to stop.

Oh Lord, as I sit here at Barnes and Noble coffee shop, I am looking out the window at the clouds and pondering the following questions:

- *Does the place already exist for Nathan?*
- *Are we to help design and build a place for Nathan and others like Nathan?*
- *Or will You lay it on other people's heart to design and build the place?*

If Bob and I are to help design and build the place for Nathan and other disabled people, please give us Your strength and Your wisdom in doing this. Bring just the right people and the right resources at the right time to do this.

As I think about the possible project I have been writing about, I feel somewhat overwhelmed. I know I can't go through a long drawn out process like we had in building our addition. Father, I don't even know if I have enough energy to even talk with others about this possible project.

This same day, as I was almost to the exit door of Barnes & Noble, I saw my friend Jean from church who also has a son with disabilities. I asked her if she had a few minutes to talk with me. I then shared my idea about designing a residential center for Nathan and other disabled people in our church. Jean said that this was not a need for them at this time and that she and her husband were focusing their energies on creating a business opportunity for Lee, their special needs son.

July 15, 2003

Carolyn called us to let us know about her conversation with Doris, the admissions director of the Virginia Home. Soon after Carolyn talked with us, I called Doris. The Virginia Home sounded like a really good place, and so I was looking forward to seeing it in person.

July 23, 2003

Justin and I drove to Richmond to visit the Virginia Home for the very first time. My observations gave me a growing hope as Doris guided us around the home. I was impressed with the various in-house therapy departments, the gym, and the indoor swimming pool. Also, I took notice of how warm and friendly all the staff seemed.

In the midst of the tour, I asked, "Do you happen to have a courtyard with a fountain?" Doris pulled up a window shade and said, "Look!" I saw a beautiful brick courtyard with trees and flowers surrounding it. I was in awe of how the Virginia Home exceeded what I had even dreamed of for Nathan!

July 25, 2003

Is the Virginia Home where you want Nathan to live? If it is, when do you want him to go there to live? Calm my anxious heart about the waiting list/ availability issue.

Also, I pursued some other options. I called the Central Virginia Training Center and talked with the admissions counselor. He indicated that the Virginia Home had a reputation for being the best setting for residents who are in wheelchairs. Then I called the Western Carolina Center. The admissions counselor discussed, at length, with me why the center there in North Carolina would not be an option for Nathan.

August 1, 2003

If Nathan is to make the Virginia Home his place to live, please enable him to like it the very first time he goes, if it is Your will. This would be a big help to me emotionally, I think, Father.

August 11, 2003

I thank You and praise You, Father, for giving Bob, Nathan, and Justin a wonderful day going down to Richmond on Saturday. Nathan really enjoyed the tour. He asked me to make the doctor's appointment for the required physical and I have (August 26, 2003 at 2:30pm). Will his enthusiasm wane any? I don't know.

September 7, 2003

Father, when should we get all the paperwork done for Nathan applying to the Virginia Home?

September 10, 2003

Oh Lord, today has been hard for me emotionally. I cried and cried after I got off the phone talking with Dr. W.'s nurse, about Nathan's physical.

September 19, 2003

When should we turn the paperwork in to the VA Home, Father?

October 13, 2003

Nathan turned his paperwork in on this day while Bob, Justin, and he visited the Virginia Home.

Kristen's Future

October 15, 2003

Kristen called today; she asked if she could come over to talk with Bob and me. She shared with us that she has started the initial process of applying to go overseas as part of a 2-year program for young adults. Kristen explained that during her summer trips to Berlin, she had experienced an increasing desire to spend a longer period of time serving overseas.

Father, please enable me to joyfully flow with Kristen as she prepares to move to another country, if it is Your will for her to do this. Lord, I have such a mixture of emotions. I'm not sure if I can identify them all now. The spiritual part of me is so very happy Kristen is gifted in such a special way to minister to so many different nationalities and cultures. The mother in me, though, desires for the next big change in Kristen's life to be marriage, not moving across the globe. However, the same nurturing energies and skills I believe will make Kristen a wonderful wife and mother are also connected to the giftedness she has in ministering to a wide range of people groups. May Your will be done, Father.

CHAPTER 30

Timely Transitions

December 2003

Creative Outlet for Me

After doing special features at several stores, I began to seriously think about getting a booth at an antique mall. Having to put up and take down my displays, all in one afternoon, no longer seemed like a good use of my time and energy. If I had a booth, my displays could stay up as long as I liked.

I believe it was early December or late November when the manager told me I could have a space at the Roanoke Antique Mall. I was able to move a few things in on New Year's Eve. Then on New Year's Day 2004, I totally moved into my ten-by-ten-feet space. The first day of April, I also rented the ten-by-ten-feet space to the right of me, giving me ten-by-twenty feet of space.

The booth was such a wonderful opportunity for me. I chose this mall location because I could come and go any day of the week since they were open seven days a week. Having something fun to work on helped me with the transitions of each of my children leaving home.

I could move into the beautiful world of interior design any time of the day or night. At night, I made pillows, painted furniture, decided on what items to put together for a vignette. During the day, I shopped in thrift stores, estate sales, and yard sales. Some days, I would work on my booth for a few hours, then leave for lunch or to shop, then come back and work an hour or two more.

I enjoyed talking with other dealers, the staff, and the patrons. Hearing how my customers were going to use the items, they purchased from my booth, added to my pleasure. During this time, I was able to develop some new and fun relationships.

The downside of my booth work was the upstairs of our house became more and more of a warehouse for the furniture, pillows, dishes, lamps, etc., that I bought to use in different vignettes in my booth. Some of my vignettes were arranged to show off a certain style of decorating while other vignettes were arranged to highlight a certain color scheme.

To help promote my business, I held social events in my booth. For example, I had an ice cream social to introduce designing outdoor rooms. Also, I had a cheese and sparkling juice party to introduce my French Provincial vignettes. At each one of my events, I had notebooks filled with pictures of the particular style I was emphasizing.

During the time I had my booth, I was invited to three different women's groups to do presentations about decorating topics. Also, I had a client, Dorothy, whom I worked with in her home. Dorothy was somewhat younger than me and really fun. She wanted me to help her make her home more comfortable and add some special touches. Being a high school teacher, she desired her home to feel a like a refuge the minute she walked through the door in the afternoon. During the initial consultation, Dorothy liked my suggestions, and she asked me to implement them. At the end, she was very happy with the results.

August 31, 2004

One after another, almost all of our personal assistants have resigned because of other obligations in their lives. I understand this, but I still feel sad and concerned for Nathan's future. Justin is ready to go away to college, and we have almost no one to help us with Nathan. As a result of all this, I am crying a lot again. I know it is time to talk with my doctor.

Also, our whole family realizes that we need to do something bold and very transparent to let people know about our situation. So together, we wrote a letter, this past Friday, to share our needs in detail with friends and acquaintances. After we finished our letter, I addressed the envelopes. On Sunday night, I sent out the first batch of letters. The date on the top of the letter was August 27, 2004, and Nathan's photo was in the middle to the right of the date.

Dear Friends,

The Rossbacher family would like to update you on Nathan's life. He graduated in 2000 from Cave Spring High School. After that, God provided several people to be his personal assistants. They have helped him to do a variety of activities such as crafts, games, and the writing of children's books. Also, they have enabled him to do community service at schools, the Crisis Pregnancy Center, and at the Ronald McDonald House.

Nathan desires to live more independently, apart from his family. Therefore, in the summer of 2003 he placed himself on the waiting list for the Virginia Home in Richmond, VA. After much research and several visits to Richmond, we decided the VA Home seemed to be the best fit for Nathan. However, the waiting period for the VA Home could be anywhere from six months to six years.

Overtime, our pool of personal assistants has greatly reduced. Nathan really needs activities that stimulate him throughout the week. This could happen in a variety of ways, either adding more personal assistants and/or by Nathan being able to participate in a day program. The Options program, run by DePaul Family Services, offers weekday therapeutic activities. The cost is $68.54 per day. Most participants' fees are paid through a Medicaid waiver. Nathan has been on a waiting list for a Medicaid waiver for two years, but has not yet been approved.

To enable Nathan to participate in this day program, we believe that God has given us the idea of approaching individuals, groups, and businesses to sponsor Nathan. We are praying for God to provide at least one person to organize this effort.

Until Nathan can enter the Options program, we need people to spend quality time with him. We are also praying for someone to be willing to recruit and coordinate the volunteers and paid workers.

These needs are very urgent! Judy no longer has sufficient emotional and physical reserves to plan and coordinate Nathan's life. In addition, Justin may leave Roanoke in the near future to attend college and/or work. Thank you for your continued prayers and interests in Nathan's life.

If you are interested in helping or have other ideas regarding Nathan, please contact Bob or Justin.

May God manifest His power and glory as He continues to meet Nathan's needs.

Love,
Bob, Judy, Kristen, Nathan, and Justin

Adjustment in Medication

Early in September, I had my annual physical with Dr. W. Since I knew that it would be difficult for me to talk without crying, I asked Bob to come with me. We told him I was crying a lot again. Then I handed him a copy of our letter about Nathan. Dr. W decided to add a new medication for me to take along with the antidepressant. It was not long before I could tell a significant difference in how I felt. I noticed I was better able to deal with the upcoming changes in our family.

Good News

September 20, 2004

We heard from Doris P. today that there is now an opening for Nathan at the Virginia Home! What a miracle God has done for us! How interesting it is we would receive this news only three weeks after we sent out the letter asking for help from our friends regarding Nathan's future.

October 2, 2004

Our family gave Nathan a going-away party tonight. As we prepared for the celebration, I thought long and hard and prayed as to how to pace myself. Kristen wrote out the guest list with Nathan. Bob, Justin, and Kristen did the inviting by phone. Also, we asked each person to bring a dish so we would have enough food for the event. Before the party, I bought potted chrysanthemums, medium-size pumpkins, and gourds. I placed the chrysanthemums on the deck, patio, and steps. A few days later, I planted the plants in the soil.

October 5, 2004

Father, thank You for how wonderful the party went on Saturday. Thirty-three people came. Justin videotaped them saying such wonderful things about Nathan to him.

We are not taking Nathan to Richmond tomorrow because there still is more paperwork to be done. Please enable the paperwork to all go through so we can take him next week, if it by Thy will, Father. I'm glad we have a few more days to get Nathan and his things ready for the move. Give us wisdom as to what things we need to buy for him.

Taking Nathan to His New Home

October 13, 2004

The process of my deciding how to best participate in Nathan's moving was difficult for me. I prayed about making wise decisions in this matter.

Finally, we came up with the plan that Justin and I would leave at a later time in the morning. Bob left about 6:30 a.m. with Nathan. By the time Justin and I arrived, all the preliminary work was completed and Nathan was in his room.

Bob and I left about three or so hours later. We drove one hour to Charlottesville where Bob had a room reserved for us at a Hampton Inn. Justin stayed with Nathan until 8:00 p.m. and then he went to a friend's house in Richmond. He spent a few days in Richmond so the Virginia Home could call him if there was a problem.

October 14, 2004

Father, we moved Nathan in yesterday at the Virginia Home. When Bob and I left his room, the admissions director, Doris, walked with us. I was crying hard when we got to the elevator. My head dropped over on Doris' shoulder. I said to her, "Please take good care of Nathan." I continued crying all the way to the car and even as we drove out of Richmond.

Thank You, Lord, for the grace and strength You gave me as we left Nathan's room. I am so glad that I did not cry in front of Nathan. I am so grateful that Justin stayed on for a while. I did not want to be the last to leave and to say good-bye.

Kristen's Future

October 21, 2004

Kristen recently went for the final part of her application process to go overseas for 2 years. Some of the countries she is considering are not the safest places to live. Please, dear God, only send Kristen to the country of Your choice. I am concerned about her safety. Probably my worst fear at this time is the possibility Kristen could be kidnapped, raped, and/or tortured. I fear this more than death for her.

Father, I entrusted Seth to You and he died. Lord, I entrusted Nathan to You and he suffered brain injury. I know my thinking is twisted-because the spiritual part of me knows that You had a higher calling for Seth from the very beginning and You had a higher calling for Nathan from the beginning. Please enable me to trust You in this whole area, especially since my past feelings of being betrayed by You are cropping up a little tonight.

It helps me to think, perhaps, there is one person or several people You want Kristen to minister to that her particular gifting and temperament will be used by the Holy Spirit to bring them into a close relationship with You through Jesus Christ.

October 25, 2004

Thank You for giving me more grace as I process this upcoming big change in Kristen's life and therefore in the life of our family. Father, to my surprise, recently I felt up to asking Kristen some questions about her possible assignment choices.

I am going to miss Kristen so very much! My heart aches as I think about the possibility of her being away for two years. I have really enjoyed having Kristen live nearby for the last 4 1/2 years; we have been able to do so many fun things together. However, it doesn't seem right for me to supersede her desires with my desires, Father. As a mother who loves her daughter so very dearly, may I want for her what she wants, if it all falls within Your direct will. Enable me, Lord, to do what You command in Romans 12:9-10 . . . "Be kindly affectionate one to another with brotherly love, in honor preferring one another."

The VA Home

AT MY NEW HOME, I SWIM AND GO TO CHAPEL, THE ADULT CENTER, AND TO PARTIES. I HAVE A LOT OF FRIENDS, AND I CAN DRIVE MY CHAIR TO VISIT THEM IN THEIR ROOMS. SOMETIMES, THEY COME TO VISIT ME.

November 1, 2004

Coffee time was really nice, today, here in the recreation therapy department. Thank You, Father, that Justin was able to get Nathan's wheelchair working and Nathan was able to get down here for the end part of coffee time. It means a lot to me for Nathan to participate in the wonderful activities here at the Home.

Now, I am sitting in a room next to the big multipurpose area in the recreation therapy department. In a few minutes, music therapy begins. It sounds like they are going to be making instruments today.

I am enjoying listening to the music therapist's very relaxing voice. She is using stickers for the residents to decorate cardboard tubes, which will be made into shakers. The residents are to pick out pictures of what their favorite music etc. is. The music therapist just asked what Nathan's favorite music is and he said, "Silent Night" and she wrote down Christmas music.

This is very interesting because Tim shared, at Nathan's Farewell Party, about singing with Nathan. He said Nathan's favorite song was "Silent Night." At the party, we all sang the first verse of Silent Night. It was very comforting that You, O Lord, allowed me to hear how Nathan's old life at home was connecting with his new life at the VA Home.

Family Changes

In the months that followed, we celebrated many events together as a family. Nathan came home for several days during the Christmas holiday. Then in January, we all went to Richmond for Nathan's birthday and stayed in a hotel. In February, we did the same thing for Kristen and Justin's combined birthday. Then in May 2005, *Kristen* left Roanoke to live overseas. During her two years, she lived in three different countries where she ministered to people's physical and spiritual needs. *Justin* left the same month to attend at Liberty University. So Kristen had moved halfway around the world, Justin had moved one hour away from Roanoke, and *Nathan* was living three and half hours away in Richmond. We were officially empty nested!

Bob and I are now well-adjusted to being empty nested; we enjoy eating a simple supper in the family room. We eat at a round oak table, in the family room, and wait for the *Incredible Hulk* reruns to come on TV. We both feel a strong calling to minister to the people God places in our lives. Bob loves to do this through teaching Bible classes at our church, and I really enjoy using my decorating skills to encourage and teach other women. Bob and I treasure any time that all three of our children can be with us. We love to just sit around and talk and laugh. We enjoy anything that we can do as a family: solving puzzles, watching movies, playing games, having cookouts, etc.

Nathan in an elevator at the mall

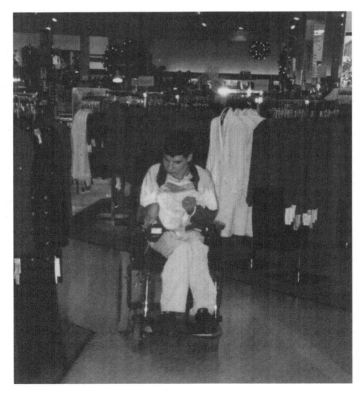

Nathan driving in a department store

Bob placing our memorial brick in the patio

Entertaining our neighbors on the patio

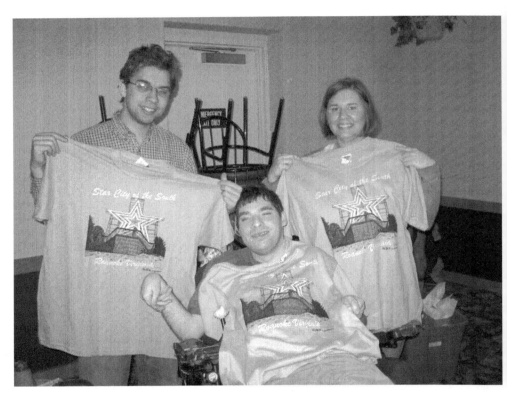

Sibling birthday party; matching Roanoke shirts from Mom

Nathan at his graduation with Justin and Kristen

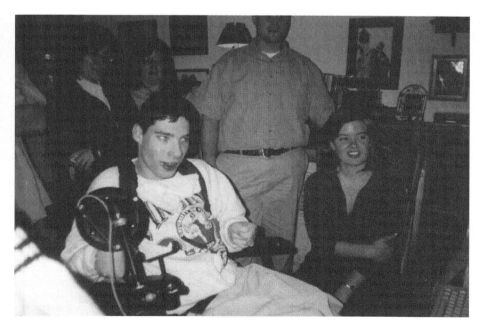

Nathan demonstrating his typing skills to Kim's OT class

Nathan at the Ronald McDonald House

Our family singing carols at the Ronald McDonald House

Nathan plays a game with Tim R.

Nathan volunteering at the Duck Class at the CDC

Nathan guest speaking with Gretchan

The students listen attentively to Nathan

Aunt Kathy and Nathan at Bonsack Elementary

Carolyn helps Nathan sponge paint

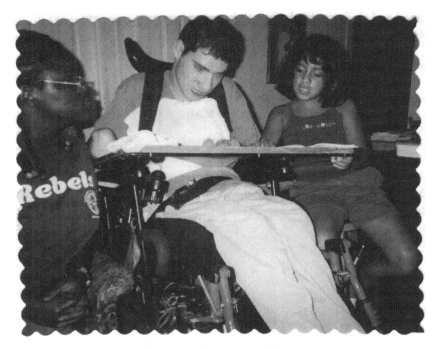

Dolores, Nathan, and Leis

Nathan playing the keyboard

Nathan typing using his Big Red Button switch

Nathan painting a birdhouse with Dolores

Judy in her booth at Christmas time

Judy and Nathan in his room at the Virginia Home

Cathy and her children Leis and Eric visit Nathan at the VA Home

Nathan participating in a swimming marathon at the VA Home

Nathan loves being in the water!

Kristen, Judy, and Bob congratulate Nathan after the race

Nathan holds Patrick, his cousin Joel's son

CHAPTER 31

The Making of the Quilt

When using old garments to make quilts, it makes no difference whether there are holes or rips in the fabric because it will be cut up into geometric shapes. Then these pieces are sewn together with other pieces. In fact, in quilting, the smaller the pieces are, the more intricate and beautiful the design. So it is with the pieces of my broken dream of raising two healthy twin sons: they are sewn together with pieces of my other broken dreams to make a beautiful quilt top.

A Broken Dream:

After I was told Seth was born dead, I knew this garment was shredded and I did not have the strength to look down. I knew that if I looked down, I would see *one garment of my twin pregnancy was, in fact, destroyed.* There was nothing I could do to change what had happened. It was an irreversible situation. At this time, I was unable to focus emotionally on what I had lost. So I began to focus on Nathan and his many needs.

It was not until later that I began to actually work through grieving Seth's death. As I processed through each aspect, I learned to reuse the raw materials in a new and different way. This has helped me to make something beautiful for Seth's portion of the quilt top.

My focus has primarily been to make a positive difference in preserving the lives of unborn babies and to encourage those who have lost babies due to miscarriage, stillbirth, early infancy death, adoption, and abortion. Some of the ways I have done this are as follows:

+ Using my nurturing love by buying parenting videos for the CPC
+ Using my regret through purchasing books for the Post-Abortion Traumatic Syndrome Group
+ Using my unmet expectations in prayer to comfort and pray for those who have lost babies
+ Using the meaning of Seth's name through furnishing and decorating a counseling room at the CPC in his memory

Ministering at a Women's Retreat

One way I was able to recycle the hurt of Seth's death was by guest speaking at a women's retreat called Balancing Life's Ups and Downs. After the Friday-evening session ended, a woman came up to me and told me she also delivered twins some years ago. One twin died after a few days and the other lived. She had unresolved issues regarding the birth of her twins. We sat and talked about her experience and prayed together.

On Sunday afternoon, I received a phone call from one of the attendees telling me that a young pregnant woman who had been a part of the retreat was in the hospital. After Sandra got home from the retreat on Saturday, she went to the hospital because she was not feeling her baby move. At the hospital, Sandra and her husband were told that their baby daughter was dead.

A few weeks later, Bob and I gave a gift of money to the CPC in memory of Sandra's and Lee's baby girl. In the thank-you note Sandra sent me, she told me hearing my story had helped her with the grieving process. Also, as a result of my story she and Lee went to the SHARE support group meetings.

Speaking at SHARE Support Group

For several years, Bob and I attended the SHARE memorial service held for family members to remember the babies they have lost. The program is planned and presented by the parents who are or have been in the group. Sometimes, the main speaker is one of the group members who shares his or her personal experience.

In 1999, I was the speaker for the service. For me, to do this was a culmination of an era. Gradually, I had worked up to this point. One year I read the scripture, another year I gave the benediction prayer. Then one year, I was able to do the talk when the planned speaker was unable to come.

The night of the service, I read some of my journal writings, including my Mother's Day letter from Seth. I knew it was going to be hard for me, so I had Bob stand beside me to take over reading my words if I lost my composure. Our entire family was there, and we went up together to light Seth's candle. Afterward, Sandra, whom I had met at the women's retreat, came up to me and said that the idea of creating a ministry in memory of her baby really stood out to her.

Ministering to Individuals

The Lord also allowed me to encourage many others over the years through individual conversations with them. For example, one weekday morning, I was making my way to the church office when I saw Allie, our minister to students, in the hallway. Allie and his wife, Ann, had experienced the loss of their premature daughter Jessica. As Allie and I hugged, I said, "Allie, I am very sorry about the loss of little Jessica." Allie replied, "What you shared with Ann last year about your experience of Seth's stillbirth was such a help to us in dealing with the death of Jessica." Allie asked, "Were you afraid to be pregnant again after your pregnancy with the twins?" I responded, "There was some fear, but my desire to have another baby was much greater than my fear." Allie then shared, "I think that is how Ann and I will feel, and we will try again to have a baby." I rejoiced with Ann and Allie when their daughter Alexandra was born the next year.

An Epiphany

In the spring of 1999, I was standing in the lobby of the Crisis Pregnancy Center when a counselor opened the door to the counseling section of the building. She came through the door with a client. As they passed through the doorway, I could see into the hallway of the counseling section, and the doors were open to the two rooms our family furnished and decorated. Looking at the two rooms located across from each other, I felt a joy and awe similar to the day I was told I was carrying Seth and Nathan, side by side, in my womb.

When I first started this project I was using the meaning of Seth's name, "the appointed"; when our family finished the rooms, I realized I had used each piece of the broken dream of having twins. By decorating the two counseling rooms opposite of each other, I had recycled the regret of not seeing Seth and was able to honor Nathan's life.

Dedication of the Rooms

When I started my counseling sessions with Martha F. in 2003, I, once again, was crying a lot when I talked about Seth. Martha commented it would be hard for me to be an effective platform speaker if I was crying a lot when I gave my presentation. I told Martha I had done a lot of activities to work on healing, but the one planned activity I had not done yet was to dedicate the counseling rooms, as a family, by having a special service.

This time of dedication was finally able to take place one evening in January 2004. One of our pastors, Chris L., and the director of the CPC, Tom, joined Bob and me and our children, Kristen, Nathan, and Justin. In each room, our family read the verses I had selected. I read my letters to Seth and Nathan. Pastor Chris spoke briefly in each room about the biblical view of the sanctity of life. I hung a plaque in both rooms: one in memory of Seth and the other in honor of Nathan. Also, Pastor Chris put oil over the doorways of each room to anoint them; next, he prayed the rooms would be places of healing for many people.

In Seth's room, I knelt with my head on the seat of the counseling chair. Pastor Chris anointed my head with oil; he, Bob, and Tom prayed for my emotional healing in regard to Seth's death. As they prayed, I wept. The chair was literally anointed with my tears. In Nathan's room, Pastor Chris anointed Nathan's head with oil and Bob, Tom, and Chris all laid their hand on Nathan. They prayed for God's blessing regarding his future.

Dedicating the two rooms provided closure for me in terms of grieving for Seth's death. In many ways, it was more beneficial to me than moving Seth's grave to Roanoke would have been. This is because the counseling rooms are a living memorial that can have an ongoing positive impact on others.

Political Involvement

Another way I was able to bring significance to Seth's short life and honor Nathan was through becoming more politically active in helping to preserve the lives of unborn babies. Our entire family got involved in the political process to help elect leaders who respect the sanctity of human life and family values. It was very special to be able to work together as a family in this way.

In 1997, the last year of Governor Allen's governorship, our family was invited to the signing of the Parental Notification Bill and to the Governor's Mansion along with many other families. This bill was an important victory for the family and the sanctity of life; it states that before an underage girl can have an abortion, her parents must be notified. Justin and I drove to the state capital building in Richmond, Virginia, to witness the signing of the bill by

Governor Allen. I had wanted us to go as a whole family, but that did not work out. Kristen was away at college and Bob was sick that day. So only Justin and I went because I did not want to take Nathan without Bob's help.

The signing ceremony took place on the front lawn of the state capital building. It was a beautiful sunny day, and the temperature was just right. The atmosphere was full of celebration: choral groups sang patriotic songs, American flags decorated the entire area, and hundreds of families gathered together on the lawn. After the signing celebration, Governor and Mrs. Allen greeted each person who visited the Governor's Mansion.

Seth's Quilt Square

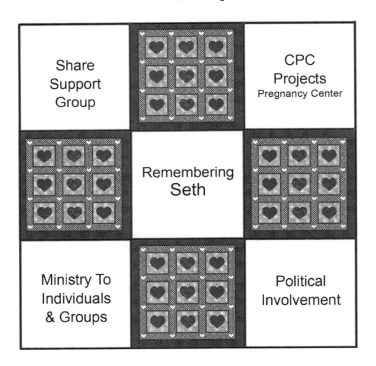

Broken Dream:

When I heard Nathan's diagnosis, it was as if I was looking down and *seeing the other garment of my twin pregnancy that I thought was whole, slashed, and lying on the floor.* I did not know how severe the cutting was, and I wanted to do everything spiritually and physically possible to mend the slashed garment.

Nathan's blocks of the quilt are blessings from God our family has had as a result of Nathan's disability:

- The patterners
- The teachers, school staff, and therapists
- The special families
- The personal assistants
- And, most of all, the special relationship among the siblings

Patterners

It is difficult for me to come up with the words to express how special it was to have the patterners come into our home and be such an intricate part of our lives. The patterners bestowed many, many acts of kindness upon us during the years of our carrying out Nathan's stimulation program. Not only were the patterners such a blessing to us, but God used our family to be a blessing to many of them as well.

Jerry

For example, one patterner, Jerry, became a very good friend. She was always smiling, brought treats over, and even invited our family over for pizza. Jerry also offered to mend my clothes before we traveled to Philadelphia. After Justin was born, she came over every morning to get Nathan ready so that I could focus on my newborn baby. Jerry and her family became so special to us. In fact, we gave Justin the middle name Ty in honor of her eldest son.

Nadine

Several years after we stopped patterning Nathan, a former patterner, Nadine, came to visit me. She wanted to tell me about how her journey of coming into a personal relationship with Jesus Christ. There were many people who had been a part of her journey, but our family was the only one she knew how to contact in order to thank in person.

Nadine started her story many years before when she lived in California and was working at a convenience store. She shared with me about an incident that had made a positive impact on her life. A regular customer, whom she knew was a Christian, came back to the store and returned some change he had been overpaid. Nadine was impressed with the fact that what he said he believed was displayed in his actions.

Later, she met a Christian woman who was sitting next to her on an airplane. This lady shared with her verses from the Bible, which explained how a person can have a restored relationship with God through Jesus Christ. They exchanged addresses and began corresponding through the mail. Nadine was so touched by the personal interest this woman took in her life.

In the midst of her journey, Nadine came once a week to our house to pattern Nathan. She observed how our family had a deep love for Jesus Christ and for one another. She saw how our faith was lived in our daily lives.

Then when she was living in another city in Virginia, she was invited to attend a Bible study. It was during this time that she came to believe Jesus was the only way back to God. She realized she was a sinner and separated from a holy God. Studying the Bible, she became convinced that Jesus came to earth, lived a perfect life, and died on the cross to take the punishment for our sins. Not only this, but he also rose again on the third day conquering sin and death.

Nadine shared with me how becoming a believer in Jesus Christ influenced every area of her life. The forgiveness and redemption she had found in Christ made a difference in how she interacted with her family. She had a new way of viewing life as she now used the Bible as her guide.

Educators and Therapists

The years of praying and patterning Nathan did not bring about the physical mending we desired, so we moved into the world of special education. Our goal, then, became to take what Nathan had and make the most of it. While Nathan was in the school system, we worked with many different professionals: teachers, instructional assistants, occupational therapists, physical therapists, and speech pathologists. They are some of the sharpest and kindest professional people I have ever known.

Nathan's second year in high school started with him being very uncomfortable in his wheelchair. This was particularly difficult because, at the same time, I was going through menopause. God graciously provided Janey to be Nathan's occupational therapist that school year. She worked faithfully in making changes to his wheelchair, enabling him to be more comfortable in his seating system. God gave me an extra measure of grace through Janey.

Her personality, demeanor, and professionalism enabled me to tell her that I was having a difficult time emotionally. She was very understanding and compassionate. As we talked further, I discovered that she was a Christian and a woman of prayer. This was a great encouragement to me.

At the end of the school year, Janey told us she no longer would be working with Nathan because she and her husband, Dave, were adopting a child. Our family prayed about this opportunity for them and rejoiced with them when Luke arrived. On a lovely Sunday afternoon, our family went to visit Janey and to meet Luke for the very first time. Nathan so enjoyed meeting the little boy that he had been praying for throughout the adoption process.

Even though Janey was no longer Nathan's OT, she remained a friend to our entire family. At this time, Kristen was a recent graduate from occupational therapy school and was in the process of looking for a job. Janey was a great encouragement and help to her during this important phase of her life. Also, Kristen helped Janey and her husband out by house-sitting and dog-sitting occasionally for them.

Special families

Over the years of our striving to help Nathan, we have met many special families through the following:

- The Institutes in Philadelphia, Pennsylvania
- The schools, churches, and the community of Roanoke, Virginia
- The Kluge Children's Rehabilitation Center in Charlottesville, Virginia
- The Ronald McDonald House in Charlottesville, Virginia
- The Virginia Home where Nathan lives now

The memories of our interactions with these families are so very precious to me. One of these families I would like to share specifically about is Terri S. and her family. Whenever I asked Kristen who her favorite elementary schoolteacher was, she always said it was her first grade teacher, Terri S. The year Kristen was in the first grade was very significant for me because it is when I reached the bottom of my burnout. Each time I visited Kristen's classroom, Terri's soft voice and sweet way with the children ministered to me; I felt like water was being poured into my dry soul.

It meant a great deal to me for Kristen to have Terri as her teacher. Also, it was such an encouragement that she was in a Christian school environment. Every morning, Kristen, along with the other students, had the opportunity to express their prayer concerns to God and with one another.

When Kristen was seventeen years old, our family found out Terri and her husband, Ron, had just learned that their four-year-old son, Evan, had muscular dystrophy. I wrote Terri a note telling her how she had indirectly ministered to me during Kristen's year in her classroom. Also, I shared with her I was available to help her in any way she needed. Later, Terri called Kristen and asked her for any insights regarding being the older sister to a younger brother with a disability. This was particularly important for Terri because Evan had an older sister, Erin.

Quite a few years later, in the summer of 2000, we learned that a group of people had joined together to raise the money, supplies, and workers to build an addition for Evan on the back of the family home. Because of Evan's age, size, and progressive loss of motor functions, the need was very great.

Our family wanted to be a part of this project to help the S family. As we talked and prayed, we decided to fix one meal a week for the family for the rest of the summer. Each week, one person in our family planned the menu and told the others what to do. Also, we sent a special treat each week such as fresh flowers, a video, or a framed encouraging Bible verse.

Helping with this project allowed me to use, in a positive way, the disappointments and frustrations I had experienced during the process of building our addition. It had taken us over nine years to finish our room/bathroom addition for Nathan. Since we started when Nathan was five years old, this meant we did not have it ready until he was a teenager. Evan did not have this kind of time.

Personal Assistants

One of Nathan's personal assistants was a very special woman named Gretchan. She is a Christian and has such a sweet and gentle way about her. Before her marriage, Gretchan had worked in many different capacities with disabled adults and children. She carried out everything I asked her to do with Nathan with great creativity and capability. Gretchan and Nathan did a wide variety of activities at the house; plus, they went out to do projects in the community.

It was such a blessing to me and to Nathan for him to have Gretchan as a personal assistant. As well, Gretchan's entire family became friends with our family. Nathan really enjoyed spending time with her husband, Tony, and her children, Scott and Anna. We continue to keep in touch with Gretchan and her family.

Another wonderful Christian woman who made such an impact on our lives was Judy B. She was a retired schoolteacher who was one of Nathan's personal assistants. Judy always had a huge smile on her face and her vivacious personality brought out the best in Nathan. Still to this day, Nathan gets a huge grin and his face lights up whenever he sees Judy. The following is a poem that Judy composed for Nathan's birthday.

January 6, 2002

From Judy B.

> *Nathan, I see your family's love in your radiant smile. I hear your family's love in your bodacious laugh! And I know God's love when I look into your glowing eyes. I'm so glad God introduced us, Nathan Rossbacher!*

The Siblings Perspective

I know having Nathan as a part of our family has had an impact on his siblings. It is interesting that both Kristen and Justin, when they were in the fifth grade, had a writing assignment about family difficulties. They both included having a brother with a disability as a part of their compositions, and so I have included their work in this section of the book.

Kristen's Fifth-Grade Writing Assignment

Family Difficulty

> *Our family has really had one big difficulty with Nathan. When my parents first found out that he was brain-injured, they must have wondered, "Why us?" But God worked everything out for good in the end. You see, when we patterned Nathan, some of the helpers became Christians. Also, our family is very close and probably more loving towards each other. Nathan is really a sweet, obedient brother and a joy to baby-sit. We are different from other families, but yet we're special and unique. God made all families! So, I guess that's what helped us threw [through], knowing that God is in control and planning our lives.*

Justin's Fifth-Grade Writing Assignment

Problems

> *When I wasn't born yet, Nathan, my brother, was just finishing patterning and my parents didn't know where to send him [to school]. But they worked it out. Later, after I was born, we started an addition onto the house for my sister. She needed*

it because her room was very tiny. We also needed it for my brother so he get out of my room and I could have my own room. It took ten years to build it all, but it was worth it . . . Now even a little later, my dad got laid off his job. So, we prayed and prayed for a good job. Now, he works at the VA Hospital and it's an even better job. You can see that we are under God's protection. The End

Also, recently I asked Kristen and Justin to write about their perspectives on our family now that they are adults. I asked them to include any particular impact having Nathan as a part of our family has had on them. Their responses were very interesting and encouraging to me.

Kristen

October 1, 2010

I have always loved being Nathan's older sister! It has been such a huge part of who I am and it has, undoubtedly, helped shape me into the person I am today. I praise God for the uniqueness of our family and for all God has taught us through Nathan. I cannot imagine our lives without him and his joyful, inquisitive spirit.

Even though I was only three years old when Seth died and Nathan was born, I remember so much from the days that followed. I have very vivid memories of the patterners who worked with Nathan. It seemed normal to me to have so many people coming and going from our house every day. We all celebrated any little bit of progress he made; when he reached a milestone, we did fun things like have skating parties or make homemade ice cream on the front porch. One might think I would have struggled with being jealous of all the focused attention Nathan received; but in actuality, I got a lot of attention too. The volunteers who came poured out love on our whole family. Sometimes, they brought fun treats like candy; other times, like at Christmas, they brought gifts of books, toys, or clothes. Many of them would spend time reading and playing with me. My mom has, often, said she thinks part of the reason I am very social and enjoy people so much is because of all my interaction with those volunteers at such young age.

Some of my favorite memories with Nathan are when we snuggled together in the bed or on a sofa, which is something we still like to do to this day. I love this position because it puts us cheek to cheek and on the same eye level. When we hang out like this, sometimes we giggle about silly stuff and other times he asks me a million questions about his favorite topics: schools, weddings, babies, and calendars. Also, I remember one particular time when we cried together in my parents' bed. Nathan was asking me questions like: why could he not walk like me, why did he not get to drive like me, and why was he not able to go to college like me? I did not have any real answers for him; so, we just cried together and then I prayed with him.

Nathan being a part of our family, definitely, taught us more about working together as a team. Due to his disability, each family member had to contribute more, provide extra help, and learn not to be so self-focused. Even from the time Justin was young, he learned to take on more responsibility. I can remember certain moments when I became more aware of the stark reality of just how dependant Nathan was on us.

For example, one summer day, when I was 12 years old, I rolled Nathan in his wheelchair out the backdoor and onto the deck. In the time it took me to turn around and shut the back door, Nathan rolled off the deck and his wheelchair landed sideways on the black asphalt driveway!! I quickly ran to him; however, I could not turn the chair right-side-up because the driveway was extremely hot and I was not wearing any shoes! Unsure of what to do next, I ran inside screaming. Fortunately, my cousin Joel was over visiting; he immediately came out and helped me get the wheelchair upright. By this time, my mom had heard the commotion and came downstairs. She was concerned that Nathan might have some broken bones or some burns from the hot asphalt, so we called 911. Except, my mom and I were crying so hard, Joel had to be the one to tell them our address over the phone. Soon after this happened, Dad built a wooden edge all the way around the deck and down the ramp as a safeguard against Nathan's wheelchair ever rolling off again. To this day, I am still extremely thankful that Nathan did not have any physical injuries from that dreadful incident. However, I remember, for years after that, Nathan would get really nervous if I was the one to roll him out the back door; his fear was a reoccurring reminder of his total dependence on us to take good care of him.

We are such a tight-knit family and for that I praise God. Going through trials and challenges presents an opportunity for people to either become closer or farther apart. By God's grace, we have been able to "grow together" through crying together, praying together, talking things out together, and working together to solve problems. I am praying, if God blesses me one day with a family of my own, my husband and I will be able to model for our children how to always grow together through the joys and sorrows of life.

Justin

June 14, 2010

There are so many factors which have been in my life that have made me into who I am today; though, I would say family is the primary factor. Some people ask me if it was hard growing up with a disabled brother. I used to respond with, "No, it is not hard, I haven't known anything else." However, this is my tendency to just look at a situation analytically. But I have come to realize the interpersonal factor is absent from that statement. If I really look at it, it comes down to this: Nathan is a joy and my whole family is awesome!

It is impossible to say what one's life would have looked like if circumstances were different, but I can say this: Nathan has been a core part of the very joy of our family. I am thankful I have parents who responded in love to the realities of a disabled child. It was due to their example my sister and learned to be selfless as well. This is not to say we were perfect little selfless angels growing up; but, it is to say there is a wonderful unity and closeness my family has and continues to experience. I do not dread family trips or long conversation with my family; instead, I look forward to them. I never fear one bit my family will be critical as they look at me. Mom and Dad, always, treated us with dignity and respect, even as we were being corrected and disciplined. It is likely this has contributed to the fact that we can talk about almost anything as a family.

We are in this thing called life together. Growing up this way was exemplified in how we all pitched in to help with Nathan's needs. I wish I could say due to these experiences I have learned perfect selflessness, but I cannot. Yet I can say that my life, my family's life and so many around our family have been hugely blessed by Nathan.

Nathan's Quilt Square

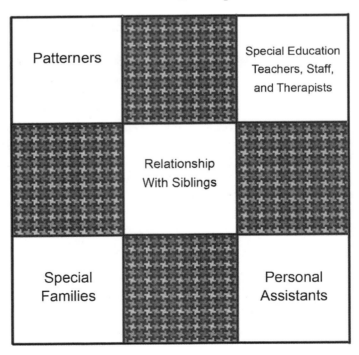

308

Broken Dream:

At this moment, it was if I was looking down at the floor and *seeing the garment of my personhood cut into pieces.* I did not know how many pieces were barely hanging together and how many pieces were lying on the floor. I did not know if I ever would feel like my old self again, emotionally whole and stable. Would I ever be able to talk with friends without crying? Would I ever be a vibrant wife again for my husband, Bob?

I have often felt discouraged about how long it is taking me to recover from my emotional infirmities. Over the years, God has gradually taught me one lesson after another, giving me time to soak in each individual lesson. Sometimes, God has led me back to former lessons adding even more insight. Deep extensive healing takes time.

Progressively, I have seen both Seth's and Nathan's parts of my broken dream of raising healthy twin sons are sewn into every area of my life. In retrospect, I see buying the large basket of sunflowers for Nathan's room at the CPC led me to develop a garden theme for the room. This led me to look up verses in the Bible, which talked about our lives being transformed from being like deserts to being like gardens.

Looking up these verses then led me to the idea of developing the yard so we could minister to our neighbors. This idea led us as a family to build our patio. My love of decorating the patio and planting flowers led me to the idea of teaching garden-style decorating classes. My enjoyment of entertaining people on our patio led me to teach a class on garden-style entertaining.

Buying the painting of lighthouses for Seth's room at the CPC led me to develop a seaside cottage theme for the room. Thinking about the light that lighthouses give to ships led me to look up verses about God bringing us from the darkness into the light through His Son, Jesus Christ. Later, we decided to use these verses about light in the dedication service.

As well, I love to use light as a medium for decorating and entertaining. I use little white lights to welcome our guests onto the front porch. As our company walks through the front door, the entire first floor has accent lamps and lit candles to give all who come a feeling of coziness. Also, the deck on the back of the house has little white lights to lure our visitors out to enjoy the romantic ambiance of the patio.

My favorite weather for entertaining is spring and fall. When planting seasonal flowers, I like to strategically place some of the flowers where they can be seen from the inside of the house. When the air temperature is nice, I can more easily leave the doors open to facilitate the flow of people between the indoors and outdoors. It is such a joy for Bob and me to open our home; we love being able to make use of the addition and patio that God allowed us to build.

My sister-in-law, Phyllis, is a consummate hostess. When she and Wayne invite people into their home, she strives to create an atmosphere that encourages her guests to relax and have a good time. Phyllis realizes many people are dealing with stress; consequently, she desires for them to have a reprieve for the time they are in her home. This is also my primary motivation for using my hospitality skills.

For our twenty-fifth anniversary, our children surprised us with a party and a Thomas Kincaid painting. This painting is of a cottage; it is so special to me because it is full of lovely flowers and accents of light. In fact, Thomas Kincaid is known as the painter of light. We hung this beautiful piece of artwork in our living room so people can see it when they first enter our home. It fits so well with my garden-style decorating and use of accent lights. The painting reminds me of my desire for our home to be a place of refuge for us and our guests. Also, it is a constant reminder to us of these biblical truths: God brings us into His light and He renews us like a lush garden.

Relationship with Bob

There was a period of years that I wondered whether I would ever be a vibrant wife for Bob again. The sparkle I have brought to our marriage, in the later years, is different in many ways than before. In the earlier years of our marriage, I was always cooking for Bob and doing things like serving breakfast by candlelight. Now to put zest in our relationship, we do things like plan little getaway trips together. I particularly enjoy when we go to a bed-and-breakfast, also known as a B & B. At first, I would be the one to look through various brochures to find interesting places to go where there was a B & B. Then later, Bob became the one to plan our excursions. He researched bed-and-breakfasts online and made the reservations for us. Something I love about B & Bs is that each one is different in its ambiance, decor, and furnishings. One of my favorite things to do is sit and relax in different places all throughout the house and then on the porch as well. Also, Bob and I both enjoy exploring the grounds and doing some sightseeing in whatever town is nearby.

Then in 2006, Bob and I were able to take a big trip! We traveled to Cairo to meet Kristen for vacation. We did things like visiting the Great Pyramids, seeing ancient mummies in the Egyptian museum, and riding a sailboat called a *faluka* on the Nile River. For the first few days, I felt like I was a character in a movie. I could not even believe I was actually there experiencing all this history and culture. We also tried Egyptian food, rode on public transportation, and learned some basic words in Arabic. It was an amazing adventure and helped strengthen not only my relationship with Bob but also with Kristen.

Friendships

During my burned-out years, I did not have enough emotional reserves to make new friends or even maintain relationships with my longtime friends. However, as I continued to heal emotionally, I began to invest more time and energy into building relationships outside my family. Finally, by His grace, God brought several special women into my life with whom I was able to develop a deeper relationship with over time.

Rahno

One morning in 1988, I met Rahno and her husband, Bob, while I was standing in line to place my order at a fast-food restaurant. When Rahno commented about the notebooks I had in my arms, I said, "I am working on writing a book." Rahno and Bob became regulars in the mornings at this restaurant. Whenever I saw Rahno and Bob after this, they would ask how my book was coming along. We had the nicest little chats on the mornings we saw each other. During our interactions, I discovered they were also Christians.

One morning, after Rahno's husband, Bob, left, I shared with Rahno about my emotional struggle with the church area of my life. The way Rahno listened to me made me feel very safe in sharing my story. She said she would pray for me.

When we decided to begin attending a new church, we made plans to visit the church where Rahno and Bob were members. Rahno was a tremendous help to us in making the transition. On one particular Wednesday night, she helped me scope out the best way to get the wheelchair into the church and introduced me to the various midweek activities.

Debbie

A very interesting thing happened to me the evening that Dr. Henry Blackaby spoke at our church about his Bible study called Experiencing God. After the service, I went up front to talk with him. I wanted to ask Dr. Blackaby if, in his travels, he had come across very many burned-out Christians.

However, there was a long line of people waiting, so I turned to walk back up the aisle. As I turned, I saw Debbie, our pastor's wife. As we talked, she said, "Judy, when we had lunch together when I first came to Roanoke, you asked me if I had ever experienced an emotional burnout, well, now I know what you were talking about."

Debbie and I started meeting every few weeks. I shared with her what I had learned about stress management and the importance of having creative outlets. At this time, Debbie did not have any ideas about what would be good creative outlets for her. So we began to do a wide variety of fun activities and prayed together that God would show her ways to replenish her emotional reserves.

Rahno helped me at a very pivotal time in my life. I helped Debbie at a very pivotal point in her life. Each relationship grew into a long-term mutual friendship.

Also, I have been gradually renewing and strengthening old friendships. I reconnected with Julie and Jan, two friends whom I had not seen in a very long time. We have been getting together for coffee or lunch and keep in touch by telephone. I am looking forward to reconnecting with more of my long-lost friends!

Judy's Quilt Square

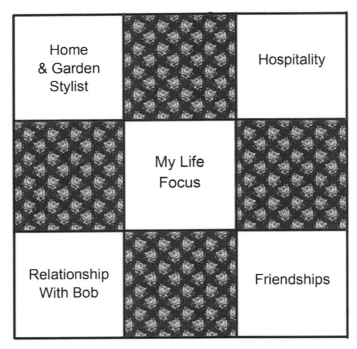

Broken Dream:

My dream of raising four children was broken! Not only was I not able to do with Justin all the things I had done with Kristen and Nathan, but also there were days I could not even make it through dinner with my family without crying. The day I cried in the bathroom, it was as if I was looking down at the garment of my motherhood and seeing the mother I had once been seemingly cut into small pieces.

It seems that God has used my burnout and recovery as a means of helping my children develop wisdom. Over the years of my learning how to manage the stressors in my life, I have shared a lot with my children about what I have discovered. Also, Bob has woven scriptural principles into our daily lives as a family. He always seems to have just the right verse for whatever situation is at hand. I am so thankful that even though I cried a lot when the children were younger, God used the steadiness of Bob's temperament to give stability to our home.

Kristen and Justin have grown into adults who live their lives with purpose and passion. Whatever they feel God has called them to do, they put their entire heart into it. However, they know the importance of pacing themselves and taking time to regroup when needed.

In his own way, Nathan, has grown into a mature man. As I reread my old journals, I found a prayer entry on October the 8, 1979, where I said, "My desire, my dream, Father, is that Nathan could develop into a mature man: spiritually, mentally, socially, and physically." At that time, I was picturing Nathan growing up to be similar to how Kristen and Justin are now. However, his maturing has been in a different way. Spiritually, Nathan has a tender heart for the needs of other people and to pray for them. Mentally, Nathan can write using a special computer system. Socially, Nathan greets everyone with a warm smile and a cheery hello. He enjoys having conversations with people and asking them questions. He is a delight and an encouragement to everyone he is around. Physically, Nathan can drive his wheelchair up and down the hall to visit his friends. They, in return, come to visit him in his room. Although Nathan has many limitations, it is wonderful to see him make progress in each of these developmental areas.

I praise God that all three of my children love people, have a high appreciation for the value of life, and have a heart for God. Now I can go to Justin or Kristen and ask for their opinions about decisions I need to make.

I greatly value their input, and I know they will pray for me. I ask Nathan regularly to pray for me.

I realize now that as I have carried out special projects in memory of Seth, I have been in a sense "rearing" him. This means that I *am* the joyful mother of Seth and, therefore, the joyful mother of *four* children! I praise the Lord like the psalmist in Psalm 113:19 that He has settled me in my home as the "happy mother of children."

Family Quilt Square

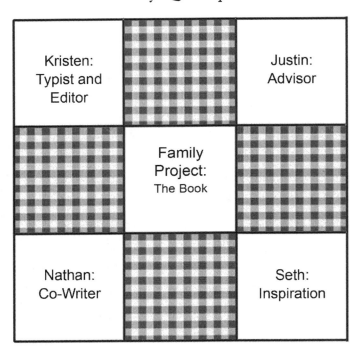

Broken Dream:

Not only was our dream to be missionaries in Europe shattered, but also I was not emotionally able to be a part of our church that I had loved so dearly. It was as if I was looking down at the garment of my church involvement, except the torn pieces were so small that I did not even recognize what it had been originally.

Even though Bob and I did not become career missionaries, each person in our family has developed a mind-set for being involved in missions and discipleship as a lifestyle:
- In our individual neighborhood
- In our individual cities
- In our state
- In our nation
- In our world

In Acts 1:8, Jesus is teaching about these spheres when He tells us the Holy Spirit will give us power to be witnesses in Jerusalem, Judea, Samaria, and even to the remotest part of the earth.

Many of the opportunities each person in our family has had for being involved in missions and discipleship has come from being in our current church. My burnout was the vehicle God used to move us from one church to another. Both churches have had a tremendous impact upon our lives. Through the teaching of our first church, we developed a strong foundation for our faith in God and His Word. During the difficult years of our life, friends from this church ministered to our family in so many special ways. We praise God for both churches!

Kristen

Kristen had many opportunities through our church's youth program to actively participate in reaching out to others. She went several times with the youth group to Cleveland, Ohio, to help work with inner-city children. Each summer, the amount of responsibility Kristen had was increased. These experiences helped her to learn more about the world around her and how she had been uniquely gifted by God to serve other people.

Then when Kristen was a senior year in high school, she traveled out of the United States for the first time. She went with her Spanish class to Costa Rica for educational and service-oriented purposes. During this particular trip, God placed a deep burden on Kristen's heart for the peoples of the world. It was just the beginning of a life journey around the world and back again.

Kristen has ministered to people in many parts of the world: Central America, Europe, the Middle East, and North Africa. She has traveled in fourteen different countries. In college, she went with her campus ministry to Guatemala for a summer. Then while she was working as an occupational therapist, she went on five consecutive summer trips to Berlin, Germany, to work with refugees from many different countries. This led to Kristen deciding to live overseas for two years.

After returning to the States in March 2007, Kristen lived with Bob and me for five months. During this time, she prayerfully considered what her next big step in life would be. We loved having her home with us!

Then in August 2007, Kristen started working on a master's degree in intercultural studies at Southern Seminary in Louisville, Kentucky. During her years in Louisville, God opened up doors for Kristen to help international immigrants and refugees as they adjust to life in America. She has been able to use her language and cultural experiences, which she learned overseas, right here in the States.

Kristen graduated with her master's degree on December 11, 2009. I was so excited that all four of us were able to attend her graduation ceremony! Currently, she is using her degree to help meet the physical and spiritual needs of the refugees living in Kentucky. Kristen's life focus is to help people of various cultures and backgrounds to become disciples of Jesus Christ by addressing their physical, emotional, social, intellectual, and spiritual needs.

Kristen's Quilt Square

Costa Rica Guatemala		Refugees In Berlin Germany
	Kentucky Refugee Work	
North Africa		Middle East

Justin

Justin's first mission trip out of the country was to Romania at age thirteen with Bob. When he was in high school, he had the opportunity to go with his youth group to do home improvement projects in Nashville and Atlanta. Justin has also helped work with children living in the inner city of Roanoke. As well, he has been to El Salvador two times where he made documentary films about La Casa de mi Padre (My Father's House), a ministry which helps to take care of children without homes. Justin co-teaches a Sunday school class for young single adults and helps in leading the class to do various community projects. He has a mind-set of missions that carries over to every area of his life.

Since high school, Justin has had a passion for producing quality films. Consequently, he has continued to develop his skills as a producer throughout the years. In May 2007, Justin graduated with a bachelor's degree in speech communication. Since Kristen was in the United States, our whole family, including my mom and sister, was able to attend Justin's graduation. It was a very special time for us to all be together!

After graduation, Justin and two other Liberty graduates, Judd and Won, formed a production company called Abandon Films. Through the love of Christ, they seek to make films that reflect God's character and that will provoke conversations about *truth*. Justin and his two business partners live in Lynchburg, Virginia, which is one hour away. They have worked very hard to develop their company. Through it, they have had the opportunity to serve all types of clients around North America. Their long-range goal is to make quality full-length feature films.

Justin's Quilt Square

317

Bob

Over the past twenty years in our church, Bob has taught many discipleship classes. In recent years, he has taught adult Sunday school classes on Sunday morning. It is beautiful for me to see Bob use his gift of teaching as he draws people into discussion by the questions he asks and the affirmation he gives. Bob has the names and phone numbers of each of his current class members in his cell phone and regularly calls them to see how they are doing. I now see the pastoral gifting that Bob has as he visits members in the hospital and those who are recuperating at home. He truly lives out his life verse, Colossians 1:28-29 (Phillips): "So, naturally, we proclaim Christ! We warn everyone we meet, and we teach everyone we can, all that we know about him, so that, if possible, we may bring every man up to his full maturity in Christ. This is what I am working at all the time, with all the strength that God gives me."

Bob's Quilt Square

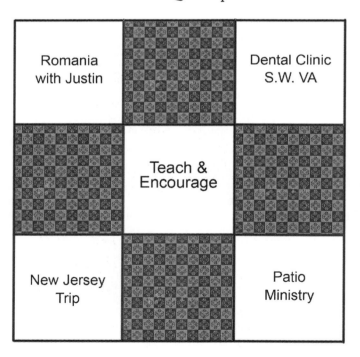

Romania with Justin		Dental Clinic S.W. VA
	Teach & Encourage	
New Jersey Trip		Patio Ministry

Lighting our candles in memory of Seth at the SHARE memorial service

Justin and Judy at the signing of the Parental Notification Bill

Kristen in the room dedicated to Nathan at the Crisis Pregnancy Center

Judy in Seth's room at the CPC

Jerry, a patterner, and her son Ron giving a Christmas gift to Nathan

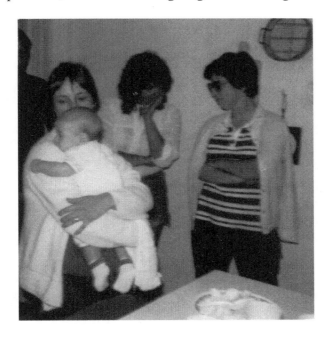

Nadine, another patterner, and her baby
at an ice cream party to celebrate Nathan's crawling goal

Nathan next to his former OT, Janey, who is holding her new baby Luke

Our friend Terri S. and her son Evan

Nathan and Gretchan, one of his personal assistants

Nathan and Judy B. making Christmas cards

Kristen and Nathan get in some "sister/brother time" in the pool

Justin and Nathan hang out with a friend from ACE camp

A relaxing weekend trip for Bob and Judy at a country inn

Bob and Judy sightsee with Kristen at the Great Pyramids

Celebrating with our close friend Rahno
at the surprise anniversary party our kids planned

Judy's good friend, Debbie, surrounded by her lovely family

Not only mother and daughter, but good friends

Giving Nathan a big birthday hug

Cheek to cheek to with Justin

Kristen travels in the Middle East

Have therapy ball, will travel

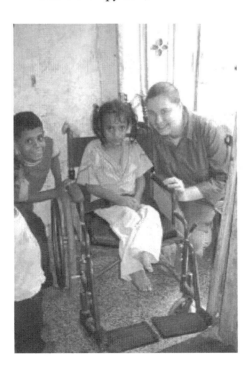

Working with special needs kids across the globe

Experiencing African food and hospitality

Gypsy children Bob and Justin met in Romania

The chapel that that Justin and Bob helped to build

The team in Romania

Bob, Judy, Nathan, and Justin with the mission team headed for New Jersey

Bob teaching adult Bible study in NJ

Justin and Bob cutting vinyl for the repairs on the church

Chapter 32

Final Thoughts

In December 1998, I had a group of women from church over to my house for dinner. I took the women upstairs to show them some furniture I had recently purchased at an estate sale. One of the women, Leigh Ann, was admiring the quilt I had on my bed. As we stood next to my bed looking at the quilt, I shared with her how I had used this quilt on several occasions for a backdrop when I present my talk—Broken Dreams, Beautiful Quilts. I explained that God has enabled me to take the pieces of my broken dreams and make a beautiful quilt from the raw material of the original dreams.

Leigh Ann asked me, "Do you think God gives children with disabilities to special families, or do you think having a child with disabilities makes you a special family?" I responded, "Children with disabilities are born into all kinds of families. One can resent the situation and become bitter. Or one can accept the situation and prayerfully make the most of the circumstances and, in a sense, become special."

As Leigh Ann and I walked down the stairs together, she shared with me that when she was pregnant with her third child, she became concerned that something was possibly wrong with the baby. Fear had gripped her. She had thought, "How will I manage?" She shared that one Sunday morning, she looked at our family and saw how happy we were, and her fear lifted. She knew she would be okay if her third child was born with some type of disability. (Her third and fourth children were born healthy.)

Quilts are not only beautiful to behold; they are also functional. During the cold winters, quilts keep us warm at night as we pull them up over our bed sheets. In a sense, the Rossbacher family quilt had given warmth to Leigh Ann while she was pregnant.

As fellow travelers on the road of life, may we help one another sort through the pieces of our broken dreams. May we encourage one another to seek God's help in taking the remnants and making beautiful quilts. As we do this, may we lend a listening ear, give words of affirmation, put our arms around each other, and pray for one another. Then, let us lift the quilts of our lives toward heaven in praise and thanksgiving to God, our Heavenly Father! Amen and amen.

A Special Message to the Reader

My motivation in writing this book, *Broken Dreams, Beautiful Quilts*, is to get Nathan's and my story out to more people around the world. My hope is that those of you who read our book will receive insight into your own personal journey of recycling broken dreams. In addition, I pray this book will help you learn how to live a more balanced, joyful life in Christ Jesus.

You may say, "Judy, a balanced, joyful life is what I want, but how do I get started?" First, you need to make sure you have a personal relationship with God through Jesus Christ. Then come before God and ask Him to guide you step by step in your journey of healing and growth. It might be helpful to use a journal to record your thoughts, prayers, and meaningful Bible verses. If needed, seek a doctor's help if you are struggling with depression and/or anxiety. Also, you may benefit from seeing a Christian counselor.

The rhythm of life is up and down. Learning to graciously handle life's joys and sorrows is a necessary skill for living a more balanced life. If you are on the upside of life, I challenge you to notice and be particularly encouraging to people who are on the downside. Here are some ideas of things you can do—give a warm greeting using the person's name, send a personal note in the mail, offer to babysit for a family with young children so the couple can go out, provide a gift certificate to a restaurant, or take by a homemade meal. Then if one day you find yourself being the one who is downcast, do not suffer alone in silence. Make sure to reach out and ask for help from others. Share your struggles with friends and allow them the opportunity to walk along side you.

Most of all, I implore you to seek the Lord; He is the One who has the power to transform your life. Be encouraged by 2 Peter 1:3 (TLB): "For as you know him better, he will give you, through his great power, *everything* you need for living a truly good life: he even shares his own glory and goodness with us!" May God receive the glory as He continues to bring healing and balance to our lives.

How to Have a Restored Relationship with God

---

1. **Admit** you are separated from God because you are a sinner.

   For all have sinned, and come short of the glory of God. **Romans 3:23**

   But your iniquities have made a separation between you and your God, and your sins have hidden His face from you so that He does not hear. **Isaiah 59:2**

2. **Realize** the way to God is through God's son, Jesus Christ.

   Jesus said to him," I am the way, and the truth, and the life; no one comes to the Father but through Me." **John 14:6**

   (Jesus said) ". . . I came that they may have life, and have it abundantly." **John 10:10 b**

3. **Believe** that Jesus is God the Son who paid the wages of your sin.

   For the wages of sin is death (eternal separation from God); but the gift of God is eternal life through Jesus Christ our Lord. **Romans 6:23**

---

4. **Call** out to God.

   If you confess with your mouth Jesus as Lord, and believe in your heart that God raised Him from the dead, you will be saved. **Romans 10:9**

5. **Know** God desires to have a personal relationship with you.

   For God so loved the world, that whoever believes in Him shall not perish, but have eternal life. **John 3:16**

   But as many as received Him, to them He gave the right to become children of God, even to those who believe in His name. **John 1:12**

If you would like to receive more information about new life in Christ call 1-888-JESUS-2000 or visit the website www.thegoodnews.org

Made in the USA
Lexington, KY
26 July 2011